The Hollywood Connection

The Hollywood Connection

The Influence of Fictional Media and Celebrity Politics on American Public Opinion

Edited by Heather E. Yates
and Timothy G. Hill

LEXINGTON BOOKS
Lanham • Boulder • New York • London

Published by Lexington Books
An imprint of The Rowman & Littlefield Publishing Group, Inc.
4501 Forbes Boulevard, Suite 200, Lanham, Maryland 20706
www.rowman.com

6 Tinworth Street, London SE11 5AL

British Library Cataloguing in Publication Information Available

Library of Congress Cataloging-in-Publication Data Available

ISBN: 978-1-4985-7047-3 (cloth : alk. paper)
ISBN: 978-1-4985-7048-0 (electronic)

∞™ The paper used in this publication meets the minimum requirements of American National Standard for Information Sciences—Permanence of Paper for Printed Library Materials, ANSI/NISO Z39.48-1992.

Printed in the United States of America

For Stephanie, Xander, and Katherine,
who keep my world spinning.
—TGH

For Mom, Dad, Heath, Chunfang, William, and Catherine
—HEY

Contents

Acknowledgments

The inspiration for this collection emerged from our participation on a few panels at the Midwest Political Science Association annual meeting back in 2015 and 2016. We had the opportunity to meet and network with scholars who were pursuing compelling research questions about the role of popular culture and fictional media in politics. After many stimulating discussions, we thought it important to gather research like what we were seeing and create this edited collection.

This book would not be what it is now without a community of scholars to nurture it. We would like to thank those who played an integral part in helping this book become a reality. We would like to extend a special thank you to Philip Habel, Emily Syndor, and Mark Ludwig who chaired the Midwest panels where this all started. Thanks also to all the panelists who participated in great discussions and provided constructive feedback on preliminary drafts of work that eventually got included in this book.

We extend our gratitude to Lexington Books, the editorial board, and the numerous people who worked behind the scenes to make this book a reality. A very special thank you to Emily Roderick, Courtney Morales, and Alison Keefner for their receptivity to the project and reliable assistance during all stages of its development. We would also like to thank Mark Harvey who was instrumental in helping us network with scholars for this project, many of whom became contributors. We appreciate each author for their hard work and contribution to this collection; without them, it would not be possible. We would like to thank our home institutions and personal social networks, which provided many forms of support.

Tim Hill would like to thank Doane University for providing institutional support. And special thanks to Stephanie, Xander, and Katherine Hill for providing all the other kinds of support. Life without you would be an endless gray fog.

Heather Yates would like to thank the University of Central Arkansas for providing support so that I could travel to conferences to present my research that became a part of this book. And to my friends and family who provided the necessary life balance, and at times, welcome distraction, that enabled me to see this project to completion.

Chapter 1

Introduction

Defining the Hollywood Connection

Timothy G. Hill and Heather E. Yates

During the heyday of his program *The Daily Show*, Jon Stewart conducted an interview with conservative commentator Bernard Goldberg in which he opined about the fundamental similarity of Hollywood and Washington, DC. "I've been to LA," Stewart said, "and I've been to Washington. They're the same city. The only difference between LA and Washington is, they think they have power in LA. They don't. . . . But in Washington they actually do have power" (2005). Stewart is no doubt correct that policy decisions have more impact on people's lives than decisions about which TV pilots get picked up. But if there is an underlying presumption in this comment that the entertainment industry and the celebrities who are a part of it have no influence on American politics, that thought is misguided.

Hollywood is a political place. As the most globally prominent and recognized entertainment industry in the world, its actors have become celebrities and have used that platform to participate in political commentary, satire, and activism since the inception of its first movie studio in 1911. Hollywood studios have exploited their production platforms to create films and television entertainment addressing political, social, and cultural problems. The comedians Will Rogers and Bob Hope are the shoulders on which Jon Stewart and Stephen Colbert stand, and even before the mass production of fictional media and satirical news programming, Hollywood and politics were connected. This collection attempts to illustrate that point: politics and Hollywood are not estranged associates.

The business of production in popular entertainment is innately political. The Hollywood-politics connection has roots in the politics of censorship during what is referenced as its "pre-code" era.[1] The politics of the Motion Picture Production Code entangled production studios, policymakers, and public opinion. Politicians and cultural critics realized the influence that popular entertainment could have on audiences and the potential influence on the direction of popular culture and social morality. In the 1930s, elite actors organized an actor's labor union that became the Screen Actors Guild (SAG), which remains to this day one of the most visible Hollywood unions. Celebrities organized to advocate for guaranteed wages and improved working conditions, and thereby established arbitration rules that allowed members to negotiate with studio executives and have better control of their careers and contracts (May 2000). Immediately after World War II, the House Un-American Activities Committee (HUAC) put the Hollywood industry on trial for alleged promotion of communist propaganda. It prompted many high profile celebrities (including Charlie Chaplin and Orson Welles) to flee the country or to retreat into anonymity, producing work under pseudonyms. Most infamously, it also resulted in the so-called "Hollywood blacklist"[2] that prevented many Hollywood actors and writers from working, which permanently altered Tinseltown (McGilligan and Buhle 1997; Shaw 2007).

Presidents and politicians have also had long-standing connections with Hollywood and its celebrities; many connections were established through personal friendships, which later served as political alliances. In the 1950s, Hollywood celebrities openly and actively engaged electoral politics and began lending their personal endorsements to presidential candidates. Hollywood Republicans campaigned for General Dwight Eisenhower in 1952, and Frank Sinatra famously lent his voice to the soundtrack of John F. Kennedy's 1960 presidential campaign. Hollywood executives urged presidential candidates to incorporate more "glitz, glamour, and media" into their campaigns as early as Herbert Hoover's White House bid. Hollywood studios reimagined the way they cast presidents as characters, portraying him as America's leading man (Brownell 2014). It could be argued that Hollywood made the presidency a celebrity status.

Hollywood, at times, has also inserted itself into global politics as America's defender and advocate for the American identity. Hollywood has often used its platform to promote political ideas salient to the era. During World War II, for example, the US government actually commissioned director Frank Capra to make a series of films collectively titled *Why We Fight* (1942–1945), which were shown to the public in an effort to maintain support for the war. During the Cold War, Hollywood responded to the global environment with everything from dramas such as *The Red Menace* (1949), *The Manchurian Candidate* (1962), and *Fail Safe* (1964) to comedies like *Dr. Strangelove* (1964) and *Spies like Us* (1984). Nor has the industry been averse to cultural commentary. The counterculture movement was given visual articulation in its various phases in films from *Rebel Without a Cause (*1955) to the motion picture version of the Broadway rock musical *Hair* (1968) to *Easy Rider* (1969).

The link that brings together politics, celebrities, and audiences for effect is what we call the *Hollywood Connection*. This Hollywood connection to our politics is one that scholars have largely ignored until relatively recently.[3] While journalists and pundits write almost daily takes exploring the latest Hollywood trend or scandal and its alleged impact on elections or policy, those ideas have rarely translated into systematic empirical tests. Only in the past decade and a half or so has this hole in the literature begun to fill.

It is the contention of the collected authors of this book that political science should pay more attention to the roles of celebrity culture and fictional media as sources of political influence. The theoretical reasons to do so are significant. First, in terms of fictional media, there is simply *more* of it: most of the media content produced is entertainment rather than news, and people spend more of their time consuming entertainment media than news media. Some shows, such as the television series *24*, discussed at length in chapter 8 by Heather Evans, devote their entire run to the depiction of a single issue domain; others may devote an entire episode or season to a given issue. This kind of deep dive is a luxury news programming cannot afford, since news will break in a wide variety of areas on any given day. And while the medium privileges entertainment value over accuracy,[4] Delli, Carpini, and Williams (1996) found that fact does not necessarily mean the topics are covered less thoroughly or accurately than they are in similarly-focused news broadcasts.

Journalists also cannot afford to tell only one side of the story, at least under the current norms of the profession. The series *24*, by contrast, can depict a counterterrorism policy in which torture and civil rights violations are the only way to "get results" without fearing accusations of bias because balance is neither a goal of the creators nor an expectation of the audience. Thus, the opportunities for influence are greater in a fictional media context than in a news media one.

Moreover, while viewers watch television news for information, they watch fictional media for entertainment and an outlet for escapism (Holbert, Kwak, and Shah 2003). As a result, they tend to watch with their defenses down, and so are less likely to argue with the ideas presented in fictional media than they are with the arguments presented on hard news programs (Mulligan and Habel 2013). Viewers also develop "parasocial" relationships with characters of their favorite television shows (Giles 2010; Horton and Wohl 1956), providing an additional path to influence: if viewers feel like the characters are friends, they are more likely to adopt their ideas as they would a friend's. And focus group research suggests that, indeed, citizens are just as likely to cite fictional as nonfictional sources when providing support for their expressed political views (Delli Carpini and Williams 1994).

A similar set of parasocial relationships governs the mass public's interactions with celebrities, which means that when Beyoncé declares herself a "FEMINIST" on a lighted backdrop larger than she is (Blair 2016), there is reason to believe the cause benefits from her association with it. Moreover, that message is more likely to get through, since she is not tied to a political party to which members of the public might feel an immediate tribal identity or animosity (Achen and Bartels 2016) as talking heads interviewed on the news are likely to be, which may increase her credibility. Finally, while journalists must for the most part wait until events happen to cover a given issue, celebrities can create the events that generate that coverage. Celebrity culture is governed by flash and by a cultivation of a sense of relationship with a given personage. It is a regular feature of contemporary life to see them leverage these tools to influence consumer choices and to further their own careers. It is at least plausible, then, that they can leverage those same tools in service of a political cause.

The need to pay greater attention to these areas gained additional urgency after November 2016 when Donald Trump, a brand-licensing mogul and reality television personality with no political experience, was elected to be the forty-fifth president of the United States. This is hardly the first time the two worlds had collided, however: Ronald Reagan, who himself had made it originally as an actor, was elected to the same post over thirty years prior. While Trump certainly helps make the argument for studying this area more carefully, then, he is only the exclamation point at the end of that sentence.

In recent years a small literature has begun to address this deficit in our understanding. While this literature has successfully demonstrated that the Hollywood connection matters, however, it is only just beginning to reckon with the more interesting questions: Under what circumstances does it matter more or less? What are the mechanisms by which its influence on political attitudes or behavior is felt? How do questions of identity, such as gender or race, affect how these messages are received? Might even ostensibly nonpolitical entertainment (that is, entertainment artifacts without an overt political valence) nevertheless have political consequences? As typically happens in a scientific pursuit, the more we learn about the Hollywood connection, the more we realize we do not know.

This book represents our attempt to move the conversation in this literature in the direction of some of these harder, more nuanced questions. We contend it is past time to do so: while establishing the baseline was important to convincing the larger field of public opinion that this connection was worth studying, that baseline is long since established. Our task is now to dig deeper to uncover more of the structure of the relationship between the main industries of the two cities Stewart mentioned.

The chapters in this volume are a diverse lot: they cover a wide variety of topics and use an array of theoretical frameworks to do so. They use methodologies from case study, to survey, to laboratory experiment. What unites them more than anything else is an attempt to push the envelope of the kinds of information we know about the Hollywood connection—and the kinds of information we have available to know about it—in a way that has not been attempted before. This introduction will attempt to set the stage for them first by briefly reviewing the fictional media and celebrity influence literatures as they currently stand and then providing some detail on how the following chapters will add to that understanding. Finally, we will provide a plan of the book that explains the logic of how the chapters flow from one to the next.

WHAT WE ALREADY KNOW

While news media has long been accepted as a source of influence on public opinion (e.g., McCombs and Shaw 1972; Iyengar, Peters, and Kinder 1982), fictional media and the celebrities it creates have until recently been largely dismissed as a source of mass opinion. For that reason, studies that entertained the possibility of an effect generally centered on cultural events, such as the miniseries *The Day After* (Feldman and Sigelman 1985), the miniseries *Amerika* (Lenart and McGraw 1989), the Oliver Stone film *JFK* (Butler, Koopman, and Zimbardo 1995) and the Spike Lee film *Malcolm X* (Davis and Davenport 1997). The assumption was that only such cultural phenomena would have enough of an impact to bend public opinion. It was only in the 2000s that scholars began to think differently about the questions regarding fictional media and thus, to discover more widespread effects. To discuss the extant literature, we will first review the demonstrated impact of the media sources themselves, and then outline the findings regarding the impact of celebrities outside of the characters they play on television and in movies.

Fictional Media

The impact of news media is well-established to be more powerful in shaping the conversation than in influencing specific attitudes. In his 1972 book *The Press and Foreign Policy*, Bernard Cohen supplied perhaps the most succinct articulation of this phenomenon in the whole of the public opinion literature. "It may not be successful much of the time in telling people what to think," he wrote of the press, "but it is stunningly successful in telling its readers what to think *about*" (13, emphasis in original).[5] It was an experimental demonstration of this assertion of the news media's agenda-setting powers (Iyengar, Peters, and Kinder 1982), coupled with survey research to demonstrate effects outside the laboratory, that launched the public opinion field's study into news media in earnest. The study by Iyengar et al., however, focused not just on agenda-setting but also on priming. As applied to media research, priming is a phenomenon in which certain considerations become more robust in providing general assessments than they would be without the prime. A surfeit of news stories about terrorism, for instance, could lead to general assessments of presidential performance riding more on assessments of the president's performance on combating terrorism, relative to other issues. We should note that the theory is agnostic as to whether this over-weighting will lead any individual to approve of the president more or less; that depends on what s/he thinks of his performance on the highlighted issue.

Since fictional media research often looks to its more established sibling for inspiration, much of the earliest work in the area took these findings and went looking for the same effects in a fictional context. Feldman and Sigelman (1985) found both priming and "issue salience" (agenda-setting by another name) effects regarding questions of nuclear war in the aftermath of the miniseries event *The Day After*, which imagined the impact of a nuclear exchange with the Soviet Union on everyday people in the American heartland. Holbert and his colleagues screened an episode of the Aaron Sorkin drama *The West Wing*, and found that the positive portrayal of the president in that show primed viewers to rate certain aspects of presidential leadership as more important, and even to revise upward their assessments of presidents Bill Clinton and George W. Bush in those aspects they had previously found lacking.

The problem of determining causality bedevils both of these studies, however. Feldman and Sigelman are working with survey data; thus, it is equally plausible that people with a strong concern about nuclear holocaust were drawn to the miniseries as it is that the miniseries itself changed their minds. Holbert et al. use a more controlled, laboratory environment and included a pretest-posttest design, a definite improvement on the methodology of Feldman and Sigelman. Inexplicably, however, they do not include a control group. Holbrook and Hill (2005) attempted to rectify these issues by aping the original dual methodological approach of Iyengar and his colleagues in a study examining crime dramas versus family-oriented ones. Using both experimental methods and survey data, they demonstrated that those who were exposed to crime procedurals were more likely to see crime as an important issue facing the country. Moreover, assessments of George W. Bush's overall job performance were disproportionately affected by assessments of his performance on crime among those who watched crime dramas, but not among those who did not. Taken together, then, these studies provide significant evidence that agenda-setting and priming, effects well-established in the news media literature, obtain just as readily in a fictional as a nonfictional context.

Such results are noteworthy, but not altogether surprising. After all, Iyengar and his colleagues explained these effects as a matter of accessibility: that mentioning one issue out of proportion to others resulted in that issue being "top of mind," and thus more likely to be called upon when asked these separate but not wholly unrelated questions.[6] In theory, there is no reason why fiction could not perform the same function. More interesting is that fictional media research has now collected a broad range of findings that suggest fictional media is capable of achieving an effect news media has not: that of changing the attitudes of individual viewers.

The earliest evidence for such persuasion effects comes not from political science but from the communication studies led by George Gerbner, which developed cultivation theory in the 1970s and 1980s (e.g., Gerbner and Gross 1976; Gerbner and Signorielli 1979; Gerbner et al. 1980, 1982, 1984). Leveraging the difference between "light viewers" (those who watch relatively less television) with "heavy viewers" (those who watch relatively more), cultivation theory posits that certain themes recur in fictional media which the audience picks up on without even being fully aware of it. The presumption is that since heavy viewers have more exposure to these themes, they will adopt them more completely. Perhaps the most famous of these themes is the "mean world" thesis: since crime, and especially violent crime, is much more prevalent on television than it is in real life, those who watch a great deal of television will internalize these representations and so be more likely to see the world as a dangerous, crime-infested place. This is hardly the only theme which Gerbner and his colleagues identify, however. Heavy viewers are also more likely to be Democrats, to identify as politically moderate, to believe in gender- and age-based stereotypes, and to disapprove of interracial marriage (though other measures of segregation were inconsistent). More generally, they find that heavy viewing promotes what they call "mainstreaming": the movement of people with putatively different worldviews toward a common set of attitudes (which is to say, the set implicitly endorsed by broadcast TV).

To these results we can add further evidence of crime-related attitude shifts, as well as two areas the Gerbner team did not explore, trust in government and ideology. Holbert, Shah, and Kwak (2004) proposed a two-step model in which certain kinds of programming influence support for police and fear of crime, which in turn influences attitudes toward capital punishment and gun ownership. Pfau, Moy, and Szabo's (2006) model was more straightforward.

They found that watching such conspiracy-minded fare as *The X Files* and *Millennium* could significantly erode one's trust in government. Similarly, Lenart and McGraw (1989) found that watching *Amerika*, a miniseries about a Soviet takeover of the United States, moved its audience in a more conservative direction with respect to Cold War politics, made them more likely to endorse positive stereotypes of Americans (though not more likely to endorse negative stereotypes of Soviets), and reduced their fear of war.

As with the agenda-setting and priming studies, however, the survey-based methodologies of these studies should give us some pause. We should not dismiss them completely, of course: the very diversity of issue domains in which researchers have recorded effects argues in their favor. Nevertheless, the causality questions at the heart of this research cannot be waved away. Perhaps being afraid of crime induces one to stay inside, so one is able to watch more television. Perhaps those with an already low opinion of government are disproportionately attracted to shows like *The X Files*, which reflect that view back to them. The correlation is not enough to suggest with confidence that these effects are real.

Laboratory experiments, then, have been indispensable in the effort to discover what effects fictional media may or may not have on the mass public. Those effects have been robust and impressive. Showing participants an episode of *Law and Order* influences their impressions of the criminal justice system, including a statistically significant impact on support for the death penalty (Mutz and Nir 2010). Exposure to the movies *300* and *V for Vendetta* induced participants to be more authoritarian and anti-authoritarian respectively, with consequences for attitudes such as immigration and military service as a condition for citizenship (Glas and Taylor 2018). Viewing *The Cider House Rules* influenced participants to be more pro-choice in cases of incest (Mulligan and Habel 2011). And watching the satire *Wag the Dog* pushed participants to be more likely to suggest that the plot of that movie—a presidential PR team stages a fake war to distract from a sex scandal—was likely to happen in the future and even that it already *had* happened (Mulligan and Habel 2013).

Effects on such visceral issues as capital punishment and immigration, or on such far-fetched conspiracy theories as appear in *Wag the Dog*, strongly suggest that the persuasion effects of fictional media are real. Accordingly, scholars have begun the process of pushing the boundaries on these effects for more than simple confirmation of their existence. Two such studies stand out. First, Adkins and Castle (2014) randomly exposed participants to one of two healthcare-related films, *As Good as It Gets* and *The Rainmaker*. Both groups experienced a leftward shift in their attitudes regarding health care with respect to a control condition with no health care content (the Tom

Hanks comedy *That Thing You Do!*). Moreover, *The Rainmaker*, which had the stronger and more overt message, pushed attitudes further than did the less strident film. The more noteworthy aspect of Adkins and Castle's work, however, is that they reinterviewed their participants a week later and were able to demonstrate that the shift that had taken place remained statistically significant. This finding is particularly important, since all previous published laboratory work only measured attitudes in the direct aftermath of the stimulus. Their work, then, is our first indication that fictional media's impact on mass attitudes is other than ephemeral.

As important as their contribution is the work of Swigger (2017), which considerably expands the scope of content worth examining. A common element of every study listed previously is that they examine a movie, television show, or genre that has a fairly simple connection to politics. *The West Wing* and *Wag the Dog* are centered on political operatives. *The Rainmaker* and *The Cider House Rules* are overt in their political messaging. Crime procedurals connect in an obvious way to crime as a political issue. Swigger, however, examines episodes of two situation comedies that are generally uninterested in politics but portray romantic relationships in sharply different ways. By exposing participants either to an episode of *Parks and Recreation* or *How I Met Your Mother*, he influences their attitudes not just on the appropriate gender dynamic in a heterosexual relationship but also on access to abortion and contraception. As this finding suggests that fictional media content need not be political in nature to have political consequences, it opens up vast new areas for fictional media research to explore.

Celebrity Politics

The evolution and personalization of technology has intensified the culture of celebrity politics. The entertainment-politics nexus has grown closer with the advent and wide proliferation of personal technologies (Wheeler 2014). The culture encompassing the connection between the entertainment industry and politics has evolved beyond celebrities involving themselves in politics to politicians themselves achieving celebrity status (West and Orman 2003). This connection has also developed beyond Hollywood actors lending their personal endorsements of political candidates to include musicians, sports figures, and comedians all weighing in with their personal political preferences.

Celebrity endorsements of political candidates have become routine, effectively blurring the lines between entertainment and politics. In the 2016 presidential election, celebrity endorsements of both Donald Trump and Hillary Clinton were more commonplace than any traditional political endorsements. Celebrities appeared at both party nominating conventions to use their platform for politics. Among some of the celebrities lending their personal endorsements were Scott Baio (who appeared on the stage at the Republican National Convention) and Katy Perry (who performed a musical set for the Democratic National Convention). Nor was this the first presidential election to exploit the influence of celebrity culture.

From the inventions of the radio, to television, to the internet, all platforms changed the manner in which audiences perceived access to celebrities. That said, the perceived social distance between the common private citizens and celebrities is closer now than it has ever been. Studies suggest the intensification of the celebrity culture of politics is rooted in the personalization factor, including technology aiding the personalization of politicians through more appearances on soft-news television shows, entertainment programs, and social media platforms (Coen 2015; Street 2012; Wheeler 2014). Celebrity theory also suggests that appeals to the audience (e.g., social media) play a role in democratizing celebrity influence (Wheeler 2014). Technology is credited for de-emphasizing party platforms and substantive policy in favor of candidate personalities. Intensified focus on the politics of personality invites spectators, audiences, and voters to accept or reject political arguments based on who made them rather than by policy preferences (Coen 2015).

The literature demonstrates that celebrities and politics are not public spheres independent of each other. As noted earlier in this chapter, Hollywood has always been a political place, entertainers have routinely advocated for philanthropic and humanitarian causes, and political candidates, with time, have achieved celebrity status (West and Orman 2003). More recent literature, much of which is featured in this collection, examines questions about how those who are celebrated for social attention translate that fame into leadership on social and political topics. As American politics has become increasingly centered on candidates and personalities, entertainers have had more room to play the role of advocate and officeholders have had more room to play the role of celebrity. The studies featured in this volume ask questions about this ability to influence public perception and popular opinion. We explore a few of the myriad ways this influence is achieved. At core of the numerous research questions engaged here is how power and celebrity politics intersect. Officeholders possess varieties of legislative authority to draft policies that impact practical aspects of daily life, whereas celebrities and entertainers use their platforms of fame to raise awareness of specific issues, topics, and critiques. When these activities intersect, it is reasonable to expect they will influence the society in which they are viewed and consumed.

PLAN OF THE BOOK

The present volume attempts to expand on the above literature in three main ways. First, it provides the beginning of a focus on issues of identity that has been conspicuously absent in the literature to this point. Second, it suggests that celebrity politics may matter in a broader array of settings than has been heretofore widely acknowledged. And finally, it attempts to identify previously undiscovered mechanisms and modalities by which fictional media influence American politics.

First, as our literature review might suggest, one area that has received relatively little attention from fictional media and celebrity politics scholars is that of identity; questions of gender, race, sexual orientation, and the like have been generally absent from studies to this point. One could easily fill an entire volume with material just trying to fill in the gap on any one of those areas of identity and come nowhere close to completing the task. Our desire here, then, is merely to provide an opening in which those conversations can begin. To that end, two of our sets of authors (Yates and Kirkpatrick, and Stoutenborough) organize their chapters explicitly around questions of gender and feminism, while a third (Mulligan) explores a wider set of identity markers.

Second, the work on celebrity politics labors to expand the scope of the area in which such research is performed. Notably, the methodology and focus of each piece is different. Kirkpatrick and Stoutenborough use survey data to explore how celebrities affect the way Americans think about feminism, DeWitt uses his own dataset to focus on the policy success of celebrities, Harvey uses his own dataset to observe the way celebrity status confers power, while Nownes's survey-based experiment examines the way a president who has leveraged his celebrity status since long before he entered politics himself can be helped by the aura of other celebrities' goodwill. Interestingly, two of these chapters (Harvey and Nownes) center on Donald Trump, an indication of how the study of celebrity influence in politics has been affected by his ascension to the Oval Office.

Finally, the fictional media research presented here follows the example of those recent studies that attempt to do more than simply document an effect. Like the chapters on celebrity politics, they try to provide additional context that pushes forward our understanding of the impact of the area, be it through a new mechanism (Hill and Van Fleet), a previously unused methodological technique (Mulligan, Yates), or a longitudinal comparison of similar cohorts (Evans). Each of these innovations opens new ground for future scholars to explore.

The book itself proceeds in three broadly thematic sections, which correspond to the three goals we have just outlined. Of course, some of the chapters serve more than one goal, so we have arranged them in the way that seemed most intuitive to us, in the hope that the reader will find a certain flow from one chapter to the next. First is a short section on identity, followed by four chapters examining the role of celebrities in politics, and then another short section that provides new context for studies on fictional media. We end with a brief conclusion in which we attempt to provide some suggestions on the way forward for research in these areas.

We open with a short section of just two chapters. In chapter 2, Kenneth Mulligan looks at time series data to examine the effect of media consolidation on representation of women, racial and ethnic minorities, and LGBTQ individuals, and finds little impact. In chapter 3, Heather Yates uses a different methodological approach, that of the qualitative case study, to explore the gender dynamics of satire. In both cases, the authors' work engages questions about representations of identity and leaves us with important questions to pursue going forward.

The emphasis on questions of identity continues into the next section, which focuses on new ideas in the realm of celebrity politics research. Chapter 4 serves as our bridge here. In that chapter, Kellee Kirkpatrick and James Stoutenborough apply the relatively new theoretical structure of narrative policy framework to the question of how one defines feminism. This provides a context in which the theory has not been applied before, as it is one in which multiple narrators exist. They find that in that situation, many of the assumptions of the theory appear to break down (though they are cautious about concluding as much), but that naming someone famous as being representative of feminism is correlated with pro-feminist attitudes. In chapter 5, Darin DeWitt uses data he previously collected with a colleague to ask whether celebrity appearances at congressional hearings result in a more favorable atmosphere for moving legislation through the process. He finds that they do, by multiple measures. In chapter 6, Mark Harvey collected original data of his own to compare the various forms of power Hillary Clinton and Donald Trump had before each ran for president in the 2016 election season. Intriguingly, he finds that the forms of power Trump's celebrity afforded him may have given him an edge in the contest once it arrived. And in chapter 7, Anthony Nownes performs a survey experiment that indicates that attaching Trump to the celebrities who have publicly endorsed him and his politics, gives him a boost in his job approval ratings over the version of the question that does not provide that information to the public. It seems, then, that even a celebrity president can be aided by the endorsement of other celebrities.

The final section is also shorter, and attempts to take the fictional media research in new directions. In chapter 8, Heather Evans explores the impact of watching *24* on attitudes toward torture for two separate cohorts seven years apart. She finds that the context matters: in her first cohort taken in 2010/2011, the effects are fairly strong, but when she reexamines the question with participants in 2017, they have greatly dissipated, possibly due to the change in the larger political context. Finally, in chapter 9, Timothy Hill and Ashley Van Fleet apply affective intelligence theory to the world of fictional media to suggest that horror films without any obvious political valence may nevertheless impact political attitudes by impacting the mood of those viewing them. Their results here are mixed, but the theory provides ample fodder for future research.

Those studying fictional media or the impact of celebrities on politics have spent most of their time up to now simply trying to legitimize their areas as reasonable ones to study. They have accomplished this goal through a series of works demonstrating an impact of these areas on the political process; most often, that impact was on mass opinion. In recent years, it has become apparent that the time for such simple demonstrations was past, and that greater nuance and more creative thinking about how and under what conditions these impacts happened was called for. The eight substantive chapters in this book represent an effort to move these areas of research more firmly in that direction. As such, we see them as only the beginning of a much greater endeavor. If they begin some deeper conversations about the directions in which these literatures should go, we will count this volume a success.

NOTES

1. This era is reference to the brief period between 1929 and 1934, when there was no enforcement of rules or regulations of content in films. Content was largely negotiated on a local level or between studios and production teams, and popular opinion rather than a regulatory body was the final arbiter. The motion picture production code supplied the censorship guidelines from what can and cannot be presented in motion pictures. For more about this history see Doherty, Thomas. 1999. *Pre-Code Hollywood.* New York: Columbia University Press.

2. Actors, writers, and producers were placed on the "Hollywood blacklist" typically as a punishment for refusing the answer the HUAC questions about having associations with the Communist Party or engaging in un-American activities. Since HUAC committee hearings were not criminal proceedings, no criminal actions were taken or threatened.

3. We use "Hollywood connection" here as a catch-all term to refer to both the impact of fictional media and the impact of celebrities in politics.

4. Arguably, of course, news media have similar incentives.

5. It is not actually required by law for political scientists to reference this comment whenever agenda-setting comes up, but it might as well be.

6. Miller and Krosnick (2000) argue that the mechanism for agenda-setting is not accessibility but a form of persuasion: the news organization has taken precious time in its broadcast for this issue, so it must be important. If that interpretation is correct, it complicates the picture for fictional media only slightly, as one could make a similar argument about, for example, the proliferation of crime procedurals.

REFERENCES

Achen, Christopher H., and Larry M. Bartels. *Democracy for Realists: Why Elections Do Not Produce Responsive Government*. Princeton, NJ: Princeton University Press, 2016.

Adkins, Todd, and Jeremiah J. Castle. "*Moving* Pictures? Experimental Evidence of Cinematic Influence on Political Attitudes." *Social Science Quarterly* 95, no. 5 (2014): 1230–44.

Blair, Olivia. "Beyoncé Explains Why She Performed in Front of the Word 'Feminist.'" *Independent* (London, UK), April 5, 2016.

Brownell, Kathryn Cramer. *Showbiz Politics: Hollywood in American Political Life*. Chapel Hill, NC: University of North Carolina Press, 2014.

Butler, Lisa D., Cheryl Koopman, and Philip G. Zimbardo. "The Psychological Impact of Viewing the Film *JFK*: Emotions, Beliefs, and Political Behavioral Intentions." *Political Psychology* 16, no. 2 (1995): 237–57.

Coen, Sharon. "The Age of Celebrity Politics." *Psychologist* 28.5 (2015) 372–75.

Cohen, Bernard C. *The Public's Impact on Foreign Policy*. Boston: Little, Brown, and Company, 1972.

Davis, Darren W., and Christian Davenport. "The Political and Social Relevancy of *Malcolm X*: The Stability of African American Political Attitudes." *Journal of Politics* 59, no. 2 (1997): 550–64.

Delli Carpini, Michael X., and Bruce A. Williams. "Methods, Metaphors, and Media Research: The Uses of Television in Political Conversation." *Communication Research* 21, no. 6 (1994): 782–812.

———. "Constructing Public Opinion: The Uses of Fictional and Nonfictional Television in Conversations about the Environment. In *The Psychology of Political Communication*, edited by Ann N. Crigler, 149–76. Ann Arbor: University of Michigan Press, 1996.

Feldman, Stanley, and Lee Sigelman. "The Political Impact of Prime-Time Television: 'The Day After.'" *Journal of Politics* 47, no. 2 (1985): 556–78.

Gerbner, George, and Larry Gross. "Living with Television: The Violence Profile." *Journal of Communication* 26, no. 2 (1976): 173–99.

Gerbner, George, Larry Gross, Michael Morgan, and Nancy Signorielli. "The 'Mainstreaming' of America: Violence Profile No. 11." *Journal of Communication* 30, no. 3 (1980): 10–29.

———. "Charting the Mainstream: Television's Contributions to Political Orientations." *Journal of Communication* 32, no. 2 (1982): 100–27.

———. "Political Correlates of Television Viewing." *Public Opinion Quarterly* 48, no. 1 (1984): 283–300.

Gerbner, George, and Nancy Signorielli. "Women and Minorities in Television Drama, 1969–1978." University of Pennsylvania, Annenberg School of Communications, 1979.

Giles, David C. "Parasocial Relationships." In *Characters in Fictional Worlds: Understanding Imaginary Beings in Literature, Film, and Other Media*, edited by Jens Eder, Fotis Jannidis, and Ralf Schneider, 442–56. Berlin: De Gruyter, 2010.

Glas, Jeffrey M., and J. Benjamin Taylor. "The Silver Screen and Authoritarianism: Popular Films Activate Latent Personality Dispositions and Affect Political Attitudes." *American Politics Research* 46, no. 2 (2018): 246–75.

Holbert, R. Lance, Nojin Kwak, and Dhavan V. Shah. "Environmental Concerns, Patterns of Television Viewing, and Pro-Environmental Behaviors: Integrating Models of Media Consumption and Effects." *Journal of Broadcasting & Electronic Media* 47, no. 2 (2003): 177–96.

Holbert, R. Lance, Owen Pillion, David A. Tschida, Greg G. Armfield, Kelly Kinder, Kristin L. Cherry, and Amy R. Daulton. "'The West Wing' as Endorsement of the US Presidency: Expanding the Bounds of Priming in Political Communication." *Journal of Communication* 53, no. 3 (2003): 427–43.

Holbert, R. Lance, Dhavan V. Shah, and Nojin Kwak. "Political Implications of Prime-Time Drama and Sitcom Use: Genres of Representation and Opinions Concerning Women's Rights." *Journal of Communication* 53, no. 1 (2003): 45–60.

Holbrook, R. Andrew, and Timothy G. Hill. "Agenda-Setting and Priming in Prime Time Television: Crime Dramas as Political Cues." *Political Communication* 22, no. 3 (2005): 277–95.

Horton, Donald, and Richard Wohl. "Mass Communication and Para-Social Interaction: Observations on Intimacy at a Distance." *Psychiatry* 19, no. 3 (1956): 215–29.

Iyengar, Shanto, Mark D. Peters, and Donald R. Kinder. "Experimental Demonstration of the 'Not-So-Minimal' Consequences of Television News Programs." *American Political Science Review* 76, no. 4 (1982): 848–58.

Lenart, Silvo, and Kathleen M. McGraw. "America Watches 'Amerika': Television Docudrama and Political Attitudes." *Journal of Politics* 51, no. 3 (1989): 697–712.

May, Lary. *The Big Tomorrow: Hollywood and the Politics of the American Way*. Chicago, IL: The University of Chicago Press. 2000.

McCombs, Maxwell E., and Donald L. Shaw. "The Agenda-Setting Function of the Mass Media." *Public Opinion Quarterly* 36, no. 2 (1972): 176–87.

McGilligan, Patrick, and Paul Buhle. *Tender Comrades: A Backstory of the Hollywood Blacklist*. New York: St. Martin's Press, 1997.

Miller, Joanne M., and Jon A. Krosnick. "News Media Impact on the Ingredients of Presidential Evaluations: Politically Knowledgeable Citizens Are Guided by a Trusted Source." *American Journal of Political Science* 44, no. 2 (2000): 301–15.

Mulligan, Kenneth, and Philip Habel. "An Experimental Test of the Effects of Fictional Framing on Attitudes." *Social Science Quarterly* 92, no. 1 (2011): 79–99.

———. "The Implications of Fictional Media for Political Belief." *American Politics Research* 41, no. 1 (2013): 122–46.

Mutz, Diana C., and Lilach Nir. Not Necessarily the News: Does Fictional Television Influence Real-World Policy Preferences?" *Mass Communication and Society* 13, no. 2 (2010): 196–217.

Pfau, Michael, Patricia Moy, and Erin Alison Szabo. "Influence of Prime-Time Television Programming on Perceptions of the Federal Government." *Mass Communication and Society* 4, no. 4 (2001): 437–53.

Shaw, Tony. *Hollywood's Cold War*. Amherst: University of Massachusetts Press, 2007.

Stewart, Jon. "Interview with Bernard Goldberg." *The Daily Show with Jon Stewart*. 2005; New York: Viacom, 2005. Original air date: July 13.

Street, John. "Do Celebrity Politics and Celebrity Politicians Matter?" *The British Journal of Politics and International Relations* 14, no. 3 (2012): 346–56.

Swigger, Nathaniel. "The Effect of Gender Norms in Sitcoms on Support for Access to Abortion and Contraception." *American Politics Research* 45, no. 1 (2017): 109–27.

West, Darrell M., and John Orman. *Celebrity Politics*. Upper Saddle River, NJ: Prentice Hall, 2003.

Wheeler, Mark. "The Mediatization of Celebrity Politics through the Social Media." *International Journal of Digital Television* 5, no. 3 (2014): 221–35.

Chapter 2

Media Ownership Concentration and Minority Representation in Prime Time Entertainment Television

Kenneth Mulligan

Media companies—the corporations that make and distribute popular media—are big and getting bigger.[1] At the same time, the biggest of the big appear to be controlling more and more of the media that people watch, read, and hear. This has occurred despite the fact that, in this century, advances in technology, including especially digital media and the internet, as well as the scaling back of government regulation, have expanded radically opportunities for new entrants into the media marketplace. Yet if recent events are any indication, the trend toward growth, consolidation, and concentration appear hardly to have slowed down. In 2017, the largest TV station operator, Sinclair Media, sought to extend its reach to more than 70 percent of American homes with its bid to acquire Chicago-based Tribune Media. A year later, in the summer of 2018, AT&T, the largest telecommunications company in the United States, absorbed America's biggest media-producing firm, Time Warner, at a cost of about $85 billion. About the same time, and at the time this was written, Comcast, the nation's biggest cable firm and largest internet service provider, was in a bidding war with Walt Disney Co., the nation's third largest media company, over who would merge with 21st Century Fox, the fourth largest media firm in the United States. Separately Comcast and Disney are also battling over which company will acquire Sky, the largest pay–TV operator in Europe. The total cost of the 21st Century Fox and Sky mergers will likely top $100 billion.

These are just the most recent of an ongoing string of massive media mergers and acquisitions. As these and other corporate conglomerates expand, integrate, and swallow up competitors, critics say the trend is problematic because it restricts the range of voices in the media marketplace. As fewer companies produce and control a greater share of popular media, it is argued, it diminishes the diversity of ideas, perspectives, and content of popular media, and these corporations' power and influence over the public grows. Furthermore, they argue, this poses problems for a free society, because, in the US in particular, theorists, politicians, regulators, and courts have long subscribed to the principle that a vibrant marketplace of ideas is essential to democracy. This apparent concentration of media power into fewer and fewer hands has led to greater scrutiny of media companies and calls for re-regulation and deconsolidation.

As serious as these concerns are, arguments against media concentration are themselves problematic for several reasons, both theoretical and empirical. Much of the evidence of the supposed negative effects of media concentration on "the marketplace of ideas" is based on assumptions, anecdotes, unrepresentative case studies, loose analysis, and conjecture, rather than objective, empirical, systematic, and representative, research. As it happens, the empirical research on the effects of media concentration is mixed. Moreover, it turns out "the media" are not just one market, but many. Equally important, conceptions and measures of media diversity are themselves varied. Perhaps for these reasons, what little quantitative research there is on this topic is time-bound or context-specific.

There has been little research on the effects of media concentration over time, and even less on its relation to diversity of content in popular entertainment media. It is important to evaluate media concentration dynamically in order to assess its consequences. It is also important to study the consequences of media concentration for entertainment media, not just news, because most people are exposed to vastly more popular entertainment media than news. Entertainment is fertile yet largely untilled ground for media studies in general and concentration research in particular. Scholars have long known that entertainment media present a distorted view of the world, and these media representations affect people's perceptions of reality. In the present context, if media concentration diminishes content diversity, this could distort consumers' perceptions of reality beyond their immediate experience. The present study seeks to address whether concentration of media is associated with diversity of minority representation in entertainment media. Specifically, it is an exploratory analysis of the effects of media concentration on the representation of racial and sexual minorities in prime time entertainment television from the 1970s through the first decade of the twenty-first century.

MEDIA OWNERSHIP CONCENTRATION AND THE MARKETPLACE OF IDEAS

Media ownership concentration occurs when a relatively few number of companies control a majority of the market. In a media industry in which market shares are spread across many companies, the market is said to be competitive. But where there are few companies who together control the market, the industry or market is lacking in competition and thus concentrated. Media ownership concentration is potentially problematic for at least two general reasons. The first is economic. Media industries, and in particular those producing digital content, due to economies of scale and scope, as well as the related benefits that come from vertical and horizontal integration, are prone to concentration (Doyle 2013). According to mainstream economic theory, market ownership concentration can lead to higher prices, less innovation, and less product differentiation.

The second potential problem relates to the consequences of media ownership concentration for democracy. Elites in the US, schooled in the basics of classical liberal democratic theory, have long subscribed to the assumption that a healthy democracy requires what Justice Oliver Wendell Holmes (1919) once called a vibrant "marketplace of ideas." "[The First] Amendment rests on the assumption," the Supreme Court reasoned in *Associated Press v. United States* (1945), "that the widest possible dissemination of information from diverse and antagonistic sources is essential to the welfare of the public." The implication of this reasoning is that citizens need access to a wide variety of sources of information to be informed and participate effectively in democratic decision making. Similarly, where media content is constrained, people's perceptions of the social and political world may be similarly biased or truncated. This assumes that media ownership concentration constrains or limits diversity of media content.

Critics say that the media today are concentrated and with negative consequences. As early as the turn of this century McChesney (2000) claimed that only a half dozen corporations controlled half or more of the mass media. Just four years later Bagdikian (2004) claimed that the number had dropped to five. A year later, Winseck (2008, based on 2005 data, 37) said that "the 'big 10' global media firms account for just over 80% of all revenues." Critics say that this high level of concentration puts enormous power into the hands of just a few firms who limit the diversity of ideas and other forms of media content, which ultimately makes them bad for democracy. They call for stronger antitrust regulation to provide more voices in the media and choices for consumers.

Regulating Media in the Public Interest

The federal government addresses these problems in two ways. First, the economic problems are dealt with through antitrust laws and regulations enforced by the Federal Trade Commission (FTC) and Department of Justice (DOJ). The goal is to prevent undue concentration that will result in enhanced competition, and, in turn, provide a variety of high quality media product choices at competitive prices for consumers. Large mergers and acquisitions of media firms are reviewed by the FTC and DOJ. Either agency can go to court to block a merger that it thinks will "substantially lessen competition" (FTC n.d.).

Second, potential problems related both to competition and the marketplace of ideas are addressed by the Federal Communications Commission (FCC). In addition to competition, the FCC's public interest mandate has led the agency to promote localism and diversity. Localism helps to ensure that broadcast media serve the interests of communities. Diversity helps to ensure that a variety of voices and perspectives are represented in media.

Media Ownership Concentration Reconsidered

Media concentration has received widespread attention in the popular press. However, despite these alarming statistics, questions of whether media are too concentrated and the effects of concentration on content are far from settled. In their review of the empirical literature, Ho and Quinn (2009, 789) say that "scholars have come to no agreement on basic questions of whether consolidation has happened, and if so, whether it has any connection to viewpoint diversity." First, the question of how much competition or concentration there is in media is complicated because there are different ways to conceptualize and measure markets and concentration and different standards of how much concentration is too much. These questions are important but largely beyond the scope of this chapter. Suffice it to say, though, that "the media" are not one industry, but many. And partly because of this, frequently cited statistics about media concentration are often based on data that are misleading, unreplicable, and with questionable or untenable assumptions. To date, the only study to quantify media concentration in the US objectively, carefully, and thoroughly is Noam's (2009) *Media Ownership and Concentration in America*. In it the author finds that whereas many media industries are concentrated (including cable TV providers and film production, for example) or recently concentrated (perhaps most notably, radio stations), several others are not, by traditional standards, concentrated (including news media, whose concentration level has changed hardly at all over the past thirty years). Moreover, Noam finds that media industries in the US tend to be less concentrated on average than most other American industries. Noam does not argue that US media are unconcentrated, or that media concentration is without implications for consumers or democracy. But his results give reason to reconsider unsubstantiated and broad claims about concentration and the need for renewed government regulation.

Linking Ownership Concentration and Content Diversity

Second, it is also warranted to reconsider the consequences of ownership concentration for media content. For most of the past century, regulators and courts took it for granted that competition in media markets leads to content diversity. It was assumed that each corporation speaks in one voice, and fewer market players means fewer perspectives, and less diversity of content. With Justice Holmes's dictum in mind, keeping media concentration at bay was considered essential to democracy. Toward the end of the twentieth century, however, changes in technology, regulation, jurisprudence, and consumer tastes collectively began to transform the media landscape. The emergence of the internet and the crumbling of conceptual and technological barriers between categories of media (e.g., print, video, and audio) led to reconsideration of obsolescent classifications and regulations, most emblematically in the Telecommunications Act of 1996. Concomitantly, courts began insisting on empirical evidence to support the link between ownership concentration and content diversity. Such evidence was, for the most part, lacking, and courts began to strike down ownership restrictions for want of justification.

Since then the evidence has been mixed at best (Aslama et al. 2007; Ho and Quinn 2009; Horwitz 2005; Napoli 2011; Noam 2009). A study of newspapers following the mergers and acquisitions of the 1990s showed that differentiation within markets and variety in the topics covered by the newspapers actually increased (not decreased) following the merger (George 2007). Ho and Quinn (2009) studied editorial positions of newspapers following mergers and found no evidence of convergence. McDonald and Lin (2004) looked at changes in program diversity on television following the introduction of cable TV. They found that the new competition increased diversity overall but not among the big three (at the time) broadcast networks (ABC, CBS, and NBC), which continued to appeal to the median viewer. Other research around this time examined government regulations intended to increase programming diversity (the FCC's financial interest and syndication or "syn-fin" rules) and found that the big three's programming was no more or less diverse after syn-fin than in the 1960s (Einstein 2004). With respect to the music industry, at least one study suggests that increased market concentration is associated with more (not less) diversity in popular music (Burnett 1992).

Deregulation, and to a lesser extent concentration, were perhaps most pronounced with respect to radio. Ownership limits were progressively relaxed beginning in 1984 and eliminated entirely by 1996. The changes in market structure and academic attention to radio ownership that resulted prompted Noam (2009, 55) to say that "radio has become the poster boy for media concentration. Most public discussions of media trends refer to the developments in radio and its lessons for public policy." Following the deregulation and ownership concentration in the late 1990s, one radio study suggested that ownership concentration diminished program diversity (Chambers 2003), but others found that it increased diversity (Berry and Waldfogel 2001; Jeziorski 2014; Sweeting 2010), and still others found no appreciable relationship between ownership concentration and content diversity (Polinsky 2007; Williams, Brown, and Alexander 2002).

Part of the problem of identifying consistent effects of ownership concentration on content diversity is the myriad ways that diversity can be conceptualized and measured when it comes to media (see Napoli 2009 for a review). In his review of media diversity, van Cuilenburg (2007, 27) defines it as "the extent to which media content differs according to one or more criteria." In media research, diversity is often used interchangeably with pluralism. The myriad uses and connotations of these terms sometimes carry "political, economic . . . cultural . . . and ideolog[ical]" connotations (Valcke, Picard, and Sukosd 2015, 1). Here, however, these connotations are set aside in favor of a simple definition of diversity that means, essentially, variety.

Van Cuilenburg (2007) discusses at least three diversity concepts that are relevant to media policy: social diversity, media diversity, and information/opinion diversity. Social diversity is about the different types of people that reflect variation in society. Media diversity relates to heterogeneity in media content. And information/opinion diversity refers to different perspectives, viewpoints, and opinions in society. The three types of diversity can be thought about as a causal chain, with social diversity reflected in media (content) diversity, which impacts information/opinion diversity. This study is loosely related to the connection between all three. As a point of departure it begins with the observation that there is diversity in the US with respect to race, gender, and sexual orientation. If van Cuilenburg is correct, then one would expect these dimensions of diversity to be portrayed in popular media to greater or lesser degrees. One would expect that diversity in race, gender, and sexual orientation on TV and elsewhere would reflect the diversity of these traits in society.

Content Diversity and Cultivation Theory

To the extent the above expectation is true, it might affect the third link, information/opinion diversity, by influencing people's perceptions of diversity in the real world. Decades of research on how popular media influence people show that systematic media messages often lead to predictable effects on perceptions and attitudes. Perhaps, most relevant for the present study, is Gerbner's cultivation theory (Gerbner and Gross 1976). The cultivation literature shows that media—and in particular, entertainment television—frequently present depictions of the world that are unrealistic in any number of ways (Morgan, Shanahan, and Signorielli 2013). For example, many cultivation studies show that TV depicts the world as more dangerous and filled with crime than occurs in actuality. The cultivation literature calls this the "mean world effect," in which people who are exposed to heavy doses of television tend to perceive the world as more dangerous than it actually is. In the present context, dealing with race, gender, and sexual orientation, if ownership concentration diminishes content diversity, then this distorted lens on the social world might affect consumers' perceptions in systematic ways. For example, if convergence of ownership causes convergence of content that appeal mainly to the median consumer, but not minorities, this may result in media that is increasingly white, male, middle class, and heterosexual. To the extent this is true, cultivation theory suggests that it could distort people's perceptions of reality.

This study examines quantitatively the effects of media concentration on diversity in prime time television programs over the course of about thirty years. The literature on the link between ownership concentration and content diversity is inconsistent—some studies show a positive relationship, others a negative one, and others no relationship at all. Because of this, and because I have not laid out a strong theoretical basis for expecting an effect of concentration on diversity in prime time, this study simply tests for associations without attempting to make strong causal arguments.

DATA AND MEASURES

The measures used are concentration of media ownership and representation in prime time of, respectively, African Americans, Latinos, women, and lesbians and gays. Each is discussed in turn.

Media Ownership Concentration

The measure of media ownership concentration comes from a methodological study by Vizcarrondo (2013). It taps ownership concentration using the Herfindahl-Hirschman Index (HHI) of US media firms. The HHI is an index of the degree of competition within an industry.[2] One benefit of the HHI as a measure of industry concentration is that it weights firms by size, so larger firms have greater influence on the overall index than smaller ones. The HHI is one of the most widely-used measures of industry concentration. It is used by regulatory agencies, including the FTC and DOJ, to evaluate mergers and acquisitions in enforcing antitrust law.

As an index of concentration, the validity of the HHI hinges on the notion of substitutability (FTC n.d.). Substitutability is the extent to which competing media would be a suitable substitute for what is chosen. For the present analysis, this matters with respect to whether one considers substitutability to be relevant only within a given media platform or across platforms. For example, is a movie a viable substitute for a TV show? How about a video game? Traditionally, scholars and regulators have considered substitutability only within industries. That is, they assume that a person might be willing, for example, to substitute one broadcast TV show for another broadcast TV show, but not that the consumer would substitute some other form of entertainment (such as streaming or other on-demand video). However, as media types, such as, but not limited to, television, internet, movies, streaming videos, and music-on-demand, are rapidly converging, and used interchangeably by consumers, some argue that substitutability should be applied across, not just within, platforms. Media companies increasingly own multiple platforms, and consumers face an ever-widening arrangement of choices. For instance, at this writing AT&T and Disney are planning launches of new streaming services. To the extent that media choices are substitutable across platforms, one assumes that consumers choose among a variety of options. Depending on tastes and availability in the home, a person sitting in front of the TV set could choose among, for example, watching broadcast TV, on-demand video from Netflix, Amazon, or Hulu, or streaming YouTube, or playing a video game.

The HHI used here adopts this cross-platform approach. It includes "those [media] companies in the business of creating, distributing, or owning content for consumption by mass audiences" (Vizcarrondo 2013, 190). Operationally, these are mainly the "Sector 51" firms of the North American Industry Classification System (NAICS).[3] This approach taps concentration across media industries rather than within a single industry. Based on Vizcarrondo's index, media concentration declined from the mid-1970s through the 1990s and has increased this century to a point similar to the early period of the index. Based on this measure, the trend has not been one of rapid consolidation. A word of caution is in order, however, because it is generally true that the broader the range of firms in the HHI, the lower one would expect the concentration to be (Noam 2009). Because of this, some might argue that ownership concentration in this cross-media HHI could be said to be biased downward.

Minorities in Prime Time TV

Representation of African Americans, Latinos, and women are measured based on the percentage of each among the the top 10 characters, cast members, or contestants in each of the top 30 TV shows in the US in each year from the 1970s through roughly the first decade of the twenty-first century. The top 30 shows were determined by Nielsen ratings. The race or ethnicity and gender of the people in the TV shows were determined by research assistants who used internet web sites including the IMDb database and others to determine whether the characters/cast/contestants were African American, Latino, or White, as well as female or male.[4] African Americans and Latinos who are actually of mixed race were classified according to whether they present as black or Latino. Thus, for example, if a character is half-Black and half-White, but looks Black, and is described in internet media as African American or Black, then he or she is counted in our index as African American, not White.

Racial Minorities in Prime Time

The index of the percentage of African Americans in prime time is the dashed line in figure 2.1. The percentage of African Americans on TV has waxed and waned over the years, from a low of about 7 percent in the early 1970s, to a

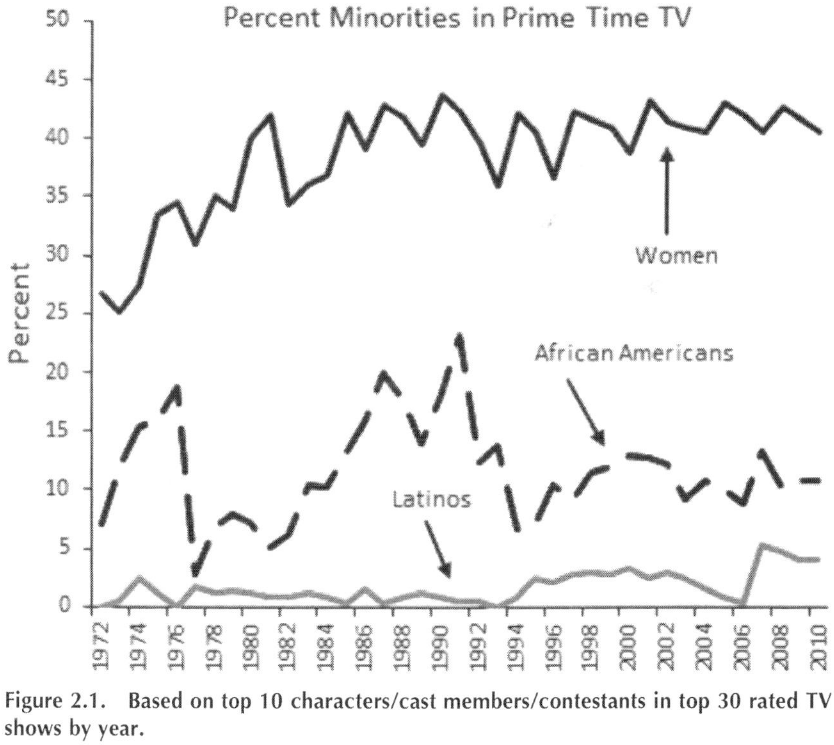

Figure 2.1. Based on top 10 characters/cast members/contestants in top 30 rated TV shows by year.

Created by the author; Adapted from imdb.com.

high of nearly a quarter of all characters in the early 1990s, but has declined to around 10 percent more recently. The measure of Latinos is the gray line in figure 2.1. It shows that Latinos have been barely represented on TV over the years. Despite currently being the largest minority group in the US, the percentage of Latinos has never risen above 5 percent during the period depicted in the figure.

Women and LGBTs in Prime Time

The percentage of women on television is the solid line in figure 2.1. It shows that the percentage of women has moved upward over the years, albeit in a somewhat seesaw fashion, from a low of about 27 percent in the early 1970s to more than 40 percent more recently. Thus women's representation on the small screen has improved over the years, although change has been slow, and women are still underrepresented relative to men.

The number of sexual minorities (hereafter LGBTs) in prime time is measured using three sources: Tropiano's (2002) *Prime Time Closet: A History of Gays and Lesbians on TV*, which includes identifiably LGBT characters in both scripted and reality programs through 2001;[5] the interest group GLAAD's yearly "Where We Are on TV" reports, which cover scripted

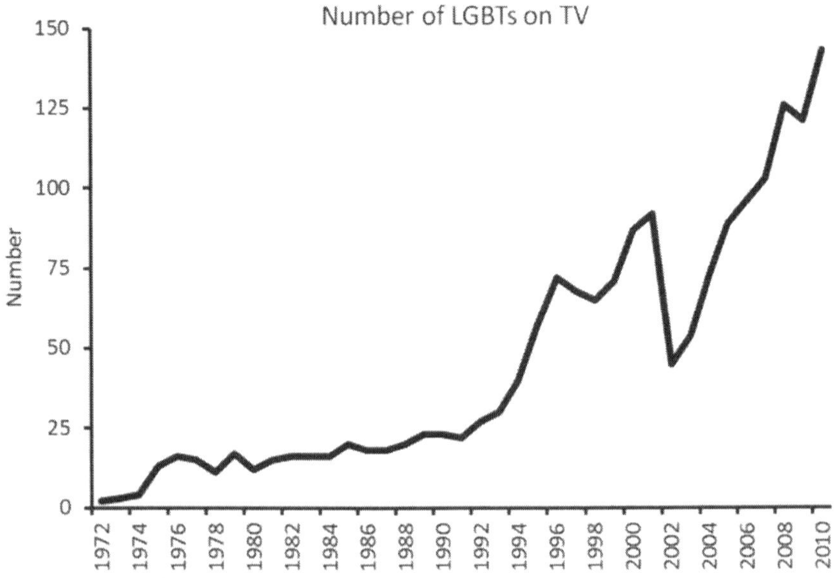

Figure 2.2. Number of LGBTs on TV.
Created by the author.

series but not reality shows;[6] and, to account for reality shows from 2002 to 2010, the *World News* "List of Reality Television Programs with LGBT Cast Members."[7] Using these sources, the combined time series, which is the number of LGBTs on TV, is presented in figure 2.2.

It shows a steady but slow increase in LGBT representation on TV during the 1970s and 1980s, followed by dramatic growth in the 1990s. The sharp drop in 2002 likely results from the loss of the Tropiano data in that year.[8] Even so, the series recovers quickly the following year, and continues its rapid ascent through the highest point, in 2010.

RESULTS

In order to assess the effects of media concentration on demographic diversity on TV, several time series models were estimated. Each of these models shows the relationship between two or more variables over time. These are a particular type of model, what economists and methodologists call the "error correction" model.[9] Among the advantages of this type of model are that it allows one to assess whether the variables move together across time, and whether there are long-run effects of one variable on another variable, and whether there are short-run effects of one variable on another.

The model of the relationship between media ownership concentration and the percentage of African Americans in prime time is presented in the first two columns of table 2.1. The variable at the top of the table, here labeled the "go together coefficient,"[10] is, in this type of model, always negative, and ranges between 0 and –1. The closer it gets to –1, the more the variables move together over time. The closer to 0, the more the variables track independently, not together, across time. Here, the go-together coefficient in the first column at the top of the table is about halfway between zero and one, and statistically significant. Substantively this implies that levels of media concentration and African American representation on TV do move together over time, albeit not in lockstep, which seems reasonable. The model also has "long-run" coefficients, which are the extent to which there is an association between two variables over the long-term. In this model, the long-run coefficient on media concentration is negative, very small, and not statistically significant by the conventional standard, which is $p < .05$. By this standard, this means that there is less than a 5 percent probability that the observed relationship between ownership concentration and African American representation on TV could have occurred due to chance alone. Here, the statistical significance of the long-run effect of media concentration on African American representation is $p = .06$. This means that there is about a 6 percent chance that the relationship between these two variables in this model happened by chance. If one is willing to allow for this probability, this long-run effect implies that, across time, as concentration increases, the percentage of African Americans in the top prime time TV shows decreases just a little bit. The short-run coefficient is the immediate effect of one variable on another, but here, for media concentration, at the top of column 2, it is not statistically significant. In addition to ownership concentration, representation of African Americans on television might also be affected by public opinion about race. For example, when the public is more liberal on race, it might also be more open to a growing presence of African Americans in prime time. To account for this possibility, the model controls for aggregate racial liberalism of public opinion in the US[11] The effect of aggregate racial liberalism is positive and significant, but only in the short term. The long-run effect is not statistically significant. This means that collective public opinion with respect to race has an immediate effect on black representation on TV, but not a longer-term influence.

Columns 3 and 4 of table 2.1 present the model of media concentration and representation of Latinos in prime time. Although the go-together coefficient is again statically significant, negative, and between zero and one, implying that ownership concentration and Latino representation on TV go together over time, both the short- and long-term effects of media concentration on Latino representation are nonsignificant. While this may seem puzzling—the variables move together across time but without any implied causation—what it likely means is that they track together, to an extent, but there are other factors, whether societal, cultural, or economic, that are probably driving these processes. Regardless, based on these results, one concludes that media concentration does not affect the percentage of Latinos on TV.

The results of the model of media concentration and women in prime time are in columns 5 and 6 of table 2.1. Although the go-together coefficient is statistically significant, as in the Latino model, the effects of media concentration in both the short- and long-term are not significant. Thus, as with Latinos on TV, media concentration does not significantly affect the percentage of women on TV. This model controls for aggregate liberalism with respect to women's rights. This is based on the supposition that when the country grows more liberal on women's issues, this may lead to a greater presence of women on TV. Conversely, when the public moves in a conservative direction on women's rights, representation of women in prime time may be reduced. The coefficient on the women's rights variable in column 5 is positive and significant in the long run.[12]This finding means that as public opinion in the US grows more liberal with respect to women's rights, the percentage of women on TV increases over the long term. The nonsignificant coefficient on women's rights in column 6 means that here there is no short-run effect.

Table 2.1. Blacks, Latinos, Women, and LGBT's in Prime Time TV

	% Blacks on TV		*% Latinos on TV*		*% Women on TV*		*# LGBT's on TV*	
	Long-Run Effects	*Short-Run Effects*	*Long-Run Effects*	*Short-Run Effects*	*Long-Run Effects*	*Short-Run Effects*	*Long-Run Effects*	*Short-Run Effects*
"Go Together" Coefficient	–.54**		–.45**		–.88**		–.35**	
	(.15)		(.17)		(.20)		(.10)	
Media Concentration	–.02	.01	–.00	.00	–.00	.01	.01	.02
	(.01)	(.01)	(.00)	(.00)	(.01)	(.01)	(.01)	(.02)
Racial Liberalism	.12	1.40**	.12	.14				
	(.18)	(.53)	(.06)	(.17)				
Women's Rights Liberalism					.32*	.05		
					(.15)	(.45)		
LGBT Rights Liberalism							3.34**	2.24*
							(.72)	(.92)
Constant	5.81		–6.97		12.78		–177.77**	
	(10.77)		(3.92)		(9.72)		(39.22)	
N	33		33		33		33	
Adjusted R-square	.50		.15		.41		.77	

** p < .01, * p < .05, two-tailed. Time series error correction models. These are OLS Coefficients with standard errors in parentheses.

The last two columns in table 2.1 show the results of the model of media concentration and the number of LGBTs on television.[13] The go-together coefficient is once again significant, but, here again, the effect of media concentration is nonsignificant in both the short and long run. The interpretation of these results is similar to that of the other columns of the table. Ownership concentration of the mass media tracks LGBT representation on TV, but the results do not imply a causal relationship between the two variables. The model controls for collective public opinion on LGBT rights, based on the idea that as the public becomes more receptive to gay rights, it might also be receptive to more gays and lesbians on TV.[14] The effect of collective preferences toward LGBT rights is significant in both the short and long run. This finding implies that as public opinion toward gay rights has liberalized, it has driven up the number of LGBTs on television.

CONCLUSION

Recent large-scale media mergers and acquisitions give the impression that ownership of mass media are becoming ominously concentrated. There is a longstanding concern that as the number of "voices" in the media marketplace declines, diversity of ideas and content is increasingly constricted. However, the empirical research that investigates the relationship between ownership concentration and content diversity is mixed. Some studies suggest concentration diminishes content diversity, others show it increases it, and still others suggest no relationship between the two.

Much of this research has dealt with radio or newspapers. Hardly any has explored the connection between ownership concentration and minority diversity in prime time entertainment television. This study used time series models to test the connection between concentration of mass media in the US and representation on TV of, respectively, African Americans, Latinos, women, and LGBTs. Overall, the results were mostly null. The analysis found no quantitative association between media concentration and representation of women, Latinos, or LGBTs on TV. There was a small long-run relationship between the concentration and representation of African Americans, but the coefficient was not statistically significant by conventional standards.

The results of this study have implication for government regulation of television. The FTC and DOJ police ownership, not just of media but all major industries, to protect the economic interests of consumers. The FCC, in contrast, has used its public interest mandate to go beyond economic considerations to include promoting localism and diversity, in addition to competition. The results of this study suggest that media concentration does not substantially affect diversity on TV, at least not in prime-time entertainment. To the extent this is true, restricting ownership concentration seems unlikely to serve the public interest, specifically, at least, with respect to entertainment TV and promoting diversity with respect to race, gender, and sexual orientation.

However, while the results are consistent with this implication, the quantitative analysis presented here should be taken with a grain of salt for methodological reasons. In this study the level of measurement used to operationalize ownership concentration was different from the level of measurement used to tap diversity in prime time. Specifically, ownership concentration was measured *across all mass media companies* while diversity was measured *just in prime-time television*. The potential problem here is that the measure of ownership concentration was broad (it includes all media companies) while the diversity measure was narrow (it included only television programs, not all types of media content). This study showed essentially no relationship between the broad measure of ownership concentration and narrow measure of diversity on TV. Future research might address this issue with a more apples-to-apples comparison of concentration of major TV networks and diversity on TV, or, alternatively, changes in diversity on TV following mergers of TV companies. Lastly, this study dealt with traditional TV going back to its heyday in the 1970s. While this longitudinal analysis is instructive, it is also true that today, while millions of people still watch live TV (mostly on cable and satellite), millions of others stream video, both live and on-demand, on other platforms, over the internet. With the rapid growth and changes in streaming and live video options, it is possible that these new technologies may have changed the landscape in ways that allow for narrowcasting and diversity that are not reflected in the top shows of legacy prime-time TV. Although these new modes of entertainment and TV viewing may not easily lend themselves to the longitudinal analysis used in this study, future research might account for them in ways that will aid our understanding of the relationship between ownership concentration and diversity in popular media.

NOTES

1. For research assistance I thank Daniel Bennett, Srobana Bhatacharyya, Emily Carroll, Chris Condry, Diep Duong, and Robin Thomas. I thank Tom Vizcarrondo for making available his data on media concentration.

2. Technically the HHI it is the sum of squares of the market shares of firms in the industry under consideration.

3. Companies classified under other sectors were also included as relevant. Also, for these, as well as international firms, "only revenues associated with media-related businesses in the United States were included" (Vizcarrondo 2013, 186).

4. Other races are excluded from the present analysis because few people on TV are identifiably of a race other than African American or Latino. Future research might expand this analysis to include other races.

5. The Tropiano book is comprehensive and considered authoritative in the field.

6. They were downloaded from http://www.glaad.org.

7. Downloaded from http://wn.com/listofrealitytelevisionprogramswithlgbtcast members/wiki.

8. It is not clear why the Tropiano and other sources do not seem to "match up" in 2002. However, there are two ways to address this. One, if the drop in 2002 is an issue of measurement error, then the error will distort the relationship with public opinion and the results will be null. From this perspective, the change in measurement simply adds noise to the data. The second way to address the issue—and the one used here—is to include a variable in the time series model accounting for the change.

9. Social scientists and statisticians would say that benefits of the error correction model include that it allows for nonstationarity, and tests for (but does not require) cointegration, and provides estimates of both short- and long-run effects (De Boef and Keele 2008).

10. Technically it is called the coefficient of cointegration.

11. The measure of aggregate racial policy liberalism comes from Baumgartner and Jones's (2018) Policy Agendas Project.

12. The measure of aggregate women's rights liberalism comes from Mulligan et al. (2013).

13. The dependent variable here is a count of the number of LGBTs on TV; however, a count model is not warranted here because, in this type of model, the DV is differenced before the model is run. Thus, technically, the DV is the change in the number of LGBTs on TV, not a count of LGBTs, across time.

14. The measure of aggregate gay rights liberalism also comes from Mulligan et al. (2013).

REFERENCES

Aslama, Minna, Els De Bens, Jan van Cuilenburg, Kaarle Nordenstreng, Winfried Schulz, and Richard van der Wurff. "Measuring and Assessing Empirical Media Diversity: Some European Cases." In *Media Between Culture and Commerce*, edited by Els de Bens. Bristol, UK: Intellect, 2007.

Bagdikian, Ben H. *The New Media Monopoly*, revised edition. Boston, MA: Beacon Press, 2004.

Baumgartner, Frank R., and Brian D. Jones. *Public Agendas Dataset.* Accessed on May 25, 2018. http://www.policyagendas.org/page/datasets-codebooks.

Baynes. Leonard M. "White Out: The Absence and Stereotying of People of Color by the Broadcast Networks in Prime Time Entertainment Programming." In *Media Diversity and Localism: Meaning and Metrics*, edited by Philip M. Napoli. Mahwah, NJ: Erlbaum, 2007.

Berry, Steven T., and Joel Waldfogel. "Do Mergers Increase Product Variety? Evidence from Radio Broadcasting." *Quarterly Journal of Economics* 116, no. 3 (2001): 1009–25.

Burnett, Robert. "The Implications of Ownership Changes on Concentration and Diversity in the Phonogram Industry." *Communication Research* 19, no. 6 (1992): 749–69.

Chambers, Todd. "Radio Programming Diversity in the Era of Consolidation." *Journal of Radio Studies* 10, no. 1 (2003): 33–45.

Compaine, Benjamin M. "The Impact of Ownership on Content: Does It Matter?" *Cardozo Arts & Entertainment Law Journal* 13 (1994): 755–80.

De Boef, Suzanna, and Luke Keele. "Taking Time Seriously." *American Journal of Political Science* 52, no. 1 (2008): 184–200.

Department of Justice and Federal Trade Commission. "Horizontal Merger Guidelines." Last modified August 19, 2010. Accessed on May 31, 2018. http://www.justice.gov/atr/public/guidelines/hmg-2010.html.

Doyle, G. *Understanding Media Economics*. Thousand Oaks, CA: Sage, 2013.

Einstein, Mara. "The Financial Interest and Syndication Rules and Changes in Program Diversity. *Journal of Media Economics* 17, no. 1 (2004): 1–18.

Federal Trade Commission. "Merger Review." Accessed on May 31, 2018. https://www.ftc.gov/news-events/media-resources/mergers-and-competition/merger-review.

George, Lisa. "What's Fit to Print: The Effect of Ownership Concentration on Product Variety in Daily Newspaper Markets." *Information Economics and Policy* 19, no. 3–4 (2007): 285–303.

Gerbner, G., and L. Gross. "Living with Television: The Violence Profile." *Journal of Communication* 26, no. 2 (1976): 172–94.

Gerbner, George, Larry Gross, Michael Morgan, Nancy Signorielli, and James Shanahan. "Growing up with Television: Cultivation Processes." In *Media Effects: Advances in Theory and Research*, edited by Jennings Bryant and Mary Beth Oliver. New York: Routledge, 2009.

Ho, D. E., and K. M. Quinn. "Viewpoint Diversity and Media Consolidation: An Empirical Study." *Stanford Law Review* 61 (2009): 781–868.

Hollifield, Ann C. "News Media Performance in Hypercompetitive Markets: An Extended Model of Effects." *International Journal on Media Management* 8, no. 2 (2006): 60–69.

Horwitz, Robert B. "On Media Concentration and the Diversity Question." *The Information Society* 21, no. 3 (2005): 181–204.

Jeziorski, Przemyslaw. "Effects of Mergers in Two-Sided Markets: The US Radio Industry." *American Economic Journal: Microeconomics* 6, no. 4 (2014): 35–73.

Lin, Carolyn A. "Diversity of Network Prime-Time Program Formats during the 1980s." *Journal of Media Economics* 8, no. 4 (1995): 17–28.

———. "Network Prime-Time Programming Strategies in the 1980s." *Journal of Broadcasting & Electronic Media* 39, no. 4 (1995): 482–95.

Litman, Barry R. "The Television Networks, Competition and Program Diversity." *Journal of Broadcasting & Electronic Media* 23, no. 4 (1979): 393–409.

Liu, Y. L. *Multiple TV Channels and Their Audiences*. Taipei, Taiwan: Shyr-Ying Publishing Company, 1997.

McChesney, Robert W. *Rich Media, Poor Democracy: Communication Politics in Dubious Times*. Champaign-Urbana: University of Illinois Press, 2000.
McDonald, Daniel G., and Shu-Fang Lin. "The Effect of New Networks on US Television Diversity." *Journal of Media Economics* 17, no. 2 (2004): 105–21.
Morgan, Michael., James Shanahan, and Nancy Signorielli. *Living with Television Now*. Mahwah, NJ: Peter Lang, 2013.
Mulligan, Kenneth, Tobin Grant, and Daniel Bennett. "The Dynamics of Public Opinion on Cultural Policy Issues in the US, 1972–2010." *Political Behavior* 35, no. 4 (2013): 807–29.
Napoli, Philip M. *Media Diversity and Localism: Meaning and Metrics*. New York: Routledge, 2009.
———. "Exposure Diversity Reconsidered." *Journal of Information Policy* 1 (2011): 246–59.
Noam, Eli. *Media Ownership and Concentration in America*. Oxford, UK: Oxford University Press, 2009.
Polinsky, Heather. "The factors affecting radio format diversity after the Telecommunications Act of 1996: Ownership concentration, stations and audience." *Journal of Radio Studies* 14, no. 2 (2007): 122–43.
Rogers, Robert P., and John R. Woodbury. "Market Structure, Program Diversity, and Radio Audience Size." *Contemporary Economic Policy* 14, no. 1 (1996): 81–91.
Schumpeter, Joseph A. *The Theory of Economic Development*. Oxford, UK: Oxford University Press, 1934.
Sweeting, Andrew. "The Effects of Horizontal Mergers on Product Positioning: Evidence from the Music Radio Industry." *RAND Journal of Economics* 41, no. 2 (2010): 372–97.
Thierer, Adam D. *Media Myths: Making Sense of the Debate over Media Ownership*. Washington, DC: Progress and Freedom Foundation, 2005.
Tropiano, Stephen. *Prime Time Closet: A History of Gays and Lesbians on TV*. New York: Applause Theatre and Cinema Books, 2002.
Valcke, Peggy, Robert G. Picard, and Milklos Sukosd. "A Global Perspective on Media Pluralism and Diversity: Introduction." In *Media Pluralism and Diversity: Concepts, Risks, and Global Trends*, edited by Peggy Valcke, Robert G. Picard, and Milklos Sukosd. New York: Palgrave, 2015.
Van Cuilenburg, Jan. "Media Diversity, Competition and Concentration: Concepts and Theories," edited by Els de Ens. *Media between Culture and Commerce*. Bristol, UK, 2007.
Vizcarrondo, T. "Measuring Concentration of Media Ownership: 1976–2009. *International Journal on Media Management* 15, no. 3 (2013): 177–95.
Williams, George, Keith Brown, and Peter Alexander. "Radio Market Structure and Music Diversity." Media Bureau Staff Research Paper, Washington, DC: Federal Communications Commission, 2002.
Winseck, Dwayne. The State of Media Ownership and Media Markets: Competition or Concentration and Why Should We Care? *Sociology Compass* 2, no. 1 (2008): 34–47.
Waldfogel, Joel. 2007. "Should We Regulate Media Ownership?" edited by Philip M. Napoli, *Media Diversity and Localism*. New York: Routledge, 2007.

Chapter 3

Laughing at Women

An Examination of How Veep's *Use of Satire Reinforces Negative Stereotypes of Women in Politics*

Heather E. Yates

Women have made strides in achieving success at educational attainment, workforce participation, and political representation. Many formal barriers preventing women from fully participating in these domains have been removed. 69 percent of Americans report that men and women make equally good leaders.[1] A majority of the American public also reports believing that it is harder for women to achieve a corporate leadership position than a political one. While women have made progress in politics, they compose only 20 percent of the US Congress, 12 percent of governors, and 25.4 percent of state legislative seats.[2] Popular entertainment has portrayed images of women as presidents of the United States and in powerful executive positions, and yet few women have actually achieved these high positions, and none have been elected to the executive branch. How do we reconcile the progressive public attitudes about women in leadership and the pervasive images of powerful women in popular entertainment with the absence of gendered parity in real life?

This chapter explores the intersection of political satire and women's political power as they are represented in the successful Home Box Office (HBO) series *Veep* by looking at how the main character, Selina Meyer (Julia-Louis Dreyfus), is portrayed through the lens of enlightened sexism. Based on a content analysis, the evidence supports three claims made about political satire's use of humor to reinforce negative attributes of women in politics. First, political satire masculinizes women's political power. Second, political satire reinforces elements of enlightened sexism. Third, political satire can turn politics-as-play into politics-as-punishment. After considering the content analysis, the chapter offers a few paths forward on this type of research.

LITERATURE AND THEORY

Is *Veep* Feminist?

Veep's creator, Armando Iannucci, is well known for the British political satire *The Thick of It* (2005), the precursor to *Veep*, which targeted British members of parliament (MPs), as well as a companion film satirizing US-British coordinated efforts toward the Iraq War, *In the Loop* (2009). Iannucci's style of edgy, at times abusive, political satire is likely best characterized by satirist P. J. O'Rouke's observation of politics: "politics is and always has been a performing art, it is ego driven, it is needy, it is narcissistic" (2017). These are many of the themes that drive the punch lines in Iannucci's satire.

When exporting his work to the American market, Iannucci was deliberate in his decision to make the lead character in *Veep* a woman. It was not a feminist decision, but an intentional one to avoid comparisons to actual US vice presidents. Iannucci explained it would be interesting to cast a woman as vice president without making it a show about a woman in politics (Burstein 2012).

Even though the scholarship examining *Veep*'s content and impact is still emerging, there are already divided conclusions about Iannucci's depiction of gender in politics. There are two identifiable schools of thought. One view is that *Veep* is a feminist text because Selina Meyer is depicted as being just as flawed as the men in politics and that men and women can be equally bad leaders (Hou et al. 2018). The other view is that *Veep* is entrenched in sexism and portrays a distinct point of view of a woman president before the country has actually elected a female president (Laflen et al. 2017). They note that there are real and practical tensions that arise when "popular culture provides visualizations of a female presidency in a country that has yet to elect a female president" (49). Further observing that such visualizations suggest that gender in the forms of sexism and misogyny are irrelevant to contemporary politics without addressing the gendered construction of political office (Laflen et al. 2017, 51; McDermott 2016). Laflen et al. observe that one of the main elements of *Veep*'s humor is that to resist sexism is a futile endeavor; Selina Meyer's capitulation to sexism (and conflict) is the driving force in the comedy. They conclude that the characters both express and are subject to sexism, misogynistic language, and stereotypes.

The central focus of this chapter's critique, examined more thoroughly below, is Iannucci's decision to gender the vice president (and president, in the show's later seasons). It may have been a pragmatic consideration to avoid comparisons with real vice presidents, but the decision seems to reflect little acknowledgment of the liabilities that accompany women in politics. *Veep*'s comedic effect relies on making fun of the unique burdens that women in politics encounter, without recognizing them as actual problems.

Enlightened Sexism

A framework which has not yet been applied to the analysis of *Veep* is Susan Douglas's (2010) "enlightened sexism." Enlightened sexism, according to Douglas, is predicated on the assumption that "women have made plenty of progress because of feminism—indeed, full equality has allegedly been achieved—so now it is okay, even amusing, to resurrect sexist stereotypes of girls and women" (9). Enlightened sexism takes the gains of the women's movement as a given, and uses them as permission to resurrect retrograde images of girls and women (10). There are six components that comprise this framework:

- Anxiety about female achievement
- A renewed and amplified objectification of young women's bodies and faces
- The dual exploitation and punishment of female sexuality
- The pitting of women against each other by age, race, and class
- Rampant branding and consumerism
- Irony and the cultivation of the ironic

There are two subtexts embedded in this framework. First, Douglas notes that embedded in this framework is the anachronistic assumption that women are fundamentally different from men and can never be equal to them. Second, enlightened sexism seeks to become the updated, hip, prevailing common sense about what women can be and do in today's world. This corresponds with Laflin et al. (2017) on the idea of "popular feminism," a concept that relies on feminism as a way to inoculate one against charges of sexism, or as Rosaland Gill (2007) explained, as something that molds feminist and anti-feminist ideas together. Therefore, the presentation of enlightened sexism in popular culture is feminist in its outward appearance, but sexist in its intent, meaning that even while it seems to support women's equality, it is dedicated to undoing feminism (Douglas, 11).

Some contemporary examples of enlightened sexism in its application to popular culture and popular entertainment are prevalent in reality television programming, such as MTV's *The Real World* or *Jersey Shore* and overtly competitive formats such as NBC's *The Apprentice* and VH1's *America's Next Top Model*. The common thread that links a majority of contemporary programming together is not its blatant representations of sexism, but its subtle delivery. Another example of enlightened sexism is Comedy Central's *The Man Show* (1999–2004). Johnson's (2007) research suggests *The Man Show* demonstrates elements of enlightened sexism in that many of the show's techniques "of marginalization and trivialization operate on an assumption that women's interests are adequately, perhaps excessively, protected by the established order" (Johnson 2007, 169), consequently making it acceptable to laugh at sexist jokes or sexism altogether. As Douglas put it, "the objectification of women is now fine; why, it's actually a joke on the guys. It's silly to be sexist; therefore, it's funny to be sexist" (Douglas 2010, 13). These examples offer the extremeness of the sexism as evidence that there is no sexism. If there is equality, there is no need for feminism, so it can be mocked and attacked without any consequence (Gill 2007). Such double entanglements as these, represented in popular culture and other media outlets, engender contradictory messages that involve the mixed use of flattery and denigration. Popular culture endorses portrayals of female characters that demonstrate a level of self-actualization and personal agency that may not really exist.

Sex Matters in Politics

It is noteworthy to emphasize the significant achievements that women and society have made toward improving the overall status of women. Since the second and third waves of the women's movement, sexist norms have gradually given way to practices promoting gender equality and the acceptance of women in many professional and educational settings (Deaux and Emswiller 1974; Klonis et al. 2005). However, these new norms in turn gave way to new attitudes among younger women who no longer see it as necessary to associate with a movement that seems antiquated and complete. This is where a highly visible distortion is established and popular entertainment has perpetuated visible fantasies (Gill 2007). The idea that women have achieved equality and therefore gender is no longer relevant to politics runs in direct contradiction to the evidence found in political science. Although more women are now represented in American political institutions, women compose only 20 percent of the US Congress, 12 percent of governors, and 25.4 percent of state legislative seats.[3] In the face of this progress, US political institutions still remain male-dominated spaces.

Despite Armando Iannucci's claim that he did not aspire to make a series about a woman in politics (Burstein 2012), political science and communication studies research reveals that biological sex matters in politics (Dittmar 2015; Falk 2008; Fox and Lawless 2011; Han 2010; Han and Heldman 2007; Huddy and Turkildsen 1993; Jamieson 1995; Kantola and Lombardo 2017; Lawless 2009; McDermott 2016; Sanchez 2009; Sheckels et al. 2012; Sheeler and Anderson 2013; Witt et al. 1995). Women are evaluated on personal traits in ways that differ from men in politics and these appraisals have been used to construct gender-based stereotypes of women in politics, in media coverage, and comedy sketches.

Evidence reveals that men and women are held to different standards in politics, women as candidates and officeholders are held to what Kathleen Hall Jamieson (1995) termed gendered "double binds." Defined as "a rhetorical construct that posits two and only two alternatives, one or both penalizing the person being offered them . . . such choices have been constructed to deny women access to power and, where individuals manage to slip past their constraints, to undermine their exercise of whatever power they achieve" (Jamieson 1995, 14). This is a socially constructed strategy to convey there is something fundamental to women that is incompatible with something the woman seeks. Jamieson identified five types of double binds:

- Women can exercise their wombs or their brains, but not both.
- Women who speak out are immodest and will be shamed, while women who are silent will be ignored or dismissed.
- Women are subordinate whether they claim to be different from men or the same.
- Women who are considered feminine will be judged incompetent, and women who are competent, unfeminine.
- As men age, they gain wisdom and power; as women age, they wrinkle and become superfluous.

These constructs are typically focused on negative, trait-based appraisals of women in politics. In application, binds draw their power from their capacity to simplify complexity. Faced with a complicated situation or behavior, the human tendency is to split apart and dichotomize it. But when this tendency drives us to see life's options or the choices available to women as irreconcilable opposites, those differences become problematic. Specifically applied to political contexts, women as candidates are challenged with achieving a harmonious balance of contradictory character traits (e.g., femininity versus toughness). For example, women are less likely to be perceived as behaving properly when engaged in strong adversarial conduct, such as an aggressive woman trial attorney or a confrontational woman candidate during a political debate. More specifically, examples of these binds have been sources of political parody on *Saturday Night Live*, targeting women in politics including Attorney General Janet Reno (portrayed by Will Ferrell in 1997), Hillary Clinton, and Sarah Palin. They were parodied on femininity versus competence frames. For example, imitations of Janet Reno and Hillary Clinton emphasized the lack of femininity and Sarah Palin was parodied on the lack of competence (Peifer 2013).

Trait-based stereotypes are generalized as expectations constructed of physical and emotional traits of women. Political communications analysis reveals that as a result of the existence of these double binds, media coverage of women candidates often focuses on topics beyond the context of the campaign itself (Bystrom 2004; Weaver, McCombs, and Shaw 2004).

Some stereotypes negate the consideration that women candidates (and later officeholders) are suited to handle issues outside of the purview of social policy and are weak on other policy domains such as the armed forces, security, or foreign policy (Carroll 2001; Pew Research Institute 2010). Women candidates often embrace their identity as a woman and (intentionally or not) end up embracing a traditional stereotype. On balance, research on recent campaigns suggests that women candidates do not de-emphasize gender or sex on the campaign trail (Lawrence and Rose 2010). For example, in 2008, Sarah Palin embraced motherhood on the national political stage, and in 2015, Hillary Clinton announced her candidacy by embracing her status as a new grandmother.

As mentioned earlier, campaign communication and media coverage aids the construction and reinforcement of voter expectations toward women candidates. Politically, the stereotyped beliefs about women are that they are more liberal than men candidates, which stem from gaps in voting behavior (women have largely voted Democratic in past elections) (Huddy et al. 1993; McDermott 1998). Most research acknowledges that political trait stereotypes stem from social ones (McDermott 1998; Panagopoulous 2004). Prior to the 2008 presidential election, the conventional assumptions about the influence of gender on voting behavior was that liberal voters would favor women candidates over men candidates and that Democrats were more likely to vote for women. On policy issues, voters who supported issues such as education, health care, government ethics, and government services would most likely support women candidates over men candidates (McDermott 1998; Thomas and Welch 2001). These assumptions were challenged by the gender dynamics in both 2008 and 2016.

Traditional social norms have usually informed the expectations of gendered behavior in politics, making it increasingly difficult for a woman in politics to embrace one identity trait to the detriment of another because both traits carry clear penalties (Jamieson 1995; Lawrence and Rose 2010). Interviews with female candidates have revealed that they feel additional pressure on account of their sex, which adds another dimension to the affairs of politics; otherwise, voters will be satisfied with the status quo of male leadership (Dodson 2001). Dodson goes on to suggest women feel a binary pressure to embrace and neutralize their gendered identities.

Satire and Humor in Politics

Satire is a long-standing companion of politics. Political satire is a type of satire that specializes in gaining entertainment from politics (Jones 2004). Historically, political satire was used with subversive intent in political regimes where speech and dissent were restricted or forbidden as a method of advancing political arguments. In more democratized and contemporary settings, satire has been used to ridicule non-normative political behavior of officeholders or to ridicule personalities, targeting character flaws and other weaknesses such as the performances observed in Armando Ianucci's *The Day Today* (1994) in the UK, Jon Stewart's *The Daily Show* (1996), Stephen Colbert's *The Colbert Report* (2005), and most recently, Samantha Bee's *Full Frontal* (2016). The satirists enjoy the protection of open speech and expression, and therefore openly mock officeholders' personalities and political issues. However, satire as a form of communication typically does not critique the more crucial economic and contemporary political structures (Day 2011). However, Samantha Bee has routinely engaged these kinds of critiques more directly in the wake of the 2016 election.

Political satire is a powerful instrument in the aforementioned programs because it has the ability to attract less politically engaged audiences across demographic cohorts (Baym 2005; Baumgartner and Morris 2011). Political satire as a method of communication is important because it is used to dissect and critique power (and those who hold it) in an entertaining fashion. Additionally, political satire has the power to recontextualize a point of view, routinely using humor to offer a different way to interpret whatever event is under scrutiny (Colletta 2009; Day 2011; Jones 2004). Political satire, more recently, though, has incurred criticism for trivializing and diminishing the seriousness of political topics and leaders (Faina 2013).

Parody, another popular device in political comedy, functions to mimic in such a way that it can normalize its caricatures of power for audiences (Sheeler and Anderson 2013). *Saturday Night Live* (SNL) has made presidential parody a corner market feature of its sketch comedy. Sheeler and Anderson (2013) found that the 2007/2008 presidential parodies skewered women leaders rather than the cultural forces that constrained them in the campaign. They noted that women as leaders were comedic targets on the basis they were women. The jokes were not meant to reveal sexism, but rather relied on sexism for their comedic effect.

The effects of humor in parodying presidentiality, especially gendered presidentiality, come from what Baym calls a televisual spectacle of aestheticized politics where political humor is handled like politics-as-play and the chafe comes when the humor itself turns from play to punishment (Baym 2007; Sheeler and Anderson 2013). Using satire to ridicule politicians is one thing, but when satire targets women politicians on the basis of sex to laugh at women's faults and foibles, this kind of laughter entails a different set of risks. When this is the case, popular entertainment does not only resurrect various sexist stereotypes and jokes relying on sexism for their effect, but also encourages the approval of them (Douglas 2010).

Mocking the Vice Presidency (and Presidency)

The 2008 and 2016 elections are reminders that the vice presidency and the presidency remain closed off to women. They remain, in effect, masculine spaces. It is also well established by previous occupants that the vice presidency suffers a credibility problem. Making the vice president a woman in *Veep* compounds this problem because it amplifies obstacles women face in politics without simultaneously acknowledging the difficulties women confront in politics. The brand of political satire in *Veep* creates a spectacle of ineffective female political leadership as source material for its jokes.

Satirizing the vice presidency is not inherently problematic since it is a constitutional post with virtually no executive power. Other than serving as the successor to the president in the event of an unexpected vacancy, the vice president only serves as the president of the Senate to cast tie-breaking votes. John Adams, the nation's first vice president, explained his role as, "in this I am nothing, but I may be everything." To further punctuate the feebleness of the office, Franklin Roosevelt's first vice president, John Nance Garner, characterized it as "not worth a bucket of warm piss" and "the worst damn fool mistake I ever made."[4] A more contemporary take came from late-night comedian Johnny Carson, who once joked that, "[d]emocracy means that anyone can grow up to be president, and anyone who doesn't grow up can be vice president."[5] The institution of the vice presidency is one bound by a contradiction, it is a political office with no official duty, but serves an important role in the constitutional line of succession. To be nothing and everything at once is the paradox that frames the setting for *Veep*'s structure.

Iannucci placed a fictitious woman in an actual institution of the executive branch, without acknowledging the difficult history gender has experienced in American politics. Creating a narrative around a fictional woman in a real political office, where no woman has yet to be elected, presents a compounded issue at the intersection of gender and politics. By their own characterization, the HBO's executive producers describe *Veep*'s plot as a naïve woman surrounded by naïve staffers who are in over their heads, struggling to be relevant in an office that possesses virtually no power. What compounds this narrative is that the jokes are reliant on negative personality traits of a woman portrayed in an office no actual woman has yet held.

The principle plot points of *Veep* attempt to establish a competent political career for its protagonist as a US senator prior to her recruitment to the post. The third season ends with Vice President Meyer becoming president by constitutional succession (not through election). The series' early premise and unfolding story is predicated on the notion that the vice presidency is a post of little consequence. HBO advertises the show as "authentic without being specifically biographical about what it is like to hold the least effectual post in the most powerful office in the World."[6]

THE CASE STUDY OF *VEEP*

Method of Analysis

This chapter expands the research on the political satire in *Veep* by conducting a theme-based content analysis of its six completed and aired seasons. Each season contains ten episodes (except for season 1, which has eight), for a total of fifty-eight episodes. The analysis applies the enlightened sexism framework and examines how satire amplifies Jamieson's gendered double binds often experienced by women in politics. Individual themes were the unit of analysis. Brians et al. (2011) defines a theme as a "particular combination of words or ideas, such as phrase, a sentence, or even a paragraph" (197). In this case the themes were located in scripted dialogue. To identify the recurring themes and patterns that structured the political satire prevalent in *Veep*, the project began with a close viewing of the first three seasons of *Veep* (Selina Meyer becomes president at the end of season 3). After multiple reviews of the early seasons, a dictionary of the dominant themes was created. Political science and gender studies literature was used to operationalize the themes in the dictionary (see table 3.1).

This same literature was used to create a four-category classification scheme for each dominant theme present in most episodes (see table 3.2). The four categories are 1) the political institution, 2) gendered agency, 3) gendered power, and 4) gendered, trait-based stereotypes. Individual themes in each episode were evaluated and coded by assigning a value using a five-point Likert scale (1 = very unfavorable, 2 = unfavorable, 3 = neutral, 4 = favorable, 5 = very favorable).[7] The values assessed for each theme were averaged for every season. Those summary values are reflected in table 3.2.

Points for Comparison

Before examining *Veep*'s portrayal of Selina Meyer as the nation's first woman vice president (and president), a benchmark for comparison needs to be established to demonstrate how the series *Veep* is distinct from other Iannucci products. While detailed content analysis of *The Thick of It* (2005) and the feature film *In the Loop* (2009) were beyond the scope of this project, some basic observations for comparison can be made.

Iannucci's brand of satire capitalizes on the notion that politics is chaotic as a result of self-serving, inept politicians and staffers, particularly the equally

Table 3.1. Operationalized Dominant Themes and Patters in *Veep*

Political Institution	
The Vice President as Inconsequential	The routine trivialization and inconsequential nature of the VP, Rossiter (1948) and Wilmerding (1953).
Intra-branch Rivalry	Visualizations or dialogue about negative, competitive tension between President and Vice President, or w/ associated staffers, office support staff, and by members of other branches such as the US Congress.
Portrayal of Staff Competence	Support staff lack managerial skills, effectiveness, organization, communication skills; Senior management lack core competency skills and appropriateness. Staffers use derogatory references toward peers, boss, or putdowns.
The Presidency	Routine negative references to the office or occupant of the presidency—references usually neutral or positive on this theme.
Gendered Agency	
Gendered Essentialism and/or Gendered social norms	"Female" as a category is mentally associated with having less status and authority (Hochschild 1973, 1017). Essentialism and gendered traits/gendered social norms (West and Zimmerman 1987).
Gendered Power	
Gendered Leadership	Sheeler and Anderson (2013), McDermott (2016), Kantola and Lombaro (2017).
Sex Role Conflict	Sex role conflict is defined as the classic fish-out-of-water narrative, driven by traditional notions of sex-based divisions of labor, where members of a particular sex category see that they are out of place, and the realization that if they were not there, their current troubles would not exist (West and Zimmerman 1987). (West and Zimmerman 1987), Double Binds (Jamieson 1995), and Double Entanglements (McRobbie 2004).
Political Office as a Gendered Space	References to the traditional path dependence of the executive in that historically, it is a masculine space, having been occupied only by men. (Judith Lorber 1994; see "Night to His Day.") Gendered assumptions about authority (Hochschild 1973).
Gendered Trait Based Stereotypes	
The Mother The Sex Object The Pet The Iron Maiden	Stereotypical categorization of women in professional settings: Rosabeth Moss Kanter (1977). *The mother* is sympathetic, nurturing, a counselor, a comforter, emotional, a compromiser and enforcer. *The sex object* is sexual competition, sexually desirable, potentially available, sexualized in imagery and interpretation. *The pet* portrays a token, child-like dependency, participates from the sidelines. *The iron maiden* portrays as tough, dangerous, rigid, rebellious, emotionless, and militant. Gendered stereotypes amplify trait-based scrutiny and assessment of women candidates. Gendered trait-based stereotypes: Shoaf and Parsons 2016, Alexander and Anderson 1993; Falk and Kenski 2006, Huddy and Terkildsen 1993, Kinder 1986, Sanbonmatsu 2002, Dittmar 2015.

Table 3.2. Likert Scores for Detected Themes in *Veep* Seasons 1 through 6

Uses of Satire in Portrayals of	*Season 1*	*Season 2*	*Season 3*	*Season 4*	*Season 5*	*Season 6*	*Summary Score*
Political Institution							
The Vice President as Inconsequential	1.6	1.7	2.6	2.2	2.9	2.8	2.3
Intra-branch Rivalry	2	2.2	3	2.4	2.5	2.8	2.48
Portrayal of Staff Competence	1	1.3	1.8	1.7	2.1	1.8	1.61
The Presidency	n/a	n/a	n/a	2.9	2.7	3.1	2.9
Gendered Agency							
Gendered Essentialism and/or Gendered Social Norms	2.5	2.1	2.4	2.2	2.5	1.9	2.26
Gendered Power							
Gendered Leadership	1.5	1.9	2	2.1	2.1	2.1	1.95
Sex Role Conflict	1.75	1.9	2.4	2.4	2.6	1.9	2.15
Political Office as a Gendered Space	1.5	1.6	2.2	1.9	2.5	1.8	1.91
Gendered Trait based Stereotypes							
The Mother	3	2.9	3	2.875	3	3	2.96
The Sex Object	2.625	2.7	2.4	3	2.6	2	2.55
The Pet	3	2.6	2.2	3	3	2	2.63
The Iron Maiden	1.875	2.1	1.9	2	2.1	1.9	1.97

Likert scale: 1=very unfavorable, 2=unfavorable, 3=neutral, 4=favorable, 5=very favorable
Figures reported are average scores calculated for each season

inept female characters that are included in both series (Hou et al. 2018). The main characters are profane, crass, and at times, abusive toward subordinates—which is where many jokes and punch lines get their comedic effect. In the film *In the Loop*, there are many carryover characters from *The Thick of It*, notably Malcolm Tucker (Peter Capaldi), a highly aggressive and domineering political director of communications. Iannucci tries to model Selina Meyer after Malcolm Tucker. Iannucci does not reveal political affiliations in any of his satire and the narrative setting involves many fictitious elements to avoid audience associations with any actual political offices or officeholders.

There are some subtle, yet notable, differences between these products that need to be accounted for in this analysis. As explained earlier about the framework of enlightened sexism, much of the contemporary sexist content in satire is delivered with subtlety. The attempt to tease out the subtle differences between *Veep* and Iannucci's British products are briefly catalogued here.

First, in *The Thick of It*, the setting is a fictitious political department named the Department of Social Affairs and Citizenship. In *Veep*, the setting is a real location in the vice president's office and later, the Oval Office. From the subjective position of the audience, its one thing to be prompted to laugh at the misadventures of a fictitious political department, but it may be another to do so at the misadventures of a woman in a real political office before an actual woman has held that office. Presenting Selina Meyer in the setting of the executive branch, fictional media potentially establishes a standard by which a real woman, running for that office, might be measured. This also permits audiences to judge the notion of a woman in the political office before she actually holds it. Only two women have been named as candidates for the vice presidency, and while women have run for president, only one has secured her party's nomination for the office. Fictional media, and political satire specifically, presents another potential liability with jokes that conflate the office and its occupant. The studies mentioned earlier (Hou et al. 2018 and Laflen et al. 2017) similarly catalogued this observation, and the same trend is detected in this analysis. In this, political science makes a distinction where political satire does not. Wilmerding (1953) distinguished this dichotomy decades ago: "still if the office is unimportant, the officer is not" (20).

Second, while satire in *The Thick of It* and *In the Loop* employs references to gendered physiology and genitalia, they are used as simile rather than categorization. The jokes do not rely on explicitly sexist remarks for comedic impact. For example, in *In the Loop*, Malcolm Tucker remarks that Simon Foster is "behaving like a tit" whereas in *Veep*'s season 5, an episode titled "C**tgate," language is used to make a classification of the president: "Selina Meyer is a cunt."

Third, in both *The Thick of It* and *In the Loop,* male characters are afforded opportunities to reclaim their agency whereas women characters on *Veep*, and Selina Meyer specifically, are not. Male characters push back against abuse, and punch lines are not reliant on sexist commentary for comedic effect the way jokes in *Veep* are dependent upon sexism for effect. For example, in *In the Loop*, the character Simon Foster, minister of international development, unintentionally makes a political gaffe on a radio media spot. Malcolm Tucker berates his subordinate for the mistake. Foster retorts, "I'm a cabinet minister! I didn't get here by screwing up every media appearance I ever had!" Able to reassert himself on a separate occasion as he was being castigated for "not toeing the line," Foster rebuffs Tucker's ridicule by saying, "we can do without the ritual humiliation." Iannucci seems to allow for male characters to reclaim agency and power in the critical moments of satire in ways female characters do not.

These points of comparison and subsequent analysis offer support for three claims offered here: 1) political satire masculinizes women's political power; 2) political satire reinforces "enlightened sexism"—deliberate or not, comedy can reinforce gendered stereotypes, effectively recontextualizing notions of women in power; and 3) political satire in *Veep* turns "politics-as-play" into "politics-as-punishment" by satirizing, and in some places, parodying workplace sexism.

FINDINGS AND DISCUSSION

It is correct that this series portrays the notion that a woman politician can be just as unsavory as a male politician, and in this, Iannucci forges a new path. The character is written in such a way that she embodies all the things that P. J. O'Rouke says politics is: she is ego driven, she is needy, and she is narcissistic. All these traits are situated within an office that has virtually no power, which is a device to help satirize the dysfunction of Washington. Portraying Meyer as an ineffective politician is not inherently problematic, but portraying Meyer as an ineffective politician because of her sex is problematic on the basis that she is insulted, demeaned, and objectified on account of her gender.

When television and film portray women as political leaders, especially as president or vice president, the portrayal assists the audience in visualizing a woman in that role. However, there is a certain risk with embracing a particular representation of a woman president (or vice president) that undercuts the value of a woman holding that office before an actual woman has had the opportunity to achieve it (Laflen et al. 2017).

The jokes and humor are effective only if there is a shared assumption that the women's movement has achieved its goals for gender equality. The particular brand of satire here communicates a denigration of women in politics while simultaneously trivializing discrimination and workplace sexism. The ramifications of popular representations of women in politics in this manner should be subjected to more research and scrutiny, but for now, the complicated themes in the series *Veep* are catalogued for how they reflect and reinforce elements of enlightened sexism. As the enlightened sexism framework asserts, humor can be used as an instrument to assert sexism as a means to claim sexism is nonexistent. Humor through satire and other various literary devices, including irony, are summarily observable in the series *Veep*.

Most of the themes across all six seasons were assessed as negative portrayals on the Likert scale. This assessment is reflective of the way satire was used to portray the first woman vice president and president negatively. Meyer's political leadership is portrayed in ways that run a risk of being oversimplified and summarily reduced to a stereotypical representation. The jokes and punch lines rely on gendered stereotypes and sexism for comedic effect.

The story begins in the vice president's office. Seasons 1 through 3 portray Selina Meyer as the vice president. Meyer is, of course, fictitious, yet jokes about the office's insignificance are not. Since the series exploits the office's reputation of being inconsequential, the storyline intersects, and often conflates, gender with the office, relying on humor as an instrument through which gendered binaries are reinforced.

In seasons 4 through 6, as Selina Meyer ascends to the presidency at the end of season 3, her appointed male vice president is subjected to aggressive and crass feminization as an occupant of the insignificant office, but through his efforts to push back and defend himself against insults, the scores (2.9 and 2.8) for the office increase in the later seasons.

Claim 1: Political Satire Masculinizes Women's Political Power

In this claim, humor functions as a mechanism to frame power as a masculine trait and norm. Selina Meyer is portrayed in a novel way in the executive branch. Humor frames this narrative as a woman getting in over her head in politics, creating chaos through clumsy decision making, which reinforces the negative gendered stereotypes while negating trait-based leadership qualities such as intelligence and competence.

A predominant pattern in *Veep* is a "fish out of water" narrative under the guise of comedic mishaps and frames an essential sex-role conflict (summary score of 2.15) with political power. The storyline demonstrates a traditional trope that political power is masculine and women operating within it are out of place and, therefore, even amusing to watch struggle with the pressures and responsibilities of political leadership. The reliance on crude, profanity-laced language to convey power and assertiveness is employed simultaneously to demonstrate that power is masculine.[8]

The jokes manifest with graphic references to male and female genitalia to convey power and weakness respectively. The figurative practice of ascribing male genitalia to Selina Meyer symbolically visualizes essential difference. The character appropriates something that she does not naturally possess in order to command power and respect. In this context, that there are two social groups (men and women) competing for recognition and ascribing male genital references to Selina Meyer to represent figurative, masculine power denotes a single category of power.

Below are selections sampled from episodes of notable dialogue that demonstrate this phenomenon. Jokes use explicit, figurative speech that equates political power with male genitalia. In season 1, episode 3, an exchange between the vice president and a character named Senator Andrew Doyle are trying to build a coalition of support for a clean jobs initiative:

> [scene: in front of her daughter for a contrast between political power and motherhood]
>
> Sen. Andrew Doyle: I was given your word, ma'am, that no one from oil was going to be on the task force, and now I got this Chuck bullshit.
>
> VP Selina Meyer: Andrew, this whole thing is so nuanced, and I have a ton of interests I have to square . . .
>
> Sen. Andrew Doyle: Twenty years ago you had no power, but you had balls. Now look at you.
>
> VP Selina Meyer: Yeah, now look at me. I have a dick and balls. . . . OK? [gestures to daughter] Can we not . . . have . . . this . . . ?
>
> Catherine: No, please don't stop on my account. This is really interesting.

This scene also implies that when women achieve high levels of political leadership, they must internalize masculine norms to be respected. Another exchange in season 2, in an episode titled "Hostages," demonstrates the same strategy to reinforce the masculinized notion of power:

> Mike (communications director): Ah, so ma'am, no word yet from the secretary of defense about joining him at the Marine base?
>
> VP Selina Meyer: Uh no, nothing from Maddox, but he knows I've got a bigger role in the White House now, which means I got a bigger dick, which means he can suck it. I am so happy about that. . . . How's my speech coming?

In season 4, episode 1, titled "Joint Session," the president prepares for her first official visit to Capital Hill for a special joint session of Congress to outline her policy agenda in an attempt to carve out her presidency:

> Meyer: How do I look?
>
> Gary Walsh (Meyer's body man): [prepping the president] Ah, beautiful, beautiful. Actually, let me take these glasses out [removes glasses from president's sheath dress pocket]. Looks like you have a penis . . .
>
> Meyer: What?
>
> Walsh: Which you could totally pull off if you had to.

For women to be considered serious contenders for political power and respected in the position, they must adopt and internalize the masculine norm of the office. In myriad exchanges between characters, the usage of figurative male genitalia inscribes power onto the female body to demonstrate the personal possession of power and respect.

Claim 2: Political Satire Reinforces Elements of "Enlightened Sexism"

This study is a new application of the enlightened sexism framework. Douglas examined the tenets of this framework in modern advertising and reality television shows. This is the first time it's being applied to a scripted television series. The empirical evidence suggests that elements of enlightened sexism are observable in *Veep*.

Making the vice president a woman appears outwardly feminist. However, the visualization of Selina Meyer as the chief executive is delivered in a tongue-in-cheek mockery of feminism, overtly making fun of feminism with extreme sexist jokes for comedic effect. For example, In season 2, episode 5, titled "Nicknames," the vice president is subject to critical public opinion, not unusual for a politician, but the nicknames directly engage Meyer's sex, including "Grizzly Madam," "Wicked Witch of the West Wing," "Dickless Van Dyke," "Blunder Woman," "Veep Throat," "Vaselina," and "She-Ra." Collectively, the nicknames attributed to the fictitious vice president is an example of sexist humor intended to demean the woman occupying the vice presidency. A caricature of the feminine vs. competent double bind is portrayed when Meyer's chief of staff (portrayed by Anna Chlumsky) says, "people attack you because they think you're beautiful and smart."

The sexism as it appears here functions the way Douglas explained: the jokes are extreme to defend against the charge of sexism. Portraying a woman as a bad political leader reinforces the enlightened sexism framework because it relies on sexism for comedic effect to convey feminism is silly and gender is not relevant to political office.

The element of irony is most evident since political satire primarily relies on it for its effect. The jokes in *Veep* rely on irony for their ability to elicit laughs from the audience. Across all seasons, the writers explore several complex themes that engage binary stereotypes. Whether intentional or not, the writers engage contradictory pressures that women in politics often encounter and negotiate, but the source of humor is how the character Selina Meyer makes blunders in navigating many of the double-binds.

Many episodes showcase other tenets of enlightened sexism in the form of pitting women against each other. The entire series of fifty-eight episodes are dotted with subtle deliveries and visualizations of this tenet. In season 1, episode 3, there is a subplot of a feud between the first lady and Meyer, and they engage in trading barbs throughout the entire episode through third party sources. "Is it true the first lady calls you 'Creepy Veepy'?" Or, "The first lady hates you because you're prettier." These quips are formulated to joke about stereotypes of women's jealously.

Fixation on physical appearance is also on display in season 3, episode 8, titled "Debate" when Meyer makes a drastic change to her appearance when she cuts her hair short. The quips about her hair and appearance specifically target gender and sexual identity in their punch lines. For example, Meyer's appearance with short hair is equated with lesbianism, she is referred to as "k.d. lang," and a search for friendly press is expressed as a "need [of] a friendly fashion reporter to avoid 'dyke' jokes." The summarizing comment is, "that's what you'll look like when you become a boy." This focus on the physical further compounds the sex object stereotype in that women's power is centralized in their physical appearances. These informal observations of themes that serve to reinforce negative perceptions of women, but are delivered with subtlety and couched in the premise that women are equal and secure, imply satire fixated on gendered appearance is harmless amusement.

Possibly one of the most visible tenets of enlightened sexism prevalent in *Veep* is the notion that women's power and agency is sourced through sexuality. While Selina Meyer is not overtly hyper-sexualized to convey notions of female power, her sexuality drives much of the conflict and the comedy in the series. In seasons 1, 3, 5, and 6, Meyer has a series of boyfriends, which serve to drive plot points. In season 3, episode 6, titled "Detroit," for instance, Meyer becomes involved with her personal trainer and the romantic relationship leads to her elevating her lover to an advisory role, which drives the comedy, but also by following his counsel instead of her advisors, leads to her looking incompetent. In season 6, episode 5, titled "Chicklet," Meyer's sexuality is used to objectify her. In this episode, the president's wax figure was made for display at Madame Tussaud's wax museum. Pictures surface on social medial of museum patrons simulating sexual acts with the President Meyer wax figure. Amy, her dejected staffer, quips, "Meyer is more famous for being sexually defiled than for service to the country." Satirizing Meyer's sexuality reveals the complexity of gender, politics, sexuality, and power.

Almost all *Veep* seasons that treat these themes are intricate and sociologically complex as many of these issues intersect. Using humor to deconstruct the complexity may perhaps be overly reductionist and give way to sex-role stereotypes and in many instances objectification. These examples convey the extremeness of the sexism and are offered as evidence that there is no sexism. If there is equality, there is no need for feminism. It can be mocked and attacked without any consequence.

Claim 3: Political Satire Can Turn "Politics-as-Play" into "Play-as-Punishment"

While political satire attempts to offer an entertaining combination of playful ridicule and dissent, politics-as-play can turn to play-as-punishment. In this particular section, the humor examined illustrates the focal point of humor is on the account of Selina Meyer's gender. Sexist humor here functions to demean, insult, stereotype, and objectify. This is particularly evident in select episodes in the series *Veep*. This notion is complex and needs to be unpacked. Playful humor becomes punishment when, potentially, audiences experience amusement from disparaging humor when they have negative attitudes toward the target (Woodzicka and Ford 2010). Can play-as-punishment influence attitudes toward the targets of humor in political satire?

Humor on several occasions operates as an instrument to deliver skewering ridicule of Meyer directly, and women in politics indirectly, to the point that it arguably blurs the line between humor and denigration. There are some select examples of this practice. In season 3, episode 2, titled "The Choice," Meyer campaigns for president and learns the sitting president has flipped his position on abortion. In the frenetic scene that subsequently unfurls, Meyer and her staff try to draft a public statement to reaffirm her own position when her staff encourages her to play the gender card. Meyer responds, "I can't identify myself as a woman. People can't know that. Men hate that and women who hate women hate that, which I believe is most women." This statement embodies the complexities associated with Jamieson's double binds. Carroll and Tollson-Rinehart (2001) also suggest women feel this binary pressure both to embrace their identity as a woman to advocate for women in politics, but equally pressured to neutralize their gendered identity. This statement also showcases the challenges women experience in lateral prejudices from other women. The joke relies on this lateral form of sexism for its comedic impact.

In season 4, episode 4, titled "Convention," a sub-plot involves Meyer's demoted chief of staff, Amy, who expresses her frustration toward Meyer's blunders and clumsy administration. The scene's setting is showcased as the staffer's emotional outburst directed at Selina Meyer:

> Amy [to Meyer]: You have two settings: no decision and bad decision. You are the worse thing to happen to this country since food in buckets, and . . . maybe slavery. You have achieved nothing a part from one thing, the fact that you are a woman means we will have no more women presidents, because we tried one and she fucking sucked!

This is an example of how politics-as-play likely turned into play-as-punishment of a woman president. First, the statement is indicative of actual pressures women have reported feeling on account of their sex, when they are the first one to achieve a benchmark, they experience closer scrutiny, and feel at higher risk for harsher consequences if policy goals are not achieved (Tolleson-Rinehart 2001). Second, it is possibly the only display of hostile sexism toward a woman president, and is potentially problematic because the statement demonstrates how fictional media may establish judgments of a woman president before an actual woman has held the office.

In season 6, episodes 2 and 10 are about the plans for Selina Meyer's presidential library. The satire is meant to ridicule Meyer's short administration by invoking doubt toward the purpose of a library for such a short administration, referring to it as a presidential "bookmobile." Other jokes made about the library rely on lateral sexism and portrays Meyer as perpetrating it. President Meyer is asking for recommendations for architects who are consequently all male. When staffer Richard suggests a female architect, Meyer quips, "Oh, we're not redesigning a kitchen here."

CONCLUSION

The portrayal of women and power in popular culture and fictional media often embraces traditional conceptualizations of women and power. Enlightened sexism as a framework promotes a distorted notion of female power and agency. Some post-feminist literature asserts this distortion is predicated on the notion that women have made progress as a result of feminism and now enjoy full equality. Therefore, enlightened sexism is practiced in the form of permissible amusement at traditional sexist stereotypes and sexist humor directed toward girls and women. These themes are visible throughout different vehicles of popular culture and mainstream entertainment based on the two assumptions that 1) gender equality is a reality and 2) using gender stereotypes for entertainment will not undermine women's equality. Furthermore, it is argued that popular feminism representations in popular entertainment promote women's power through the usage of their faces, bodies, attire, and sexuality to achieve and enjoy real power.

One principle concern presented by post-feminist perspectives of what it means to be a powerful woman (interpreting personal sexuality as the source of power and agency) stand to dismantle many benefits women have worked to achieve. Therefore, that is the reason for looking to popular culture as a possible informal barrier to women's political ambitions.

The principle concern realized by media studies researchers and feminist scholars is that popularized images of women in power that engender the tenets of enlightened sexism poses a possible danger to contemporary women candidates and officeholders. After reviewing the series *Veep* as a cultural artifact of fictional media, there are some pathways forward on this research. As important as it is to scrutinize cultural artifacts and catalogue the messages and images they promote, the next stage requires testing and measuring any effects on public opinion. Moving forward, experimental research methods will be useful to measure any potential effects satirical portrayals of women in politics has on audiences. Testing these themes with audiences is necessary to test the tenets of the enlightened sexism framework on the three claims advanced in this chapter.

The use of comedy in this fashion transmits the message that the only way a woman can assert power and be taken seriously is to internalize the masculine social norms of the office. Ultimately, humor and comedy successfully reinforce negative stereotypes of women in power by disarming audiences to the message that women cannot be successful public servants in the executive branch.

NOTES

1. Pew Research Center, 2008. Social and Demographic Trends Report, "Men or Women: Who's the Better Leader?" www.pewsocialtrends.org.

2. Center for American Women and Politics, "Women in Elective Office 2018" report found at www.cawp.rutgers.edu.

3. Center for American Women and Politics, "Women in Elective Office 2018" report found at www.cawp.rutgers.edu.

4. Horwitz, Tony. "The Vice Presidents History Forgot." *The Smithsonian Magazine*. 2012.

5. Carson, 1991. Delivered by Johnny Carson on the Tonight Show in a humorous monologue titled "What Democracy Means to Me."

6. www.hbo.com/veep.

7. A coding spreadsheet was created for every season. Themes in each episode were appraised and assigned a value. Assigned values were averaged into a summary score for each season reported in table 3.1. Themes were coded positively for notions conveying gender equity or showing the workplace in a positive light. Themes were coded negatively if they used derogatory words or phrases to put someone down or to denigrate an office. Themes were coded negatively if jokes used male or female genitalia to convey strength or weakness (respectively). Themes were coded negatively if comedic situations or words were used to put someone down, used sexist language to offer a punch line (something to laugh at), or put down the office someone occupied. When reviewing each episode to assess the observation of a gendered stereotype and the intensity in which it is reinforced (or challenged and/or dispelled), this researcher coded themes negatively (a score below a numerical value of 3) if they portrayed, a) the glorification of binary sex-role conflicts (see Jamieson's double-bind binaries and Kanter's framework—Mother, Pet, Sex Object or Iron Maiden) and b) the glorification of gendered incompetencies and qualifications (ways in which humor is used to degrade competence).

8. The HBO production studio relies on input from practitioners and political consultants and it is no secret that profanity can be legitimately classified as part of political and journalistic tradecraft in non-public spaces.

REFERENCES

Alexander, Deborah, and Andersen K. "Gender as a Factor in the Attribution of Leadership Traits." *Political Research Quarterly* 46, no. 3 (1993): 527–45.

Baumgartner, Jody, and Jonathan S. Morris. "Stoned Slackers or Super-Citizens? The Daily Show Viewing and Political Engagement of Young Adults." In *The Stewart/Colbert Effect: Essays on the Real Impacts of Fake News*, edited by Amarnath Amarasingam, 63–77. Jefferson, NC: McFarland, 2011.

Baym, Geoffrey. "The Daily Show: Discursive Integration and the Reinvention of Political Journalism." *Political Communication* 22, no. 3 (2005): 259–76.

———. "Representation and the Politics of Play: Stephen Colbert's Better Know a District." *Political Communication* 24, no. 4 (2007): 359–76.

Bostdorff, Denise M. "Vice Presidential Comedy and the Traditional Female Role: An Examination of the Rhetorical Characteristics of the Vice Presidency." *Western Journal of Speech Communication* 55, no. 1 (1991): 1–27.

Brians, Craig Leonard, Lars Willnat, Jarol B. Manheim, and Richard C. Rich. *Empirical Political Analysis*. New York: Longman, 2011.

Burstein, David D. "'Veep' Creator Armando Iannucci on the Real Comedy of Politics." *Fast Company*, April 20, 2012.

Bystrom, Dianne G. "Women as Political Communication Source and Audiences." In *Handbook of Political Communication Research*, edited by, Lynda Lee Kaid, 435–59. Mahwah, NJ: Lawrence Erlbaum Associates, Publishers, 2004.

Carlin, Diane B. and Kelly L. Winfrey. 2009. "Have You Come a Long Way, Baby? Hillary Clinton, Sarah Palin, and Sexism in 2008 Campaign Coverage." *Communication Studies* 60, no. 4 (2009): 326–43.

Carroll, Susan J. "Representing Women: Women State Legislators as Agents of Policy-Related Change." In *The Impact of Women in Public Office,* edited by Susan J. Carroll, 3–21. Bloomington: Indiana University Press, 2001.

———. "Reflections on Gender and Hillary Clinton's Presidential Campaign: The Good, the Bad, and the Misogynistic." *Politics & Gender* 5, no. 1 (2009): 1–20.

Colletta, Lisa. "Political Satire and Postmodern Irony in the Age of Stephen Colbert and Jon Stewart." *The Journal of Popular Culture* 42, no. 5 (2009): 856–74.

Day, Amber. *Satire and Dissent: Interventions in Contemporary Political Debate.* Bloomington: Indiana University Press, 2011.

Deaux, Kay, and Tim Emswiller. "Explanations of Successful Performance on Sex-Linked Tasks: What Is Skill for the Male Is Luck for the Female." *Journal of Personality and Social Psychology* 29, no. 1 (1974): 80.

Dittmar, Kelly. *Navigating Gendered Terrain: Stereotypes and Strategy in Political Campaigns*. Philadelphia, PA: Temple University Press, 2015.

Dodson, Debra L. "Acting for Women: Is What Legislators Say, What They Do?" In *The Impact of Women in Public Office*, edited by Susan J. Carroll, 225–42. Bloomington: Indiana University Press, 2001.

Dolan, Kathleen A., and Thomas M. Holbrook. "Knowing Versus Caring: The Role of Affect and Cognition in Political Perceptions." *Political Psychology* 22, no. 1 (2001): 27–44.

———. "Gender Stereotypes, Candidate Evaluations, and Voting for Women Candidates: What Really Matters?" *Political Research Quarterly* 67, no. 1 (2014): 96–107.

Douglas, Susan J. *Enlightened Sexism: The Seductive Message that Feminsm's Work is Done.* New York: Times Books-Henry Holt and Company, 2010.

Elder, Laural. "Why Women Don't Run: Explaining Women's Underrepresentation in America's Political Institutions." *Women & Politics* 26, no. 2 (2004): 27–56.

Faina, Joseph. "Public Journalism Is a Joke: The Case for Jon Stewart and Stephen Colbert." *Journalism* 14, no. 4 (2013): 541–55.

Falk, Erika, and Kate Kenski. "Issue Saliency and Gender Stereotypes: Support for Women as Presidents in Times of War and Terrorism." *Social Science Quarterly* 87, no. 1 (2006): 1–18.

———. *Women for President: Media Bias in Nine Campaigns.* Champaign: University of Illinois Press, 2008.

Fox, Richard L., and Jennifer L. Lawless. "Gendered Perceptions and Political Candidacies: A Central Barrier to Women's Equality in Electoral Politics." *American Journal of Political Science* 55, no. 1 (2011): 59–73.

Gill, Rosalind. *Gender and the Media.* Malden, MA: Polity Press, 2007.

Hall, Elaine J., and Marnie Salupo Rodriguez. "The Myth of Postfeminism." *Gender & Society* 17, no. 6 (2003): 878–902.

Han, Lori Cox. *Women and US Politics: The Spectrum of Political Leadership.* Boulder, CO: Lynne Rienner Publisher, 2010.

Han, Lori Cox, and Caroline Heldman, eds. *Rethinking Madam President: Are We Ready for a Woman in the White House?* Boulder, CO: Lynne Rienner Publishers, 2007.

Hochschild, Arlie. "A Review of Sex Role Research." *American Journal of Sociology* 78, no. 4 (1973): 1011–29.

Hou, Carrie, Nathan Stewart, and Elena Chabbi. "The Personal and Political: Exploring Comedic Masculinity and Femininity in *Veep*." In HBO's *Original Voices*, 85–98. Routledge, 2018.

Huddy, Leonic, and Nayda Terkildsen. "Gender Stereotypes and the Perception of Male and Female Candidates." *American Journal of Political Science* 37, no. 1 (1993): 119–47.

Jamieson, Kathleen Hall. *Beyond the Double Bind: Women and Leadership*. New York: Oxford University Press, 1995.

Johnson, Ann. "The Subtleties of Blatant Sexism." *Communication and Critical/Cultural Studies* 4, no. 2 (2007): 166–83.

Jones, Jeffrey P. *Entertaining Politics: New Political Television and Civic Culture*. New York: Rowman & Littlefield, 2005.

Kanter, Rosabeth Moss. *Men and Women of the Corporation*. New York: New York Press, 1977.

Kantola, Johanna, and Emanuela Lombardo. *Gender and Political Analysis*. New York: MacMillan International Higher Education, 2017.

Kinder, Donald R. "Presidential Character Revisited." In *Political Cognition*, edited by Richard R. Lau and David O. Sears. Hillsdale, NJ: Erlbaum, 1986.

Klonis, Suzanne C., Ashby Plant, and Patricia G. Devine. "Internal and External Motivation to Respond without Sexism." *Personality and Social Psychology Bulletin* 31, no. 9 (2005): 1237–49.

Laflen, Angela, Michelle Smith, Kristin Bayer, Rianna Ramirez, Jessica Recce, and Molly Scott. "Add Women and Stir: Female Presidents in Pop Culture, 2012–2016." *The Seneca Falls Dialogues Journal* 2, no. 1 (2017): 47–72.

Lawless, Jennifer. "Sexism and Gender Bias in Election 2008: A More Complex Path for Women in Politics." *Politics & Gender* 5, no. 1 (2009): 70–80.

Lawrence, Regina G., and Melody Rose. *Hillary Clinton's Race for the White House: Gender Politics and the Media on the Campaign Trail*. Boulder, CO: Rienner, 2010.

Lorber, Judith. "Night to His Day: The Social Construction of Gender." In *Race, Class, and Gender in the United States*, sixth edition, edited by Paula S. Rothenberg, 54–64. New York: Worth Publishers, 2004.

McDermott, Monika L. "Race and Gender Cues in Low-Information Elections." *Political Research Quarterly* 51, no. 4 (1998): 895–918.

———. *Masculinity, Femininity, and American Political Behavior*. New York: Oxford University Press, 2016.

McRobbie, Angela. "Post-Feminism and Popular Culture." *Feminist Media Studies* 4, no. 3 (2004): 255–64.

Niven, David, and Jeremy Zilber. "How Does She Have Time for Kids and Congress? Views on Gender and Media Coverage." *Women and Congress*. New York: The Hawthorn Press, 2001.

O'Rourke, P. J. *The History of Comedy*. Episode 7,"Politics Aside." CNN, aired August 13, 2017.

Panagopoulos, Costas. "Boy Talk/Girl Talk: Gender Differences in Campaign Communications Strategies." *Women & Politics* 26, no. 3–4 (2004): 131–54.

Peifer, Jason T. "Palin, Saturday Night Live, and Framing: Examining the Dynamics of Political Parody." *The Communication Review* 16, no. 3 (2013): 155–77.

Rossiter, Clinton L. 1948. "The Reform of the Vice-Presidency." *Political Science Quarterly* 63, no. 3 (1948): 383–403.

Sanbonmatsu, Kira. "Gender Stereotypes and Vote Choice." *American Journal of Political Science* (2002): 20–34.

Sanbonmatsu, Kira, and Kathleen Dolan. "Do Gender Stereotypes Transcend Party?" *Political Research Quarterly* 62, no. 3 (2009): 485–94.

Sanchez, Leslie. *You've Come a Long Way, Maybe: Sarah, Michelle, Hillary, and the Shaping of the New American Woman*. New York: Macmillan, 2009.

Scheckels, Theodore F., Nichola D. Gutgold, and Diana B. Carlin. *Gender and the American Presidency: Nice Presidential Woman and the Barriers They Faced.* Lanham, MD: Lexington Books, 2012.

Sheeler, Kristina Horn, and Karrin Vasby Anderson. *Woman President: Confronting Postfeminist Political Culture.* College Station: Texas A&M University Press, 2013.

Shoaf, Nicole R. Foster, and Tara N. Parsons. "18 Million Cracks, but No Cigar: News Media and the Campaigns of Clinton, Palin, and Bachmann." *Social Sciences* 5, no. 3 (2016): 50.

Thomas, Susan, and Susan Welch, "The Impact of Women in State Legislatures: Numerical and Organizational Strength." In *The Impact of Women in Public Office*, edited by Susan J. Carroll, 166–83. Bloomington: Indiana University Press, 2001.

Tolleson-Rinehart, Sue. "Do Women Leaders Make a Difference? Substance, Style and Perceptions." In *The Impact of Women in Public Office*, edited by Susan J. Carroll, 149–65. Bloomington: Indiana University Press, 2001.

Weaver, David, Maxwell McCombs, and Donald L. Shaw. "Agenda-Setting Research: Issues, Attributes, and Influences." In *Handbook of Political Communication Research*, edited by Lynda Lee Kaid, 257–82. Mahwah, NJ: Lawrence Erlbaum Associates, 2004.

West, Candace and Don Zimmerman. "Doing Gender." *Gender and Society* 1, no. 2 (1987): 125–51.

Wilmerding, Lucius Jr. "The Vice Presidency." *Political Science Quarterly* 68, no. 1 (1953): 17–41.

Witt, Linda, Karen M. Paget, and Glenna Matthews. *Running as a Woman: Gender and Power in American Politics*. New York: Simon & Schuster, 1995.

Woodzicka, Julie A., and Ford, T. E. "A Framework for Thinking about the (Not-So-Funny) Effects of Sexist Humor." *Europe's Journal of Psychology* 6, no. 3 (2010): 174–95.

Chapter 4

If "This is What a Feminist Looks Like," I Don't Like It

Kellee J. Kirkpatrick and
James W. Stoutenborough

From the cover of *Ms. Magazine* featuring President Obama ripping open his shirt to reveal the words "this is what a feminist looks like" in 2009 to Beyoncé's VMA performance featuring the word "FEMINIST" emblazoned on the backdrop in 2014, politicians and celebrities alike have been embracing the title of feminist. Sometimes referred to as the "f-word," the term feminism in recent years has become stigmatized and polarizing. Given the efforts of these politicians, celebrities, and activists to reclaim this word, it is important to understand whether these efforts have been successful and what impact their efforts have had on the public's perception of the feminist movement. Scholars of the Narrative Policy Framework (NPF) have demonstrated that the narrator of a movement's message can have a significant influence on how the public embraces or rejects the message. The NPF has yet to examine an issue where myriad narrators exist, making it virtually impossible to identify a single narrator, like the feminist message. Consequently, individuals must identify their own narrator, or, in other words, must decide who represents the feminist message to them. The goal of this chapter is to understand how these personal narrators impact individual perceptions of feminism. Using a national survey of 1,600 adults, we explore how these ambassadors of feminism are shaping public opinion toward feminism. The results of the analysis suggest that whom a person associates with feminism, whether it be a politician, celebrity, or activist, can directly influence their favorability toward the feminist movement.

IS FEMINISM A DIRTY WORD?

The word feminism, defined as "the theory of the political, economic, and social equality of the sexes," has long been a polarizing term (Merriam-Webster n.d.). A simple internet search for the word reveals that feminists have been, and still continue to be, described as "ugly, uptight, angry, aggressive, harsh, strident, demanding, dogmatic, man-hating lesbians" (Wade 2015, para. 2; Liss, Hoffner, and Crawford 2000). Perhaps the most famous negative description came from television evangelist Pat Robertson, who said, "the feminist agenda is not about equal rights for women. It is about a socialist, anti-family political movement that encourages women to leave their husbands, kill their children, practice witchcraft, destroy capitalism, and become lesbians" (quoted in Bentz 2013, para. 15). Given the negative connotations and media portrayals, it is no wonder that many refer to it as the other "f-word" (Beck 1998; Douglas 1994).

Despite the negativity surrounding the word "feminism," public opinion polls have found that since the 1980s, approximately 30 to 40 percent of women identify as feminists (Aronson 2003; Ferree and Hess 1995). From the 1980s on, the number of individuals identifying with the term feminism waxed and waned, but mostly waned from the highs of the 1960s. On June 29, 1998, *Time* magazine's bleak cover featuring photos of Susan B. Anthony, Betty Friedan, Gloria Steinem, and television character Ally McBeal asked in bold red, "Is Feminism Dead?" (*Time* 1998). Many blamed the younger generation who basked in the accomplishments fought for and won by first and second wave feminists (Aronson 2003). Scholars also started seeing similar trends among young women, particularly that they were more likely to be depoliticized, more likely to seek individual solutions rather than group solutions, and much less likely to identify as feminist (Aronson 2003; Henderson-King and Stewart 1994; Rapp 1988; Zucker 2004). Despite these findings, polls showed that despite a rejection of the term "feminist," the public had steady and often growing support for feminist ideas such as equality in pay, hiring, and politics. These seemingly conflicting opinions are often attributed to the negative stigma around the word "feminist." In fact, when "feminism" was replaced by "women's movement," scholars found increased support for many typically feminist ideals (Burn, Aboud, and Moyles 2000; Buschman and Lenart 1996; Zucker 2004). This societal stigma is frequently attributed to media framing of feminism, especially during the 1970s (Beck 1998; Wade 2015).

Some began to wonder if feminism needed a "rebranding." Starting in 2003, college feminist groups across the United States began campaigns to try to change the face of feminism, encouraging young feminists to wear t-shirts with the slogan, "this is what a feminist looks like." The t-shirts, made and distributed by the Feminist Majority Foundation, were sold to organizations on more than eighty campuses (Seligson 2006). The campaign became so popular that in 2009, *Ms. Magazine* featured on its cover the newly elected

President Barack Obama ripping back his suit and tie in superhero fashion to reveal a "this is what a feminist looks like" t-shirt underneath (Smeal 2009). President Obama has continued to be a strong supporter of feminism, and during a 2016 White House summit on women he told the crowd, "I may be a little grayer than I was eight years ago, but this is what a feminist looks like" (Carmon 2016).

President Obama is not the only public figure to support feminism. Politicians and celebrities alike have come forward to voice their support. In 2014, the magazine *Elle*, in partnership with the Fawcett Society, revived the "this is what a feminist looks like" campaign, devoting its entire December 2014 issue to the topic of feminism (Buccellato 2014). The issue gave a platform to a variety of celebrities who spoke out in support of feminism including Mark Ruffalo, Kristen Stewart, Beyoncé, Jennifer Lawrence, Lena Dunham, Emma Watson, Miley Cyrus, Zooey Deschanel, Ellen Page, Taylor Swift, and more (Team *Elle* 2015). Feminism has seen even more support on the high fashion runways, with Maria Grazia Chiuri, designing for Dior, sending t-shirts down the runway with slogans such as "We Should All Be Feminists," and "Why Have There Been No Great Women Artists?" (Ledbetter 2017). These shirts' reach has been widespread, being sported by celebrities such as Jennifer Lawrence and Rihanna.

It is hard to determine how much impact these efforts have made on public perceptions, but recent public polls do show a slight uptick in those claiming the feminist identity. Indeed, a 2016 poll by the *Washington Post* and Kaiser Family Foundation found that 60 percent of women and 33 percent of men identified as either a feminist or a strong feminist (Cai and Clement 2016). There are likely a variety of explanations for this increase, but it seems clear that celebrities are continuing to act as spokespeople for the movement.

CELEBRITY POLITICS

As this volume clearly illustrates, celebrities have a long history of becoming involved in politics in myriad fashions. Perhaps one of the most common actions performed by celebrities is to bring our attention to issues that are of importance to them (see Harvey 2018; West and Orman 2003). They use their celebrity status to inform us of issues that they believe we should know about, and hope that we will follow their lead because of their status. Indeed, Harvey (2017) clearly demonstrates that celebrities have the power to persuade people.

The potential influence of individual celebrities is not debated. Instead, we seek to better understand exactly how and why celebrities have an influence.

Perhaps more importantly, what kind of an influence do celebrities have when the spotlight is not on them or their issue of choice? Equally important, how much influence do they have in an issue area where they are one of many potential persuaders?

However, before we are able to examine these questions, it is important to define who, or what, is a celebrity. Obviously, most would agree that a television star or movie star counts as a celebrity. However, the Merriam-Webster Dictionary defines a celebrity as "the state of being celebrated" and as "a famous or celebrated person" (*Merriam-Webster* n.d.). The etymology of celebrity comes from the Latin word *celibritatem*, which meant "multitude, fame," and *celeber*, which meant "condition of being famous" (Harper n.d.). These definitions of celebrity suggest that there is much more to being a celebrity than being a thespian or an athlete.

We adopt a definition of celebrity outlined by Sam G. Riley, editor of *Star Struck: An Encyclopedia of Celebrity Culture*. In this book, Riley (2010, xiii) defines a celebrity as "a famous person who receives heavy media attention, who is popular due to personal qualities that go beyond actual accomplishments, and whose identity is suitable for some degree of merchandising." As this definition suggests, any number of individuals could be considered as celebrities, including politicians who often receive heavy media attention. West and Orman (2003) clearly make the case that politicians have moved into the realm of celebrity. They write,

> In the 1990s, the now-defunct magazine *George*, started by the late John F. Kennedy Jr., demonstrated how all politics had become entertainment and how pop culture had become political. In this era of politics *as* entertainment and entertainment *as* politics, what has become of the political process, and what has become of pop culture? In a time when the deaths of Princess Diana and John F. Kennedy, Jr. are covered around the globe, the distinction between public life and pop culture has virtually disappeared. Celebrities run for political office (or lobby those who do), and operatives such as George Stephanopoulos, Geraldine Ferraro, Oliver North, and Jesse Ventura become celebrated figures. With popular culture merging with the political system, the press has moved toward a style of reporting that emphasizes Hollywood-style gossip and scandal, to the detriment of traditional politicians and political parties. (2003, x)

It should be clear to any observer of politics that politicians have become modern celebrities, even if they do not intend to do so. In fact, one of our own former students, Kelly Cosby, helped to turn Supreme Court Justice Ruth Bader Ginsburg into a pop culture icon when she dubbed her the "Notorious RBG" in a rap parody of the Notorious B.I.G. (Ross 2015). Since that time, the Notorious RBG has participated in comedy skits with Stephen Colbert on *The Late Show* and is the subject of children's books (e.g., Levy 2016). The tabloids, which have historically focused on entertainment celebrities, now pay nearly as much attention to politicians as they do the latest actor being caught with the nanny. Coverage of Michelle Obama, Hillary Clinton, or Sarah Palin was everywhere when they were politically relevant. As West and Orman cynically state, "Politics *is* pop culture" (2003, x).

While few politicians would openly admit it, many go out of their way to be celebrities. This process was arguably put into hyper-drive the moment Bill Clinton appeared on *The Arsenio Hall Show* in 1992, playing "Heartbreak Hotel" on his saxophone with sunglasses and sitting for an interview that lasted more than thirty minutes, while he was running for president. At the time, Clinton had just secured the Democratic nomination, but he was still a relatively unknown entity outside of Arkansas, challenging a sitting president, George H. W. Bush. Many still credit this appearance as truly establishing him with a national audience and changing the way politicians engage with the public (Braswell 2016).

Further illustrating the blurring of the worlds of politics and entertainment, there were six different politicians who once appeared in a single episode of *Parks and Recreation* as themselves—Senators Barbara Boxer, Kirsten Gillibrand, Cory Booker, Orrin Hatch, John McCain, and former secretary of state Madeleine Albright. Additionally, former vice president Joe Biden and former first lady Michelle Obama appeared in other episodes of this comedy series (Chittal 2015). Learning from President Clinton, former Speaker of the House Newt Gingrich played himself on *Murphy Brown* in 1996, while presidential hopeful and former governor of New Jersey, Chris Christie, appeared on the *Michael J. Fox Show* in 2013 (Sollosi 2016). Additionally, many politicians have portrayed themselves in movies. For example, in the 2000 film *Traffic*, Senators Harry Reid, Barbara Boxer, Orrin Hatch, Charles "Chuck" Grassley, and Don Nickles filmed a scene that turned out to be improvised (McCarthy 2000). Indeed, it has become a time-honored tradition for well-known and ambitious politicians to appear on television shows and in movies as a way to reach a broader audience.

With this in mind, it is clear the lines between politician and celebrity have blurred to the point where it can arguably be difficult to distinguish the two. Both traditional entertainment-based celebrities and politicians are subjected to the same tabloid attention. Members of both groups are regularly surrounded by autograph seekers and adoring fans. There is a difference in attention given to members of both groups based upon one's relative status within each group. For instance, stars of a hit television show will get substantially more coverage than those who were on a show that was cancelled five years earlier and cannot find anything more than a guest role on another show. Similarly, politicians who hold positions of power (committee chairs, cabinet positions, leadership roles, etc.) receive substantially more attention than first-term politicians or those who were voted out of office. Because of these similarities, we argue that politicians can also be considered celebrities.

FEMINIST NARRATORS AND THE NARRATIVE POLICY FRAMEWORK

The Narrative Policy Framework (NPF) is a fairly recent theoretical approach to understanding the policy process. It explains how issues get on the political agenda, how certain policy solutions rise and fall in public support, and how decision makers choose which policy solutions to adopt. The primary contention of the NPF is that narrative, or the stories we tell, are integral to building public attention and support for policy solutions, which can lead to policy adoption (McBeth et al. 2014). In fact, scholars have found that narratives are more powerful and persuasive than facts and statistics (Shanahan, McBeth, and Hathaway 2011). As scholars of the NPF note, narrative is how individuals make sense of the world and, ultimately, renders human existence meaningful (Polkinghorne 1988).

The NPF emphasizes the role that plots, settings, characters, and morals (policy preferences) play in influencing public attitudes toward a given issue. While each of these is important, research suggests that all four parts of a traditional narrative are not necessary for a policy narrative. Indeed, Shanahan and colleagues (2013) argue that all that is necessary is for a policy narrative to have at least one character and some reference to a policy preference. This suggests that many aspects of a narrative can be implicit. For example, if there is a policy controversy concerning a local river, a policy narrative regarding the river may not actually need to explicitly name the river for it to resonate with the public, as the public implicitly understands that the narrative is about that troubled river. In situations like this, the setting may be implicit, and not explicitly stated.

This flexibility becomes important when examining real-world narratives. Kirkpatrick (2017) argues that public narratives can develop over time within societies, even when there is not a concerted effort by decision makers or policy entrepreneurs to pursue a particular policy goal. Using narratives of infertility, Kirkpatrick illustrates that these public narratives form through a variety of mechanisms and often rely on implicit references to the core narrative components. For instance, while the narrative that motherhood is implicitly tied to femininity is well known and internalized by many, there is not necessarily one narrator that this narrative can be attributed to. Rather, individuals may attribute this narrative to personal or popular sources such as family and friends or figures in popular media. As this example demonstrates, an individual has the ability to pick their preferred narrative and narrator. We argue that the same is true for feminist narratives.

As discussed above, there are several feminist narratives that have evolved over time. Some narratives portray feminism in a negative light, casting feminists as man-hating and seeking social and political domination over men. Other, more positive, narratives portray feminism simply as a movement to achieve equal treatment for men and women. As Taylor Swift told *Elle* magazine, "So many girls out there say 'I'm not a feminist' because they think it means something angry or disgruntled or complaining or they picture, like, rioting and picketing. It is not that at all. It just simply means that you believe that women and men should have equal rights and opportunities" (Team *Elle* 2015, 10).

With this context in mind, the NPF outlines several hypotheses relating to the way narratives influence individual behavior (see, e.g., McBeth et al. 2014, 234). Of particular interest to this project is the hypothesis regarding narrator trust. It argues that, "[a]s narrator trust increases, an individual is more likely to be persuaded by the narrative" (Jones and McBeth 2010, 344).

This is where celebrity politics, feminism, and the NPF converge. Since, as Kirkpatrick (2017) argues, public narratives can develop over time to which no particular narrator can be credited, an individual can pick and choose whom they perceive as the narrator of their preferred narrative among any number of possible narrators who have made arguments related to that public narrative. If an individual associates feminism and feminist narratives with a specific person (or narrator), be it a celebrity, politician, activist, or someone the individual is personally familiar with, the NPF tells us that if the individual trusts this person (or narrator), they are more likely to be influenced by the narrative.

The NPF recognizes that there are often competing narratives for any given issue. Thus, a primary focus of the framework is to understand narrative uptake, or, in other words, identify what characteristics are more likely to make a narrative persuasive to an individual. For instance, the micro-level NPF hypotheses contend that having more exposure to a narrative (narrative breach), seeing oneself in a narrative (narrative transportation), having similar/dissimilar perspectives as portrayed in the narrative (narrative congruence/incongruence), connecting to strong characters (power of characters), and having trust in the narrator (narrator trust) are all predictors of a narrative being persuasive at the individual level. As a whole, these hypotheses seem to assume that individuals primarily react to carefully constructed narratives with these components. However, as previously mentioned, there are a variety of public narratives that exist that do not necessarily have all the narrative components neatly aligned, meaning that individuals assign their own narrators to a narrative. The NPF, as is, does not explicitly address what might happen if an individual assigns a narrator that they distrust and perhaps even dislike. Given the incredible number of politicians and celebrities that have made public comment about feminism, and the variety of competing narratives about feminism, there are many public and private figures that individuals could identify as *their* narrator of feminism.

Consequently, we would anticipate that those who are predisposed to agreeing with feminist narratives will identify narrators who reinforce these positions. Meanwhile, those predisposed to disagreeing with feminist narratives will either be unable to identify a narrator, or they will be more likely to identify an individual with whom they most disagree in order to rationalize not accepting the moral of the narrative. It is an open question within the literature as to which of these are likely to happen. This also opens the door to the possibility that those opposed to the feminist narrative would strategically identify narrators with whom they disagree, which would likely result in these identified narrators cancelling themselves out. In other words, if, say, one hundred people identify a celebrity as their preferred narrator, but fifty of these identified narrators with whom they disagreed, we would expect to see the influence of celebrity narrators cancel each other out when it comes to accepting the moral of the narrative.

ANALYTICAL APPROACH

The above discussions raise several pertinent questions. First, whom does the public envision when thinking of a representative of the feminist movement? Second, are celebrities commonly identified as representing the movement? Third, can these representatives be categorized into meaningful groupings? Fourth, what predicts the likelihood of an individual identifying a certain type of representative? Fifth, does the public perceive a difference between the narratives associated with the feminist movement and the women's movement? Finally, does the envisioned narrator (the representative of the feminist movement) influence an individual's perception of the feminist movement or the women's movement?

To answer these questions, we utilize a *Washington Post*/Kaiser Family Foundation poll, the Post-Kaiser Feminism Survey, conducted from May 21 to June 17, 2015. The survey sampled adults ages eighteen and older in the United States, and it was administered via telephone, both landline and cellular. A total of 1,610 adults were surveyed, including an oversample of 495 women.[1]

To answer the above questions, three questions from the survey will be examined in greater detail to understand what predicts these views. The first of these directly identifies who an individual might associate with feminism. Specifically, respondents, or those who participated in the survey, were asked, "Can you think of anyone in the US society today who represents feminism, or no?" This was an open-ended question, allowing the respondent to provide any answer that came to them.[2] Given the history of feminism and the fact that there is no single voice for feminist issues, we operate under the presumption that the identified representatives are the narrators for these respondents. In other words, these are the people these respondents likely picture when feminism is brought up, as these were the people they thought of when asked.

In total, respondents identified twenty-five different women or groups of women who represent feminism today. From this list, which will be presented below, we categorized the reported representatives into five categories—celebrities, politicians, activists, "others," and those who reported that they did not know any modern representatives of feminism.[3] Each of these categories are coded 1 if the identified representative belongs to that category and 0 if the representative does not belong. This coding allows us to interpret any potential predictor as increasing the likelihood of identifying a representative from the group being examined (i.e., celebrity, politician, activist, etc.) This survey question will allow us to answer our first four questions.

The remaining two research questions will be examined using two additional survey questions. Our fifth research question sought to determine if there was a difference between public attitudes toward the women's movement and feminism. This is measured using an experimental treatment within the survey. This treatment randomly assigned half of the respondents to receive questions using the term "feminism." The other half of the respondents were assigned the phrase "women's movement." An analysis of the randomization process suggests that there were no concerns over the random sorting of respondents into one group or another creating a bias in the results. Specifically, the "feminism" group was asked, "In general, do you have a favorable or unfavorable impression of feminism?" The "women's movement" group was asked, "In general, do you have a favorable or unfavorable impression of the women's movement?" Respondents in both groups were given the alternatives of "favorable," which we code as 1, and "unfavorable," which was coded as 0. This coding allows us to interpret any potential predictor as increasing the likelihood of viewing either feminism or the women's movement as favorable.

In our analyses of research questions four (predictors of identifying a representative in a specific category) and six (determining if identifying a representative in one of these categories predicts favorability toward feminism or the women's movement), we estimate probit regressions.[4]

To answer research questions four and six, we needed to identify several potential predictors from the survey. It is important to control for the influence of attitudes that specifically relate to feminism, as these attitudes should directly influence both the identification of a representative and an individual's favorability toward feminism or the women's movement. The survey asked several questions related to feminism of all of the respondents, regardless of which treatment they received. Specifically, we examine the influence of five feminism attitudes. The inclusion of these attitudes allows for a tougher test of the relationship between an individual's identified representative and their favorability toward feminism and the women's movement (question six).

The first question assesses an individual's familiarity with feminism, asking respondents, "How much have you heard about feminism or the feminist movement in the past year?" It was coded from 0, representing "nothing at all," to 3, representing "a lot." This coding allows us to interpret the results in terms of increasing familiarity. We anticipate that those who are more familiar with feminism will have more developed views on the issue. In particular, we suspect those with greater familiarity will be able to identify someone who represents the feminist movement.

The second question addresses whether an individual would self-identify as a feminist.[5] It asks, "Do you consider yourself to be a strong feminist, a feminist, not a feminist or an anti-feminist?" Responses were coded from 0, representing "anti-feminist," to 3, representing "strong feminist." This coding allows us to interpret the results of our analyses in terms of increasing association with feminism. Those who identify as a feminist should be more likely to perceive the movement favorably and identify representatives of the movement.

The third feminist attitude assesses whether an individual believes women and men should receive equal pay. Specifically, respondents were asked, "When it comes to improving women's lives should each of the following be a top priority, important but not a top priority or not too important. First, should equal pay for equal work be a top priority, important but not a top priority, or not too important?" This question assesses the importance of a traditional position of feminism. It is coded from 0, representing "not too important," to 2, representing "a top priority." This coding allows us to interpret the results of our analyses in terms of increasing priority. Those who believe equal pay should be a priority should be more likely to view the movement as favorable and identify representatives of the movement.

The fourth feminist attitude addresses whether the focus of the current movement represents an individual's goals. Specifically, respondents were asked, "Do you think the feminist movement today is focused on changes you want, or not?" This question was coded such that those who said "yes, does" received a 1 and those who said "no, does not" received a 0. This coding allows us to interpret the results in terms of those who believe the movement is focused on the right things. Obviously, this would suggest that an individual who believes the movement is focused on the right things should be more likely to look favorably on the movement.

The final attitude toward feminism assesses if an individual believes the movement represents the views of all women. This question allows us to determine if an individual is able to properly identify the fact that women are not universally in favor or supportive of the feminist movement. Specifically, respondents were asked, "Which of the following statements about the feminist movement do you think are true and which are not true? The feminist movement accurately reflects the views of most women. Is this true or not true?" This question was coded such that those who responded "true" received a 1 and those who said "not true" received a 0. This coding allows us to interpret the results in terms of those who believe this statement to be true. We suspect that those who believe the movement represents all women will be more likely to view the movement favorably. These individuals should also be more likely to identify a representative of the movement.

Finally, analyses of public attitudes regularly identify demographic differences as being important predictors of an individual's attitudes. Specifically, we control for the influence of political ideology (1 = liberal to 3 = conservative), party identification (1 = strong Democrat to 5 = strong Republican), race, years of education, marital status, religious attendance (frequency of attendance), income, gender, and age. Consistent with previous studies (e.g., Bromley-Trujillo et al. 2015; Stoutenborough et al. 2014) and as a recognition of the number of models analyzed, we adopt a general expectation for each of these demographics. We anticipate that demographic differences will influence individual attitudes toward the feminist movement and the ability of an individual to identify a representative of the movement.

RESULTS

The analyses of our research questions will be divided into two parts. First, we will focus on research questions one through four, which all concern the identification of a representative of feminism. Second, we will examine responses to the evaluations of feminism or the women's movement.

Identifying a Representative of Feminism

Our first research question concerned who the public identifies with modern feminism. The results of the survey question are presented in table 4.1. As noted above, respondents were able to identify twenty-five individuals or groups of individuals they believe to represent feminism today. The most commonly identified individual was Hillary Clinton, with 344 respondents identifying her as a modern representative. The second most identified representative was feminist icon Gloria Steinem with sixty-two. Meanwhile, 885 respondents were unable to identify any representative of modern feminism.

Our second research question asked if the public would identify celebrities as representatives of feminism. Given the platform that many celebrities have begun using to argue for feminist positions, these individuals are some of the most covered advocates for feminism. Interestingly, we found that eighty respondents identified a celebrity. While not an overwhelming number of identifications, eleven different celebrities were identified, reflecting the diversity of celebrities advocating for women's rights. Among the celebrities identified, Oprah Winfrey was the most frequently named with fifteen. She was followed by Emma Watson with thirteen and Angelina Jolie, Beyoncé, and Ellen DeGeneres, who each had nine identifications.

By now, it is clear that our third research question has already been answered. Specifically, we wanted to know if we could classify identified representatives into categories.[6] We were easily able to create categories for celebrities, politicians, and activists. In total, 586 recognizable individuals were identified who belong to one of these groups. In other words, for those who can identify a specific representative of the feminist movement, 80.9 percent of them can be categorized into one of these three categories. It is worth noting that of the 586 recognizable individuals, politicians were the most likely to be identified.

We now turn our attention to the examination of research question four. This question concerned identifying the characteristics that predict the likelihood of an individual identifying a representative of feminism from one of these categories. This is an important step in understanding the nature of the role that these representatives will play as narrators of feminism and/or the women's movement.

The results of analyses are presented in table 4.2.[7] We focus on four of the five categories identified above. Specifically, we examine the predictors of identifying a celebrity, politician, activist, or being unable to identify anyone at all. We focus on these four because we will examine the influence an individual's identified representative has on their views of feminism and the women's movement below.[8]

Table 4.1. Respondent Responses to Who Represents Modern Feminism

Celebrity	*Politician*	*Activist*	*Others*	*Do Not Know*
Amy Poehler (4)	Condoleezza Rice (10)	Gloria Steinem (62)	Family Members/Friends (18)	No, No one (793)
Amy Schumer (4)	Elizabeth Warren (31)	Sheryl Sandberg (5)	Me/Myself (4)	Don't Know (92)
Angelina Jolie (9)	Hillary Clinton (344)	National Organizations (10)	Other (106)	
Beyoncé (9)	Michelle Obama (39)			
Ellen DeGeneres (9)	Nancy Pelosi (3)			
Emma Watson (13)	Ruth Bader Ginsburg (2)			
Jane Fonda (5)	Sarah Palin (9)			
Lena Dunham (3)	Sonia Sotomayor (1)			
Oprah Winfrey (15)				
Rachel Maddow (5)				
Taylor Swift (4)				
Total: 80	Total: 439	Total: 77	Total: 128	Total: 885
Overall Percent: 4.97%	Percent: 27.28%	Percent: 4.78%	Percent: 7.95%	Percent: 55.00%

Table 4.2. Determinants of Identifying a Celebrity, Politician, Activist, or Nobody as a Representative of Modern Feminism

	Celebrity		*Politician*		*Activist*		*Do Not Know*	
	Coefficient	*Prob.*	*Coefficient*	*Prob.*	*Coefficient*	*Prob.*	*Coefficient*	*Prob.*
Feminism Attitudes								
Familiar with Feminism	.307 (.121)	.011	.078 (.067)	.245	.111 (.165)	.498	–.257 (.048)	.000
Self-Identified Feminist	–.166 (.165)	.316	.255 (.086)	.003	–.100 (.192)	.602	–.159 (.073)	.030
Men and Women Equal Pay	–.106 (.741)	.885	–.612 (.268)	.022	–.626 (.523)	.231	.371 (.230)	.108
Feminism Focus	.170 (.291)	.557	.016 (.135)	.901	–.034 (.314)	.913	–.049 (.115)	.667
Represents the Views of All Women	.081 (.271)	.763	.226 (.128)	.078	.430 (.299)	.150	–.236 (.106)	.027
Demographics								
Political Ideology	–.111 (.159)	.486	–.056 (.093)	.546	–.352 (.201)	.080	.121 (.073)	.098
Party ID	–.075 (.093)	.417	–.064 (.046)	.179	.123 (.088)	.163	.038 (.038)	.312
White	.180 (.277)	.514	–.017 (.133)	.897	.399 (.403)	.323	–.148 (.111)	.184
Years of Education	.050 (.058)	.383	.096 (.029)	.001	.078 (.076)	.300	–.122 (.026)	.000
Married	–.186 (.287)	.516	–.157 (.130)	.226	.075 (.288)	.793	.136 (.107)	.205
Religious Attendance	–.010 (.007)	.166	.006 (.002)	.017	–.002 (.007)	.734	–.0007 (.002)	.762
Income	.0001 (.004)	.967	.006 (.002)	.005	.012 (.005)	.039	–.003 (.001)	.049
Female	.285 (.303)	.347	–.148 (.131)	.258	.544 (.350)	.121	.138 (.112)	.222
Age	–.036 (.007)	.000	.004 (.003)	.183	.035 (.008)	.000	.001 (.002)	.487
Constant	–1.999 (1.263)	.114	–2.881 (.593)	.000	–6.749 (1.366)	.000	1.650 (.465)	.000
Number of Observations	1024		1024		1024		1024	
Wald Chi²	55.02	.0000	66.95	.0000	50.60	.0000	128.00	.0000
Log Pseudolikelihood	–223.128		–592.219		–190.066		–637.383	

Robust standard errors in parentheses. Two-tailed test.

We begin with an examination of the predictors of an individual identifying a celebrity as being a representative of modern feminism. The analysis suggests that those who are more familiar with feminism were more likely to identify a celebrity. This suggests that celebrities are, in fact, acting as strong representatives of modern feminism. Additionally, we find that those who are younger in age were more likely to identify a celebrity. This suggests that celebrities are more likely to reach a younger population with their message on feminism.

Turning our attention to politicians, we find that those who self-identify as feminists were more likely to identify someone involved in politics as a representative of feminism. Interestingly, those who view equal pay as a higher priority were less likely to identify a politician. Additionally, those who believe feminists represent all women were more likely to identify a politician. The analysis identified three demographic characteristics that predict identifying a politician too. Specifically, we learn that those who have more education, attend religious services more frequently, and earn larger incomes were more likely to identify a politician.

Next, we examine the predictors of identifying an activist. Surprisingly, none of the feminism attitudes was found to predict identifying an activist. However, those who are more conservative were less likely to identify an activist. We also find that those with more income and those who are older in age were more likely to identify an activist.

Our final analysis of these categories examines those who were unable to identify anyone as a representative of modern feminism. Perhaps not surprisingly, those who are more familiar with feminism, those who self-identify as a feminist, and those who believe feminism represents all women were less likely to not identify any representative. The analysis also finds that those who are more conservative were more likely to be unable to identify anyone. Additionally, those with more education and more income were more likely to be able to identify a modern representative.

Narrative Choices: Feminism vs. the Women's Movement

We now turn our attention to the differences between attitudes toward narratives regarding feminism and the women's movement. As explained above, there is good reason to believe that the public will view these two competing narratives in different ways. Of the two, feminism has been far more controversial. Consequently, we expect that the public will respond differently, in terms of favorability, based on which narrative they are evaluating.

This becomes the basis of our fifth research question. To determine if the public views these two narratives differently, we estimate a simple t-test.[9]

Recall, our measures of favorability are both coded as 0 or 1, with 1 representing a favorable view. We find that 693 respondents received the feminism treatment, with 70.99 percent reporting a favorable view. Conversely, 682 respondents received the women's movement treatment, with 75.95 percent reporting a favorable view.

The question becomes whether there is a significant difference between .7099 and .7595, the decimal forms of the two percentages. The difference is .0495, with a standard error of .0237. The probability of the t-score (2.0832) is .0374. Consequently, the t-test indicates that the difference between these values is statistically significant. This tells us that the public is significantly more favorable toward the narrative of the women's movement compared to the narrative surrounding feminism. This empirically captures the fragmented and polarized competitive marketplace that represents contemporary feminism and the women's movement. Importantly, preliminary analyses find that there was not a significant difference between those who received either treatment, meaning the difference we find can be attributed to the differences in the narratives, and not the people subjected to either treatment.

This brings us to our final research question, which sought to determine if an individual's representative of modern feminism influences their favorability toward feminism or the women's movement. Before we turn to the examination, we would like to take a moment to remind the reader how we got to this point. First, recall that the NPF argues that trust in the narrator is essential for an individual to believe a given narrative. Unfortunately, it is not always easy to identify a narrator. Thus, it was important to establish and evaluate an individual's perceived narrator of feminism. This is where the question regarding who an individual sees as representing feminism comes into play. This person serves as that respondent's narrator, as the person the respondent identifies with feminism. Because there are so many possible representatives/narrators, it is not feasible to analyze the influence of each of them. This is why we categorized these representatives/narrators. Furthermore, we establish above that there are important differences in the predictors of identifying with a celebrity, politician, activist, or not identifying with anyone at all. Consequently, this information tells us that the categorizing of the specific representatives provides a meaningful indicator and that these different representatives have common predictors, despite the inherent differences between specific representatives. The question now concerns whether an individual's perceived narrator influences their favorability. This is particularly important since there is a significant difference between perceptions of favorability.

With this in mind, do narratives coming from celebrities, politicians, or activists influence an individual's favorability of feminism or the women's movement? The results of this final set of statistical analyses are presented in table 4.3.

Table 4.3. Determinants of an Individual's Favorability of Feminism or the Women's Movement

	Feminism		*Women's Movement*	
	Coefficient	*Prob.*	*Coefficient*	*Prob.*
Narrator				
Celebrity	−.712 (.429)	.097	.560 (.454)	.218
Politician	−.865 (.355)	.015	.658 (.310)	.034
Activist	−1.212 (.451)	.007	.547 (363)	.132
Do Not Know	−1.107 (.339)	.001	.443 (.316)	.161
Feminism Attitudes				
Familiar with Feminism	−.090 (.082)	.272	.032 (.078)	.684
Self-Identified Feminist	.595 (.107)	.000	.368 (.111)	.001
Men and Women Equal Pay	−.134 (.408)	.742	.932 (.372)	.012
Feminism Focus	.831 (.156)	.000	.893 (.154)	.000
Represents the Views of All Women	.430 (.153)	.005	.364 (.147)	.014
Demographics				
Political Ideology	−.351 (.103)	.001	−.247 (.109)	.025
Party ID	−.0007 (.052)	.989	−.110 (.055)	.046
White	−.176 (.168)	.294	.036 (.171)	.832
Years of Education	.117 (.038)	.002	−.045 (.035)	.202
Married	.042 (.174)	.806	−.178 (.149)	.233
Religious Attendance	−.009 (.003)	.018	−.001 (.004)	.665
Income	.00004 (.002)	.988	.006 (.002)	.029
Female	−.104 (.178)	.558	−.150 (.174)	.387
Age	.007 (.004)	.086	−.008 (.004)	.072
Constant	−1.174 (.811)	.148	−.609 (.840)	.468
Number of Observations	477		467	
Wald Chi^2	133.02	.0000	130.87	.0000
Log Pseudolikelihood	−176.880		−160.774	

Robust standard errors in parentheses. Two-tailed test.

We begin with an examination of the predictors of viewing feminism favorably. Much to our surprise, all four narrator groups are negative predictors. Specifically, we find that those who identified a celebrity, a politician, an activist, and those who could not identify any narrator were all less likely to view feminism favorably than the reference group. However, we do find that those who self-identified as feminists, those who believe the current feminist focus represents their views, and those who believe feminism represents all women were more likely to be favorable of feminism. We also find that those who are more liberal, more educated, attend religious services less frequently, and those who are older in age were more likely to view feminism favorably.

Turning our attention to our final model, which examines the favorability of the women's movement, we find that those who identified a politician as a narrator were more likely to view the women's movement favorably. While the other three narrator categories are not statistically significant, they are all in a positive direction. The model does reveal that those who self-identified as feminists, those who believe equal pay should be a priority, those who believe the current feminist focus represents their views, and those who believe feminism represents all women were more likely to be favorable of the women's movement. Meanwhile, the analysis also indicates that liberals, Democrats, those with higher incomes, and those who are younger in age were more likely to view the women's movement favorably.

DISCUSSION

We began this project with two primary goals. First, we wanted to understand the public's views on feminism and the women's movement. Second, we were interested in whether celebrities negatively or positively influenced these attitudes. To examine these goals, we outlined a theoretical framework from which we were going to approach this subject. Subsequently, we outlined six specific research questions and a strategy to answer each. Finally, we analyzed the data and reported the results. This endeavor reveals several important implications for our understanding of feminism, the narrative policy framework, and the role of celebrities on public attitudes.

First, the data establish that many within the public identify modern feminism with celebrities and politicians. What is interesting about the celebrity list is that they are all well-known liberals, except Taylor Swift who, despite self-identifying as a feminist, has remained relatively apolitical throughout her career. While it is conventional wisdom that most celebrities tend to be more liberal, it is notable that no celebrity representing conservativism was identified by the public as representing modern feminism.

This liberal bias within the identified celebrities is all the more perplexing given that none of the traditional left/right political indicators predicted identifying a celebrity. In other words, liberals and conservatives were equally likely to identify a celebrity. Likewise, we find that Democrats and Republicans, whites and non-whites, the religious and the non-religious, men and women, the educated and the less-educated, the married and the non-married, and even the wealthy and the poor were no more or less likely to identify a celebrity. This might cause one to suspect that celebrities would not influence perceptions of favorability, but that was not the case. Additional analyses are needed to dig deeper into these relationships to determine if there are sub-population influences that are hidden in the current analysis that might reveal a specific influence for, say, liberals who identify a celebrity versus conservatives who identified a celebrity. Unfortunately, this is beyond the scope of the current project.

Second, we find that our politicians were a bit more inclusive. Respondents identified both Republican and Democratic women as representatives of feminism. Both Condoleezza Rice and Sarah Palin were identified as modern, Republican feminists. Even without Hillary Clinton, however, far more Democrats were identified than Republicans. However, just as we found with the celebrity group, there were no differences in the likelihood of identifying a politician based on party identification or political ideology. Despite this, we find that this group was a predictor of both feminism and the women's movement's favorability.

Importantly, the fact that members of the public identified politicians alongside traditional celebrities reinforces our argument that these politicians should be considered celebrities in their own right. If we were to remove Hillary Clinton's 344 identifications, the number of politicians and celebrities were approximately equal, 90 to 80, respectively. Additionally, we find that there were eight different politicians identified, which is similar to what we found with celebrities. Recall the definition of celebrity was to be a famous or celebrated person. The fact that the public was able to identify these women without any prompting clearly indicates that they have achieved the status of a famous or celebrated person, which makes them all celebrities.

Third, it is surprising that all four categories were less likely to view feminism favorably. This suggests that the unmeasured group, the "others," must have been more likely to view feminism favorably.[10] To some extent, this should have been expected. If you identify yourself, a family member, or a friend as a representative of feminism, there is reason to believe that you may be more likely to view feminism favorably because of these relationships. While we do not know whom the 106 "other" results were, it is probably safe to assume they were not celebrities, politicians, or activists, as Supreme Court Justice Sonia Sotomayor was specifically itemized with only one respondent identifying her. If they are not a member of one of these groups, then they may be people like a businesswoman, a teacher, or a local leader. To be identified by a respondent, these individuals are likely to hold a stronger influence than a celebrity, politician, or activist that the respondent is unlikely to have ever met. Obviously, this is beyond the scope of what the data allow us to say with certainty, but it seems reasonable that this would explain why the "others" are more likely than the other four categories to view feminism favorably.

Importantly, it would be a mistake to interpret these results as suggesting that those who identify a celebrity, politician, activist, or nobody at all did not view feminism favorably. Indeed, all four of these categories, including those who were unable to identify a representative, had a majority of respondents identify that they viewed feminism favorably. We found that 83.78 percent of those who identified a celebrity also reported that they view feminism favorably. For politicians, this number was 77.65 percent. For those identifying an activist, we find that 66.67 percent favored feminism. Finally, even 64.88 percent of those who were unable to identify any representative reported a favorable view of feminism. While the statistics report a negative relationship, this is in relation to the "other" category, and should not be interpreted as meaning that those who identify, say, a celebrity did not favor feminism.

At first glance, these unexpected results could suggest that there are limitations for the NPF when operating in a marketplace of competing narratives. However, as noted above, this concern is not particularly supported here. Again, these negative relationships are in comparison to the "other" category, and each of the four have a majority viewing feminism favorably. While this analysis may raise legitimate questions about how well the NPF holds up in a marketplace like this, the current results do not indicate a theoretical limitation. This is an important question, though, and one that requires attention. Perhaps an analysis where a super-majority of the respondents were not in agreement would allow researchers to better test the effects of such a marketplace on NPF theory.

Fourth, there might be a relatively simple explanation for why three of the narrator groups no longer predicted favorability when analyzing the women's movement. As noted above, 75.9 percent of the respondents indicated that they had a favorable view of the women's movement. While this is only 5 percent higher than the favorability of feminism, the additional 5 percent likely eliminated the difference found between these groups and the "others" category. Importantly, a super-majority of those sampled generally view the women's movement positively, so there was not a lot of movement to be made. Importantly, losing that tie to the familiarity found within the "others" group, it appears that those who identified someone in that group were generally less likely to express favorability toward the women's movement *vis-à-vis* the other four groups, which is why they are all positive. However, we only find a significant distinction with the politicians. Perhaps this is because these are representatives who embody the women's movement because they have achieved equality in some of the most powerful governing bodies in the world. Obviously, additional research is necessary to fully understand this relationship.

Fifth, despite explaining how modern politicians should be considered celebrities, we did not combine the two categories into a single celebrity category. We believe that there is a fundamental difference between entertainment-based celebrities and politicians. The results of the analyses (presented in table 4.2) suggest that this was an appropriate decision. Despite both being considered "celebrities" under the definition of "celebrity," there are considerable differences in the predictors of those who identified either group as being representatives of modern feminism. In fact, no two variables included in our models predicted the likelihood of a respondent choosing a traditional celebrity or a politician. This means that those who identified a politician were distinctly different from those who identified a traditional, entertainment-based celebrity.

This decision to keep the two groups separate also revealed an important distinction between the two. As reported in table 4.3, we find that both celebrities and politicians decreased the likelihood of viewing feminism favorably. However, identifying a politician increased the likelihood of viewing the women's movement favorably. If we had combined these two groups, this distinction would have been lost.

Sixth, these results provide additional evidence in support of the Narrative Policy Framework. The unique nature of this study provides the first evidence of how an individual's perception of a narrator directly influences their attitudes. Until now, studies of the NPF either assigned a narrator or completely omitted the source of a narrative. In many narrative environments, the narratives are advocated by any number of narrators, whether those narrators recognize that they assumed this role or not. This study illustrates that the public is sophisticated enough to assign a narrator to a narrative when not explicitly provided one.

This is important for several reasons. First, it means that previous studies that implicitly or explicitly assumed that the trust hypothesis of the NPF could be ignored by not identifying a narrator may be incorrect. This study indicates that the public may create their own vision of who might be furthering a particular narrative and assessing the quality of that narrative accordingly. Relatedly, this may also present problems when a narrator is explicitly identified, as the respondent may picture someone else or someone completely unrelated (e.g., we saw this in terms of the "politician" category).

A second implication for the NPF suggests that this approach can greatly simplify the process of examining the influence of a narrator in policy domains where narratives have been around for a long time. By asking a respondent whom they see representing the various sides of an issue, it can become a proxy for the larger category of individuals that advocate that position. In other words, we find that simple categorization resulted in predictive patterns, and similar efforts can be made on any number of issue domains to understand the nature of narrators on public attitudes.

A third implication for the NPF is that these results indicate that individuals opposed to the moral of a public narrative are not overwhelmingly identifying narrators with whom they disagree. This is particularly telling since those who identify politicians were more likely to favorably view the women's movement despite being less favorable to feminism. The fact that this group was significant in both models, but in different directions suggests a nuance to public attitudes and that those predisposed to oppose the feminist message were not overwhelmingly identifying those with whom they disagree. As for celebrities and advocates, they were both close to statistical significance and both were positive predictors in the women's movement analysis, suggesting a similar pattern with politicians.

Seventh, as noted multiple times, we do not know who was classified as an "other" in the data. Unpacking this could lead to a better understanding of the role of celebrities on attitudes toward feminism. Perhaps there were several local celebrities that would not be well known outside of a respondent's area. Again, it is unclear. This ultimately limits our ability to fully examine the data and understand what is going on. Relatedly, it is possible that we would be able to identify the role of proximity/familiarity with a narrator on an individual's attitudes. Currently, the NPF does not explicitly outline the probability that personal experience with a narrator will have a greater influence than simply being familiar with them. However, we suspect that results related to the "others" represent this personal experience aspect. With better data comes a better understanding of this relationship.

Finally, this project adds to our overall understanding of three distinct bodies of literature. We have already discussed how this aids our understanding of the Narrative Policy Framework and how this fits within the larger research on feminism and the women's movement. The third body of literature, and the one we would like to end with, relates to popular culture and celebrity politics. While there were not an overwhelming number of respondents who identify entertainment-based celebrities or politicians, the fact that greater than 30 percent of the sample identified a representative from either group is quite impressive and illustrates the importance of celebrities within political discourse. It is important to remember that this question was asked without any pre-identified answers. In other words, it was not a case where a respondent read off a list and saw Beyoncé's name and decided to identify her as a representative. Instead, Beyoncé was the first person these respondents thought of when asked. This goes to illustrate how pervasive popular culture has become in political discourse.

These results could also have interesting implications for the future of feminism and the women's movement. As our results indicate, individuals are able to attach their own narrators to these complicated concepts. While those who wish to further women's rights may advocate for a rebranding of feminism, it seems that politicians and traditional celebrities might be creating a variety of personal brands of feminism, advocating for women's rights in their own way. Individuals in the public seem to be drawn to these different portrayals of feminism and this could in turn have a positive effect on public support for gender equality. For instance, if a person identifies Beyoncé as their personal narrator, their affinity for Beyoncé and her brand of feminism might influence the person's overall perception of feminism. This personalized approach to feminism could allow for activists to further the movement even with a loose coalition, with individuals waving their individual banners of feminism. This could suggest that the concept of feminism could now operate under a very large tent where diverse views can still work together to achieve a common ideal.

We are unaware of any analysis that asks these types of questions. As far as we can tell, this is the first analysis to determine if celebrities serve as representatives of any movement where survey respondents were not prompted with any potential names. The way this concept is measured provides a tough test for our research questions, as only those who have the strongest mental relationship with a celebrity would likely think of one on the spot. Thus, it is entirely possible, if not probable, that many of those who are categorized into the "others" and do not know groups would likely identify a celebrity if given a list of options. Overall, this indicates that the influence of celebrities on political discourse is likely greater than this study indicates, and that these influences may be longer lasting than many predict.

NOTES

1. When conducting a public opinion survey that contains an oversample, the survey research firm will set a base goal for the number of completed surveys. In this case, the goal was likely 1,100. During the survey process, every potential respondent is identified at random, meaning anyone, regardless of demographic characteristics, has an equal chance of being contacted. Once the survey research firm has met its base goal, they will introduce screening questions to the beginning of the survey to identify members of the population that is specifically being oversampled, in this case women. If the survey research firm calls a phone number and a man answers the phone, they are disqualified from the survey, and the firm moves to the next phone number. This process ensures that only those who belong to that specific sub-population are included in the oversample. In this case, the survey research firm was likely contracted to complete 1,600 surveys, with 1,100 a random sampling of adults and 500 a random sampling of adult women. The final numbers, 1,115 and 495 likely reflect the difficulty of precisely knowing how many surveys will be completed when there are a large number of survey researchers calling potential respondents at the same time.

2. Respondents were allowed to provide more than one answer to this question. We chose to use the first person identified for these analyses. Only 6.3 percent of the respondents identified a second representative, and no respondent identified more than four. From a theoretical perspective, this is the most appropriate approach, as this was the first person each respondent was able to think of, which increases the likelihood that this was who the respondent would think of when thinking of women's issues.

3. The "others" category consists of those who identified themselves, family members and friends, and those who were coded as "other" by the survey administrators.

4. Probit regressions are statistical analyses that are designed to analyze data that is coded as 0 and 1, as the above data is coded. These represent the most appropriate analytical tools to answer these questions.

5. It is important to note that both men and women can be feminists.

6. While the survey administrator had already collapsed some of these into groups (e.g., "personal family members/friends," "national organizations," and "other"), it is clear from the specific names that are recognizable, that there were three clear categories of identified representatives.

7. The easiest way to interpret the results from the tables reporting the statistical results (i.e., tables 4.2 and 4.3) is to look at the columns labeled "Prob." As a general rule of thumb, if the number reported in this column is smaller than .100, then the statistical model is reporting that there is a statistically significant relationship between the predictor (all of the characteristics listed in the rows) and the object of our evaluation (all of the questions in the columns). A statistically significant relationship tells us that these predictors are important for understanding the items evaluated (i.e., the narrator categories and the favorability questions).

8. We do not analyze the "others" because we are not completely sure what that coding category really means. Again, the results were coded by the company administering the survey, and they do not provide an explanation of what kinds of responses justified being coded as belonging in the "other" category. Accordingly, we would be unable to interpret any results from such an analysis.

9. This is a statistical technique that will test to see if there is a statistically significant, or a meaningful, difference between two averages.

10. In statistics, a model cannot include an entire list of all possible 0/1 combinations like the five identified in table 4.1 because it would cause estimation errors. Accordingly, the statistical analysis must leave at least one of these categories out of the analysis, as we did with the "others." Although rarely discussed in this manner, the technical way to interpret the results of the narrator groups in the favorability models is as a comparison to the omitted group(s). In this case, celebrities, politicians, activists, and not being able to identify anyone resulted in a respondent being less likely to view feminism favorably compared to those who identified someone classified as an "other." Again, this comparison caveat is typically omitted and assumed to be understood. This is why we can say that the "others" were likely to be more favorable to feminism.

REFERENCES

Aronson, Pamela. "Feminists or 'Postfeminists'?: Young Women's Attitudes toward Feminism and Gender Relations." *Gender & Society* 17, no. 6 (2003): 903–22.

Beck, Debra Baker. "The 'F' Word: How the Media Frame Feminism." *National Women's Studies Journal* 10, no. 1 (1998): 139–53.

Bentz, Leslie. "The Top 10: Facebook 'Vomit' Button for Gays and Other Pat Robertson Quotes." *CNN*, July 9, 2013. https://www.cnn.com/2013/07/09/us/pat-robertson-facebook-remark/index.html.

Braswell, Sean. "Bill Clinton's Great Sax Appeal." *Ozy*, June 8 2016. https://www.ozy.com/2016/bill-clintons-great-sax-appeal/69591.

Bromley-Trujillo, Rebecca, James W. Stoutenborough, and Arnold Vedlitz. "Scientific Advocacy, Environmental Interest Groups, and Climate Change: Are Climate Skeptic Portrayals of Climate Scientists as Biased Accurate?" *Climatic Change* 133, no. 4 (2015): 607–19.

Buccellato, Marcy. "*Elle*'s December Feminism Issue: We're With You, Karl: Our Feminism Issue Is Coming." *Elle*, September 30, 2014. https://www.elle.com/uk/life-and-culture/news/a23186/feminism-magazine-issue-special-december-2014/.

Burn, Shawn Meghan, Roger Aboud, and Carey Moyles. "The Relationship between Gender Social Identity and Support for Feminism." *Sex Roles* 42, no. 11–12 (2000): 1081–89.

Buschman, Joan K., and Silvo Lenart. "I Am Not a Feminist, But . . .": College Women, Feminism, and Negative Experience. *Political Psychology* 17, no. 1 (1996): 59–75.

Cai, Weiyi, and Scott Clement. "What Americans Think about Feminism Today." *Washington Post*, January 27, 2016. https://www.washingtonpost.com/graphics/national/feminism-project/poll/.

Carmon, Irin. "Obama: I am 'What a Feminist Looks Like.'" *NBC News*, June 14, 2016. https://www.nbcnews.com/politics/barack-obama/obama-i-am-what-feminist-looks-n592581.

Chittal, Nisha. "'Parks and Recreation' Features Slew of Political Guest Stars." *MSNBC*, February 11, 2015. http://www.msnbc.com/msnbc/parks-and-recreation-features-slew-political-guest-stars.

Ferree, Myra Marx, and Beth B. Hess. *Controversy and Coalition: The New Feminist Movement across Four Decades of Change*, third edition. New York: Routledge, 1995.

Harper, Douglas. "Celebrity." *Online Etymology Dictionary*, n.d. https://www.etymonline.com/word/celebrity.

Harvey, Mark. *Celebrity Influence: Politics, Persuasion, and Issue-Based Advocacy*. Lawrence: University Press of Kansas, 2017.

Henderson-King, Donna H., and Abigail J. Stewart. "Women or Feminists? Assessing Women's Group Consciousness." *Sex Roles* 31, no. 9–10 (1994): 505–16.

Jones, Michael D., and Mark K. McBeth. "A Narrative Policy Framework: Clear Enough to Be Wrong?" *Policy Studies Journal* 38, no. 2 (2010): 329–53.

Kirkpatrick, Kellee J. "The 'Not Yet Pregnant': The Impact of Narratives on Infertility Identity and Reproductive Policy." In *Narrative, Identity, and Academic Community in Higher Education*, edited by Brian Attebery, John Gribas, Mark K. McBeth, Paul Sivitz, and Kandi Turley-Ames, 111–28. New York: Routledge, 2017.

Levy, Debbie. *I Dissent: Ruth Bader Ginsburg Makes Her Mark*. New York: Simon & Schuster Books for Young Readers, 2016.

Liss, Miriam, Carolyn Hoffner, and Mary Crawford. "What Do Feminists Believe?" *Psychology of Women Quarterly* 24, no. 4 (2000): 279–84.

McBeth, Mark K., Michael D. Jones, and Elizabeth A. Shanahan. "The Narrative Policy Framework." In *Theories of the Policy Process*, third edition, edited by Paul A. Sabatier and Christopher M. Weible, 225–66. Boulder, CO: Westview Press, 2014.

McCarthy, Todd. "Traffic." *Variety*, December 11, 2000. http://variety.com/2000/film/reviews/traffic-4-1200465858/.

Merriam-Webster. "Feminism." *Merriam-Webster*, June 17, 2018. https://www.merriam-webster.com/dictionary/feminism.

———. "Celebrity." *Merriam-Webster*, June 20, 2018. https://www.merriam-webster.com/dictionary/celebrity.

Polkinghorne, Donald. *Narrative Knowing and the Human Sciences*. Albany: State University of New York Press, 1988.

Rapp, Rayna. "Is the Legacy of Second-Wave Feminsm Post Feminism?" *Socialist Review* 18, no. 1 (1988): 31–37.

Riley, Sam G. Introduction to *Star Struck: An Encyclopedia of Celebrity Culture*. Edited by Sam G. Riley. Santa Barbara, CA: Greenwood Press, 2010.

Seligson, Hannah. "Campus Women Wear Feminism on Their Chests." *We News*, February 24, 2006. https://womensenews.org/2006/02/campus-women-wear-feminism-their-chests/.

Shanahan, Elizabeth A., Mark K. McBeth, and Paul L. Hathaway. "Narrative Policy Framework: The Power of Policy Narratives in Influencing Public Opinion." *Politics & Policy* 39, no. 1 (2011): 373–400.

Smeal, Eleanor. "This Is What a Feminist Looks Like." *Huffington Post: The Blog*, February 13, 2009. https://www.huffingtonpost.com/eleanor-smeal/this-is-what-a-feminist-l_b_157531.html.

Sollosi, Mary. "17 of the Best Political Cameos on TV Shows." *Entertainment Weekly*, May 11, 2016. http://ew.com/gallery/politicians-tv-cameos/.

Stoutenborough, James W., Rebecca Bromley-Trujillo, and Arnold Vedlitz. "Public Support for Climate Change Policy: Consistency in the Influence of Values and Attitudes over Time and across Specific Policy Alternatives." *Review of Policy Research* 31, no. 6 (2014): 555–83.

Team *Elle*. "This Is What a Feminist Looks Like, and This Is What She Says." *Elle*, February 13, 2015. https://www.elle.com/uk/life-and-culture/news/g23452/this-is-what-a-feminist-looks-like-whistles-tshirt-clutch-bag-fawcett-society-charity-feminism-issue-beyonce-miley-cyrus-emma-watson/.

Time magazine. "Is Feminism Dead?" *Time*, June 29, 1998. http://content.time.com/time/covers/0,16641,19980629,00.html.

Wade, Lisa. "Where Do Negative Stereotypes about Feminists Come From?" *Sociological Images*, December 28, 2015. https://thesocietypages.org/socimages/2015/12/28/where-do-negative-stereotypes-about-feminists-come-from/.

West, Darrell M., and John Orman. *Celebrity Politics*. Upper Saddle River, NJ: Prentice Hall, 2003.

Zucker, Alyssa N. "Disavowing Social Identities: What It Means When Women Say, "I'm Not a Feminist, But . . ." *Psychology of Women Quarterly* 28, no. 4 (2004): 423–35.

Chapter 5

Celebrity Policy Entrepreneurs Expand the Scope of Conflict

Darin DeWitt

In recent decades, entertainment celebrities have become increasingly engaged in issue advocacy. To assess the impact of these entrepreneurial efforts, I ask: can celebrities leverage their star power to capture attention and mobilize engagement for their pet political causes? According to foundational theories of public policy, issue mobilization is a precondition for policy action. Specifically, by expanding the scope of conflict, policy entrepreneurs help secure their issues a spot on the policy agenda, transform the contours of debate and, when mobilization is persistent, place the issue up for a decision. While policy scholars have shown that major political leaders and parties have the power to kickstart and guide this process, they have overlooked the increasingly active role of celebrity issue advocates.

To help clear a path forward, I outline the basic features of the American policymaking process and identify prospects for celebrity influence. After discussing how to best assess the impact for celebrity political influence, I introduce three empirical tests that evaluate the ability of celebrity policy entrepreneurs to increase the participation of elected officeholders, journalists, and the mass public in the initial stages of the agenda-setting process. In combination, my results show that issues associated with celebrity policy entrepreneurs are more likely to court the type of engagement that typically disrupts policy monopolies and drives government action.

THE POLICYMAKING PROCESS IN AMERICA

In *Agendas and Instability*, Frank R. Baumgartner and Bryan D. Jones (2009, 256) argue that the principal impediment to policy change is a "scarcity of attention." This scarcity results from the fact policy issues are copious in number and each of those issues is exceedingly complex (Kingdon 1995). In addition, cognitive limits and institutional frameworks also constrain the public agenda, at any moment in time, to a small and finite number of issues. These external constraints come from three sources. First, the public has little appetite for complexity and is largely uninterested in policy (Tesler 2015). Second, journalistic norms about newsworthiness focus media coverage on a very small number of issues at any one time such that, for any issue, policy coverage is typically nonexistent but on rare occasion heavily amplified (Uscinski 2014). Finally, when it comes to public policy, members of Congress find it difficult to multitask and, as such, government action requires the focused and coordinated action of virtually all members (Fenno 1991; Smith, Roberts, and Vander Wielen 2015). For all of these reasons, the government agenda is compact and the larger political system neglects innumerable potential issues.

Why are some issues dealt with by the political system? The first step in the policymaking process involves getting an issue on the governmental agenda. In *Agendas, Alternatives, and Public Policies*, John W. Kingdon argues that an issue occupies a place on the finite agenda when it commands focused attention. This attention, according to Kingdon's empirical work, is not simply a function of context, crises, or other external events but, rather, is manufactured by policy entrepreneurs.

To disrupt the status quo and change the way in which a policy domain is dealt with, entrepreneurs must expand the scope of conflict by mobilizing the erstwhile disengaged (Cobb and Elder 1983; Schattschneider 1960). Expanding the scope of conflict is no easy task. Nearly all policy entrepreneurs fail, but a very select few succeed (Leech et al. 2007). Why are some entrepreneurs able to overcome the "scarcity of attention" problem, draw disengaged non-specialists into debate, and thereby get an issue on the governmental agenda?

To place an issue on the governmental agenda, successful policy entrepreneurs must develop a compelling policy image that captures the attention of political elites, the media, and the masses. This new policy image must redefine the issue by providing "a new understanding of the nature of the policies involved" (Baumgartner and Jones 2009, 25).[1] Successful policy images share two features. First, to capture the attention of the uninterested and the policy-averse, new policy images should strip away the inherent complexity of the underlying issue. To this end, successful entrepreneurs discuss policy in "simplified and symbolic terms" and, when seeking to mobilize the masses, highlight "highly emotional symbols or easily understood themes" (Baumgartner and Jones 2009, 26, 30). Second, the policy image must captivate the visible political actors that set the agenda, namely "those who receive considerable press and public attention, includ[ing] the president and his high-level appointees, prominent members of Congress, the media, and such elections-related actors as political parties and campaigners" (Kingdon 1995, 199).

Once an issue occupies a position on the governmental agenda and garners focused attention from political elites, policy entrepreneurs would like to advance that issue to the decision agenda, which is "the list of subjects within the governmental agenda that are up for active decision" (Kingdon 1995, 4). According to policy scholars, successful entrepreneurs do two things to spur government into action. First, they link their policy image to consensus ideals such as "progress, participation, patriotism, independence from foreign domination, fairness, economic growth" (Baumgartner and Jones 2009, 7). By connecting the policy issue to values that all political actors seek to promote, policy entrepreneurs encourage government action and minimize prospects for countermobilization. Second, once this new policy image has been fully articulated, entrepreneurs must look for and exploit a policy window, "an opportunity for advocates to push their pet solutions or to push attention to their special problems" (Kingdon 1995, 203–4). This involves exploiting or inventing "focusing events, crises, and symbols" that link an entrepreneur's policy image to the pressing event. In particular, entrepreneurs seek to create events that encourage "personal viewings of problems by policymakers and the diffusion of a symbol that captures their problem in a nutshell" (Kingdon 1995, 204).

Finally, throughout this whole process, policy entrepreneurs must act swiftly because attention is short-lived and policy windows are only open for a very brief period of time.

PROSPECTS FOR CELEBRITY INTERVENTION IN THE POLICY PROCESS

Policy scholars have focused on the role that traditional political elites—such as "elected officials, career civil servants, lobbyists, academics, or journalists"—play in developing policy proposals, shaping the governing agenda, and advancing causes through the policymaking process (Kingdon 1995, 204). These accounts overlook the entrepreneurial efforts of celebrities. This is a curious omission as Harry Strine (2004), in "Stars on Capitol Hill," shows that, throughout the postwar era, celebrities have been actively involved in issue advocacy, engaging in extensive efforts to lobby political elites and mobilize the masses.

I draw on theoretical studies of celebrity to articulate the role and potential utility of celebrity entrepreneurs in the policymaking process outlined in the previous section. My focus is on what John Street (2004, 438) labels the celebrity politician (CP2): "the entertainer who pronounces on politics and claims the right to represent peoples and causes, but who does so without seeking or acquiring elected office." As Andrew F. Cooper (2007, 131) argues in his study of celebrity diplomacy, these celebrity entrepreneurs engage in political advocacy "with an eye to persuade and shape debate among elite decision makers and mass audiences."

The government agenda consists of issues that command focused elite and mass attention. By definition, celebrities are highly visible entities that command large amounts of media and public attention (Gamson 1994; Rojek 2001; Street 2004; Turner 2014; van Krieken 2012; Wheeler 2013). The power of celebrity is the ability to turn attention to the individual "into other kinds of 'capital'—esteem, status, wealth, influence" (van Krieken 2012, 5; Gamson 1994; Jackson and Darrow 2005; Meyer and Gamson 1995). Celebrity is valuable precisely because it helps serve as a "promotional booster" for celebrity-endorsed commodities, values, behaviors, and ideas (Wernick 1991). Thus, if a celebrity makes a concerted effort to take up a cause, then that should prime the issue and help overcome the impediment of scarce attention that bedevils most policy issues (Atkinson and DeWitt 2016). Of course, the ultimate impact of a celebrity depends on their underlying level of fame such that celebrities with higher levels of star power will provide a greater promotional boost for their cause (Jackson and Darrow 2005).

For the government to deal with a policy issue in a new way, entrepreneurs must do more than capture attention. They must also mobilize the disengaged. Thus, celebrity attention capital is valuable to the extent that it does not simply grab attention, but also shapes individual behavior. Scholars clearly demonstrate that celebrities use their command of public attention to shape the cultural and economic decisions of the masses effectively (Marshall 1997; Rojek 2006; Turner 2014). However, it is not clear whether the documented celebrity ability to prime issues also promotes cognitive engagement with policy and thereby helps citizens negotiate political meanings (Baum 2003; Street, Inthorn, and Scott 2013). While the theory of post-democracy, the dominant viewpoint in celebrity politics, suspects that celebrities actively engage top political leaders but not the masses, these assertions rest on anecdotal and correlational evidence (Marsh, 't Hart and Tindall 2010). As such, the ability of celebrities to mobilize policy engagement is a question that has been left unanswered.

I argue that celebrities possess the skill set necessary to promote engagement and, thus, expand the scope of conflict on policy issues. As outlined above, policy scholars establish that a policy entrepreneur is more likely to capture attention and expand the scope of conflict if their proposed policy image is: 1) simple, symbolic, or emotional, 2) personalizes the technical issue, and 3) links reform to a consensus ideal. Qualitative studies of celebrity advocacy provide ample evidence that celebrities craft policy images that satisfy each of these criteria. Specifically, celebrities, in their issue advocacy, simplify highly technical and intricate issues (Daley 2013; de Waal 2015; Ponte and Richey 2011), present "personalized, emotional appeals" (Darr and Strine 2009; Harvey 2017), and frame their arguments in terms of mainstream values and ideas that are construed as being distinctly "American" (Apolloni, Atkinson, and DeWitt 2017). These findings are often interpreted as evidence of the trivial nature of celebrity political advocacy (e.g., Demaine 2009). However, when viewed in light of the canonical theories of policy change (Baumgartner and Jones 2009; Cobb and Elder 1983; Kingdon 1995), the traditional argument is turned on its head. Rather, by making policy more accessible and linking it to consensus ideals, celebrities are more likely to foster engagement among the elites and masses. Furthermore, the ability to simplify and personalize policy messages is likely to be a skill that celebrities command that many other elite political actors do not.[2]

Finally, pressuring the government to decide a policy question requires that entrepreneurs either invent a spectacle or exploit a focusing event. Celebrities build their image and name recognition through the mass media (Turner 2014). As such, high-profile celebrities are well versed in how to construct entertaining events and narratives that the news media feels compelled to report on and that news audiences will want to consume (e.g., Goodman, Littler, Brockington, and Boykoff 2016). Thus, celebrities who focus on political advocacy should be able to devise the type of spectacle needed to coordinate and focus attention when an issue is on the agenda and a policy window is open. To illustrate, when President Barack Obama and Congress were actively considering the security situation in South Sudan, George Clooney drew media and public attention to the issue by organizing a protest at the Sudanese embassy in Washington, DC. that would result in his arrest (Devereaux 2012). The image of Clooney being escorted by police with his hands behind his back was widely covered by news outlets. By instigating active public interest, Clooney's advocacy efforts should provoke a response from electorally motivated officeholders.

In conclusion, policy scholars assign different roles to different political elites. For instance, policy details are the domain of invisible policy specialists—interest groups, bureaucrats, and legislative staffers—and that legislative strategy is the domain of politicians (Kingdon 1995). From a theoretical standpoint, the role for celebrities is to help invisible actors capture the attention of visible political elites, to provide the kind of entertainment and star power that incentivizes politicians, the media, and the masses to take up the issue, and to provide a focal point that keeps the attention of all of these different actors focused on a single policy image when a policy window opens and policy action becomes feasible.

HOW TO DISCOVER CELEBRITY INFLUENCE

Celebrity politics scholars have long been interested in whether celebrities can transform politics by expanding the scope of conflict for policy issues through the mechanism of attracting attention for and fostering engagement with their advocated issue (Brockington 2014; Couldry and Markham 2007; Goodman, Littler, Brockington, and Boykoff 2016; Ponte and Richey 2014; Scott 2015; Street 2004; Wheeler 2013, 2014). Initial celebrity politics scholarship marshaled an array of anecdotes, correlational evidence, and case studies consistent with the claims that celebrity political advocacy mobilizes the masses and shapes the government and decision agenda (Busby 2007; Demaine 2009; Cooper 2008; Meyer and Gamson 1995; Warren 1986; West and Orman 2003). However, these claims of vast celebrity influence in directing the course of public affairs failed to survive scrutiny in further case studies (Brockington 2015; Markham 2015; Ponte and Richey 2011; Scott 2015; Wheeler 2011).

In response to this absence of clear and robust findings, the celebrity politics literature has called for empirical studies (Boykoff and Goodman 2009; Marsh, 't Hart, and Tindall 2010) with research designs that:

1. Approximate treatment and control conditions through the use of celebrity and non-celebrity comparison groups[3] (Scott 2015),
2. Focus on how audiences engage with celebrity advocacy (Brockington and Henson 2015; Doyle, Farrell, and Goodman 2017; Gamson 1994; Scott 2015; Street, Inthorn and Scott 2012, 2013; Turner 2014),
3. Comprise samples of respondents that are representative of broad populations[4] (Atkinson and DeWitt 2016; Brockington 2015), and
4. Expand the existing methodological repertoire (Brockington 2015).

In this chapter, I introduce a dataset and research design that meets each of these demands.

The empirical tests presented below rely on the Congressional Hearing Attendance Dataset, developed in collaboration with Matthew D. Atkinson (see Atkinson and DeWitt 2017).[5] This dataset compiles a comprehensive list of congressional hearings held since 1994 along with contextual variables for each hearing, including witness lists and member of Congress attendance records. Congressional hearings are a key event in the policymaking process. Committees schedule hearings to establish their issue expertise, place an issue on the agenda, and define the contours of legislative bargaining (Davidson et al. 2017; Talbert, Jones, and Baumgartner 1995). These hearings feature testimony from bureaucrats, academics, interest groups, and, on occasion, celebrities.

The Congressional Hearing Attendance Dataset constitutes a large number of comparable political events, some of which include celebrity involvement and others that do not. By comparing audience engagement with hearings featuring celebrity witnesses to those without, it becomes feasible to estimate the impact of celebrity interventions. In particular, I will examine three measures of audience engagement for hearings featuring celebrity witnesses and for hearings without celebrity witnesses: congressional attendance, news coverage, and internet search-traffic. These measures include broad audiences—for example, all members of Congress, media agenda setters, and all citizens with internet access. They also expand the methodological repertoire by assessing behavioral measures outside the laboratory.[6]

Transformative celebrity advocacy requires authenticity and extensive effort (Brockington 2015; Inthorn and Street 2011; Jackson and Darrow 2005; O'Regan and Stambough 2018).[7] The celebrity advocacy captured by the Congressional Hearing Attendance Dataset fulfills both criteria. Invitations to Capitol Hill are extended to celebrities who have a long-standing reputation for expertise and involvement in their issue area (Apolloni, Atkinson, and DeWitt 2017; Darr and Strine 2009; Larkin 2009; Strine 2004). These celebrities have spent years actively and publicly advocating on behalf of their particular issue, usually in conjunction with a major interest group in Washington, DC. Furthermore, nearly all celebrities have either a personal foundation or personal experience with the issue at hand.[8] Thus, in terms of the typology presented by Mark Harvey elsewhere in this volume, the celebrity witnesses in my study command issue-relevant authenticity (referent power), knowledge (expert power), and information in the form of logical arguments (informational power) (see also Harvey 2017, 40–57). By focusing on political entrepreneurs with these powers, I am more likely to uncover celebrity effects if they do, in fact, exist.

To appropriately isolate celebrity effects, a few key features of celebrity political events must be taken into account. Jackson and Darrow (2005, 88) identify "level of fame" as a key variable that explains why some celebrities shape political outcomes and other celebrities do not. Their study suggests that celebrity political influence is limited to the population that judges a person to be famous. By implication, a celebrity who appeals to a niche audience, such as alternative country singer k.d. lang, will shape the opinions of much fewer people than a superstar loved by broad swaths of society, such as iconic hockey player Wayne Gretzky or multi-platinum singer-songwriter Adele. Thus, when possible, I will explicitly analyze whether the estimated effects vary according to level of fame.[9]

The impact of celebrity interventions may also vary across issues. This is reflected in the fact that the celebrity politics literature tends to focus on a single domain at a time—for example, climate change (Alexander 2013; Boykoff and Goodman 2009; Doyle, Farrell, and Goodman 2017; Seymour 2018), international development (Brockington 2014; Ponte and Richey 2014), humanitarianism (Daley 2013; de Waal 2008; Richey 2015; Scott 2015), and foreign policy (Cooper 2007, 2008; Wheeler 2011). The variable impact of celebrity advocacy by issue is also revealed in Jackson and Darrow's (2005) survey experiments involving Canadian college students. They find that celebrities successfully shape evaluations of political leaders but fail to influence attitudes of Canadian youth toward American energy policy.[10] In short, to appropriately examine the ability of celebrities to move the policy needle, scholars must take into account how their impact might vary across policy issues.

This concern is of particular importance when studying mass political engagement. Citizens have less appetite for policy than do politicians and journalists. In "A Theory of Media Politics," John Zaller (2017, 25) argues that the citizens allocate time to activities that offer a "direct and certain return for the effort" they expend. This leads citizens to privilege two types of news. First, citizens prefer news that delivers "pure entertainment value" (Zaller 2017, 30; see also Atkinson, Deam, and Uscinski 2014; Street, Inthorn, and Scott 2012). Here, celebrities provide the payoff for citizens and the political content consumed is incidental (Baum 2003). Second, citizens are more likely to pay attention to news "that can tangibly improve the length or quality of their lives" (Zaller 2017, 15).

Zaller's theory provides two theoretical predictions. Since celebrities provide entertainment value, political news featuring a celebrity is more likely to engage the mass public than a comparable event without a celebrity. However, the baseline attention rates vary according to whether political news provides "direct and certain" rewards. What type of congressional hearing coverage provides such rewards? Health policy hearings fit the bill, while virtually all other types of hearings fall short.[11] To illustrate, it is implausible that an individual who engages in news coverage of congressional hearings about music licensing reform, the humanitarian crisis in East Timor, or an assessment of the US visa adjudication process could single-handedly act on that information and make much of a difference in national affairs. As such, a rational individual will allocate their time to other activities with more direct payoffs. However, when a citizen engages media coverage of congressional hearings about preventative measures that reduce breast cancer death rates or the relative contribution of nutrition and exercise toward combating obesity, they can use that information to make a dramatic change in their own personal well-being. Since the public seeks out news that it can use, Zaller's rational choice account of news consumers predicts that the baseline rate of mass interest for policy issues will be much higher for health issues than it will be for others.

CELEBRITY CONGRESSIONAL ENGAGEMENT HYPOTHESIS

The governmental agenda is set by highly visible political elites such as the president, high-ranking executive branch officials, and members of Congress (Kingdon 1995, 199). Can celebrities expand the scope of conflict and shape the government agenda by increasing issue engagement among this elite audience?

According to the study of celebrity politics, the answer is an unqualified "yes." Theories of post-democracy posit that celebrities influence politics through access to and the attention of traditional political elites (Brockington 2014; Brockington and Henson 2015; Couldry and Markham 2007; de Waal 2008, 2015; Goodman, Littler, Brockington, and Boykoff 2016; Hague, Street, and Savigny 2008; Wheeler 2014). More specifically, in discussions of celebrities lobbying Capitol Hill, the dominant scholarly, journalistic, and popular perception is that celebrities readily command legislator attention and, thus, expand the scope of conflict in congressional deliberations by turning ordinary events like committee hearings into high-profile affairs (Busby 2007; Demaine 2009; Drezner 2007; Heitshusen 2012; Larkin 2009; Meyer and Gamson 1995; Strine 2004; Warren 1986; West and Orman 2003). These arguments are used to explain why interest groups and congressional policy entrepreneurs seeking attention for their policy concerns ally with celebrity activists and bring them to Capitol Hill.

The idea in the celebrity politics literature is not implausible. A member of Congress could be more likely to attend a hearing featuring a celebrity. Doing so would allow that member of Congress the opportunity to exploit celebrity-fueled media coverage to advertise her name (Mayhew 1974), explain her Washington activity (Fenno 1978), and reach politically disengaged constituents. But a broader reading of congressional scholarship suggests caution. While members of Congress would like to spend the afternoon hobnobbing with a celebrity, they may face more immediate demands—fundraising, other committee and subcommittee work, forums with visiting delegations, partisan meetings, ad hoc groups, and receptions of various kinds (see Price 2004; Taggart and Durant 1985; Fenno 1982; Davidson et al. 2017).

If celebrities boost turnout at congressional hearings, then their entrepreneurial efforts will likely have a lasting impact on the policy process. Hearing participation is a high-cost legislative activity where members of Congress allocate scarce resources to learn about a policy problem and acquire the information necessary to exercise influence at later stages in the policymaking process (Arnold 1990; Curry 2015; Diermeier and Feddersen 2000; Gilligan and Krehbiel 1990; Hall 1996). Successful hearings set the legislative agenda, define the parameters of debate for an issue, and, by providing a forum for face-to-face interaction among members of Congress, facilitate collective action (Deering and Smith 1997; Den Hartog and Monroe 2011; Evans 1991; Fenno 1991).[12] By expanding the scope of conflict at the hearing stage, celebrities help policy entrepreneurs in building a new policy coalition that can disrupt the status quo.[13]

The Celebrity Congressional Engagement Hypothesis tests the conventional wisdom of the celebrity politics literature.[14] It posits that legislators pay more attention to celebrities than other policy experts and advocates. To evaluate this hypothesis, I examine attendance rates at 10,433 congressional committee hearings held between 1995 and 2014.[15] In this analysis, the congressional hearing is the unit of analysis and the response variable is operationalized as the percentage of committee (or subcommittee) members that participated in the hearing.

Since celebrities who testify are not equally famous and, thus, not equally alluring to members of Congress, I measure the star power associated with each hearing by counting the number of mentions that a celebrity receives in the *New York Times* in the 365 days prior to their testimony.[16] I use a time-specific measure of star power because the theoretical priors from the celebrity political literature suggest that politicians interact with a celebrity as a means of increasing their public profile and, as such, politicians will be most eager to associate with celebrities that command vast amounts of attention at the moment they testify on Capitol Hill (e.g., Strine 2004; West and Orman 2003). The analysis that follows will compare the percentage of committee (or subcommittee) members attending a particular hearing across three hearing types: no celebrity witness, ordinary celebrity witness (fewer than ten *New York Times* mentions), and superstar celebrity witness (ten or more *New York Times* mentions). To provide the reader a feel for the data, the category of ordinary celebrity includes Geena Davis, Sheila E., and Richard Simmons. And the category of superstar includes Sheryl Crow, Jeff Daniels, Nicole Kidman, and Kevin Kline.

To isolate the impact of a celebrity witness, I ran an ordinary least squares (OLS) regression that explains the percentage of committee members attending a hearing. In addition to my primary explanatory variables (*celebrity witness* and *superstar witness*), I also included a range of control variables that capture variation in baseline attendance rates across hearings: hearing transcript length as a proxy for hearing significance, committee fixed effects to capture the varying value of committee assignments,[17] hearing type fixed effects (e.g., appropriations, oversight, etc.),[18] major topic codes[19] to account for variation in interest across policy issues, and a subcommittee indicator variable.

In an OLS analysis of the combined House and Senate data, the baseline rate for committee attendance is 47 percent of committee members.[20] When an ordinary celebrity (witnesses with fewer than ten *New York Times* mentions) testifies, committee attendance declines by 4.5 percentage points to 42.5 percent of committee members. But superstar celebrities (witnesses with ten or more *New York Times* mentions) boost turnout by 4 percentage points to 51 percent.[21] In substantive terms, this means that, on the average committee in a chamber, a superstar celebrity increases Senate committee participation by one senator and House committee participation by two members.[22]

As is readily apparent, this result is much more qualified than the theoretical expectations of post-democracy. For celebrities to boost attendance, they must command a very high profile and, even then, these individuals expand the scope of conflict by only one or two members of Congress. Yet, this should not be interpreted as a null result. The participation of a single senator can make an enormous difference for a policy issue, as can House members when they occupy a seat on the appropriate committee or subcommittee (Fenno 1991; Sinclair 2006). Given the severe constraints on time that members of Congress face, the absence of other known stimuli for increasing congressional hearing attendance, and the importance of well-placed members of Congress in pushing an issue along, these effects should nonetheless be judged as nontrivial. This evidence suggests that, in a perhaps limited way, celebrities can get politicians to pay attention to the issue-relevant information developed by policy specialists.

CELEBRITY MEDIA ENGAGEMENT HYPOTHESIS

Media coverage drives the policymaking process. When a new policy image captures media coverage, increases in government attention follow, and this change improves prospects for policy action (Baumgartner and Jones 2009, 274–84).

Does the mass media amplify or mute celebrity political messages? The dominant assumption of scholars, interest groups, and the public is that the media will transmit celebrity political opinions (Cooper 2007; Demaine 2009; Goodman 2013; Goodman et al. 2016; Inthorn and Street 2011; Jeffreys 2016; although see Brockington 2014; Gamson 1994; Thrall et al. 2008). The underlying logic has two components. First, celebrities are skilled at capturing media and public interest and, as such, politicized celebrities consciously court media coverage of their advocacy efforts. Second, in a post-democratic society, elites—such as editors and journalists—are highly responsive to celebrities.

Extant studies track celebrity issue mentions in the news over time with conflicting judgments about whether the raw news numbers represent impressive levels of coverage (Boykoff and Goodman 2009; Thrall et al. 2008). Brockington (2014) points to the general problem in such work by asking: "How do you know that any story appears because of the celebrity in it?"

To isolate the impact of celebrities on media coverage, Matthew D. Atkinson and I collated an original dataset of *New York Times* coverage of Congress on the day of and day after celebrity visits to Capitol Hill (see Atkinson and DeWitt 2018). Across the 138 news days in this dataset, there are 2,007 *New York Times* articles that mention Congress. With this resource, I look for coverage of the issues discussed at all committee hearings held on days in which a celebrity testifies and evaluate the coverage rates for hearings with celebrity witnesses and for hearings without celebrity witnesses.[23]

In the period from 2007–2014, there are 613 hearings held on the 69 days in which celebrities testify on Capitol Hill. In all, 4.4 percent of issues (n = 544) discussed at non-celebrity hearings received coverage in the *New York Times* compared to 11.6 percent of issues (n = 69) discussed at celebrity hearings.[24] This means that celebrity hearings are 2.6 times more likely to receive coverage in the *New York Times*.[25] Thus, celebrities boost attention for their pet political causes. And, as a result, policy entrepreneurs interested in policy change should work with celebrity advocates.[26]

CELEBRITY MASS ENGAGEMENT HYPOTHESIS

Celebrities connect citizens to new public issues, communities of interest, and distant others (Inthorn and Street 2011; Scott 2015; Street, Inthorn, and Scott 2013). By nurturing feelings that some public issues are salient and should be addressed by society, popular culture helps "establish the potential (if no more) for engagement" (Street, Inthorn, and Scott 2013, 34). However, public awareness of an issue's existence is not enough to change the manner in which elites deal with an issue. Rather, active public engagement is a precondition for celebrity transformation of issue politics and celebrity-instigated political change (Brockington and Henson 2015). In this section, I explore this avenue of celebrity influence by asking: Do citizens actively or superficially engage with celebrity political messages?

Brockington (2014, 127) notes that this question remains untested: "[e]lite interest in and desire to work with celebrity advocates is based partly on the premise that it engages and represents the broader public interest. This is a fair assumption to make, given the way that celebrity fills so much of the news and public domain. But it remains an assumption. It is time to test it and explore how celebrity advocacy can be received."

Theoretical expectations are conflicting. Scholars of post-democracy argue that the celebrities, through their issue advocacy, transform politics by gaining access to elites and that the mass public is comprised of "largely passive witnesses to a spectacle" (Hague, Street, and Savigny 2008, 21). Yet celebrities may break through and incite a cognitively capable public to engage because they make complex policy problems compelling and accessible. In traditional interest-based theories of public opinion, scholars posit that issue activists influence the political agenda by mobilizing the mass public through the issue publics' mechanism. This mechanism holds that activists cause members of the public to care about an issue and this, in turn, incites a response from political officeholders who have an interest in appeasing voters (Delli Carpini and Keeter 1996; Zaller 2013).

I test the veracity of the issue publics' mechanism in the realm of celebrity political advocacy by asking: If a celebrity calls attention to a significant policy issue, does this translate into more tangible political acts among the masses—specifically, do members of the public take steps to become informed? To evaluate this idea, I examine Wikipedia article traffic for issues discussed at a selection of celebrity and non-celebrity hearings.[27] I use Wikipedia because scholars have shown that it is the most widespread means of gathering information and learning about a new topic of interest.[28]

Since hearings are designed to spark public interest, I cannot isolate celebrity influence without comparing the attention stimulated by celebrity and non-celebrity hearings. My celebrity cases include all 69 celebrity hearings held between 2007 and 2014. For each celebrity case, I randomly select one non-celebrity hearing held on the same day, and this set of hearings constitutes my non-celebrity comparison cases.[29] For the 138 hearings in this analysis, I rely on the full-text hearing transcript to identify the topic of discussion at the hearing, and then locate the most relevant Wikipedia page.[30] For instance, on 22 April 2008, when actress Justine Bateman spoke about the importance of net neutrality for the entertainment industry, I identified "Net Neutrality" as the most appropriate Wikipedia page. I then collected daily page views for Wikipedia's "Net Neutrality" page on the twenty days preceding and the twenty days following 22 April 2008. My randomly selected non-celebrity hearing for the day of Justine Bateman's visit to Capitol Hill, 22 April 2008, is a hearing on the role that credit rating agencies play in the American economy. Thus, I also collected article traffic for Wikipedia's "Credit Rating Agency" page. This process of identifying Wikipedia issue pages is repeated for 68 additional celebrity cases and their appropriate comparison cases.

In my empirical analysis of article traffic, the outcome of interest is daily page views for each issue discussed in Congress—both before and after the hearing takes place. To standardize the analysis across cases, the response variable—daily page views—is rescaled to reflect traffic relative to a baseline. The baseline for each issue is the average number of daily page views in the pre-period (that is, the twenty days prior to a hearing). Therefore, the page views variable takes a value of 0 if article traffic for a particular date is identical to the pre-period average and would take the value of 30 if traffic for that date is 30 percent above the baseline (or the pre-period average).

The Celebrity Political Engagement Hypothesis anticipates that the page views variable will experience a spike in the days following celebrity advocacy efforts. Political communications scholars show that persuasive political interventions have behavioral effects with a nonlinear decay rate that approximates a quadratic process (Hill et al. 2013). Consequently, I model the page views variable as a quadratic function of time and a hearing indicator variable that differentiates the pre- from the post-period. The critical test of the Celebrity Political Engagement Hypothesis is whether the article traffic data associated with celebrity hearings is different than the article traffic data associated with non-celebrity hearings.

I examine the article traffic data in three different ways—by pooling all hearings together, examining the subset of health policy hearings, and examining the subset of non-health policy hearings. As previously discussed, rational citizens have an incentive to pay attention to and engage with health policy hearings irrespective of celebrity involvement, as the information provided can be used to make a tangible difference in daily life. This is not true for non-health policy issues and, as such, I must control for this variation by conducting separate analyses for each subset of the data.

In an OLS analysis of Wikipedia page views for issues addressed by congressional hearings, the celebrity intervention produces a spike in attention—relative to control cases—in just one of the three analyses. In the aggregate and with respect to health policy, hearings—whether they include celebrities or not—boost attention at comparable levels. However, that is not true when I focus on non-health policy issues.

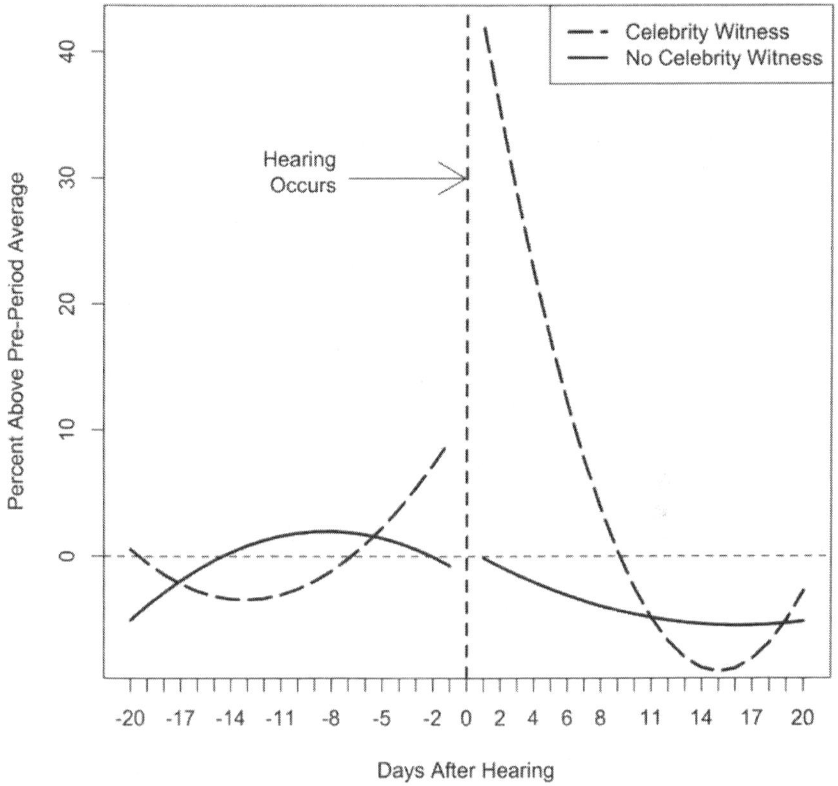

Figure 5.1. Effect of congressional hearing on issue Wikipedia page views (all major topic codes with the exception of health).
Created by the author.

When health policy issues are removed from the analysis, I find that celebrities drive public attention toward their advocated issue. Figure 5.1 plots the result. It shows that, on the day after a hearing, Wikipedia page views for issues discussed in celebrity cases increase by 42 percent (95 percent confidence interval [28.8, 54.9]) relative to the baseline (the average number of page views in the twenty days preceding a hearing). By contrast, Wikipedia issue pages associated with a non-celebrity hearing experience no spike in issue attention after a hearing is held. In figure 5.1, I estimate that, on the day after a hearing, a change in daily page views for issues discussed in non-celebrity comparison cases is essentially zero, or –0.15 percent (95 percent confidence interval [–15.9, 15.6]). In the case of non-health issues, there is strong evidence that celebrity and non-celebrity hearings have differential effects on article traffic. In figure 5.1, I also observe that the increased level of attention that follows from celebrity hearings lasts for more than one week. Is this increased level of attention big, small, or middling?

While there is no obvious way to answer this question, consider two relevant benchmarks. First, in 1991, Demi Moore became the first Hollywood celebrity who refused to hide her pregnancy from public view. Moore broke the convention in the boldest and most spectacular of ways, by appearing naked and seven months pregnant on the cover of *Vanity Fair*. "The cover became instantly iconic, mocked and replicated and spoofed in the manner of meme culture" (Petersen 2017, 113). In return, how much did *Vanity Fair* benefit from being associated with this once-in-a-lifetime celebrity spectacle? According to Petersen (2017), circulation for that issue increased by 33 percent. Second, in a field experiment published in *Science*, Gary King, Benjamin Schneer, and Ariel White (2017) find that when small- to medium-sized news outlets engage in pack journalism, social media posts in the relevant policy domain increase by approximately 19.4 percent on the day following the news media intervention, with that effect decaying to 0 percent by day six. The authors of the study argue that their news interventions have a "big impact" and, in a substantive sense, "represent important and substantial increases in national policy discussions on important issues" (King, Schneer, and White 2017, 779; Netburn 2017). Given these benchmarks, the substantive effect I uncover in figure 5.1 looks quite impressive.

Of course, searching for information online is only the starting point in the public mobilization process. Members of the mass public drive action on political issues when they constitute an issue public (Zaller 2013). An issue public exists when a group of citizens finds an issue to be important, commands basic knowledge of the issue, remains attentive to new information on the issue, and uses that information to guide their political behavior (e.g., how to vote or whether to send issue-oriented letters to members of Congress) (Krosnick 1990). While celebrities can kickstart this process, future research must determine whether and under what conditions celebrity political efforts translate into sustained attention that shapes political behavior.

Nonetheless, the data and results presented so far will help guide scholars in these endeavors. In table 5.1, I reduce the full set of 69 hearings to those that (a) include a superstar celebrity witness and (b) cover a non-health policy issue. This set of hearings covers a range of cases where celebrities are well-positioned to help traditional policy entrepreneurs expand the scope of conflict and can be leveraged to evaluate the extent to which celebrities shape subsequent stages of the policy process.

In summary, I find that when citizens can use the information in hearings to make a tangible difference in their daily lives, they pay attention and engage with the issue irrespective of celebrity participation. However, on issues

Table 5.1. Congressional Hearings Featuring Superstar Celebrity Witnesses, 2007–2014

Celebrity	*Date*	*Hearing Title*
David McCullough	Feb. 7, 2008	The Founding Fathers' Papers: Ensuring Public Access To Our National Treasures
Gene Upshaw	Feb. 27, 2008	Steroid Use In Professional And Amateur Sports
Phil Mickelson	Jul. 22, 2008	Innovation In Education Through Business And Educational Stem Partnerships
Gretchen Wilson	Feb. 12, 2009	New Innovations And Best Practices Under The Workforce Investment Act
Linda Rondstadt, Josh Groban, & Wynton Marsalis	Feb. 24, 2009	Department Of The Interior, Environment, And Related Agencies Appropriations For 2010
Steven Soderbergh	Apr. 6, 2009	Sinking The Copyright Pirates: Global Protection Of Intellectual Property
Nicole Kidman	Oct. 21, 2009	International Violence Against Women: Stories And Solutions
Jeff Daniels	Feb. 24, 2010	Interior, Environment, And Related Agencies Appropriations For 2011
John Cho	Apr. 30, 2010	The 2010 Census: Participation Of Hard To Count Communities In Non-Response Follow-Up
Mariska Hargitay	May 20, 2010	Rape Kit Backlogs: Failing The Test Of Providing Justice To Sexual Assault Survivors
Kevin Costner	Jun. 9, 2010	Deluge Of Oil Highlights Research And Technology Needs For Effective Cleanup Of Oil Spills
Stephen Colbert	Sep. 24, 2010	Protecting America's Harvest
Scott Turow	Feb. 16, 2011	Targeting Websites Dedicated To Stealing American Intellectual Property
Ben Affleck	Mar. 8, 2011	The Democratic Republic of the Congo: Securing Peace in the Midst of Tragedy
Ken Burns	Apr. 14, 2011	Interior, Environment, And Related Agencies Appropriations For 2012
George Clooney	Mar. 14, 2012	The Sudan Security, Peace, and Accountability Act
Stanley Tucci	Mar. 21, 2012	Interior, Environment, And Related Agencies Appropriations For 2013
Ben Affleck	Dec. 12, 2012	Update On The Evolving Security Situation In The Democratic Republic Of The Congo
Lee T. Miller & Rosanne Cash	Jun. 10, 2014	Music Licensing Under Title 17 (Part I & II)

where an individual cannot make a consequential difference on their own, a celebrity is necessary to provide any engagement with the issue.

CONCLUSION

Celebrity politics is pervasive but, as Street, Inthorn, and Scott (2012) highlight, "the relationship is more complex and more significant than has previously been supposed." I have examined one way in which celebrity political advocacy could matter by asking: In the United States, can celebrities promote the elite and mass engagement that is necessary to expand the scope of conflict on their advocated issue?

Relative to non-celebrity comparison cases, I find that celebrity-endorsed policy issues capture greater levels of attention and engagement among members of Congress, media agenda-setters, and the mass public. Elsewhere in this volume, Mark Harvey (2018) notes that celebrity political activists may command "reward and coercive" power, which is the power to "hold public officials accountable" by "affecting public opinion to pressure politicians to change policy." My empirical evidence suggests that superstar celebrity witnesses command such power at the agenda-setting phase. Furthermore, interest groups and political elites seeking policy change will benefit from developing ties with committed celebrity activists. The extent to which this political power remains at subsequent stages of the policymaking process is left, however, for future research.[31]

When assessing the impact of celebrity advocacy, future research must keep policy studies front and center. Scholars of celebrity politics often set the bar for celebrity influence too high—for example, demanding that celebrities change individual-level attitudes and behaviors that no person or event could likely influence (e.g., partisanship, race, religion, morality) or demanding an effect size that other well-placed entrepreneurs are unlikely to ever achieve. Given the uphill battle that any political entrepreneur faces in the policymaking process, consequential effects will often appear modest in isolation but will be far from minimal when considered in contrast to appropriate comparison groups.

NOTES

1. For example, Baumgartner, De Boef, and Boydstun (2008) find that policy change on the death penalty occurred when the policy image shifted from morality to bureaucratic error and the potential death of innocent individuals.

2. For instance, Baumgartner and Jones (2009, 9) argue: "the skills and resources useful in private negotiations may not be the same as those useful in public debates. Technical expertise, inside contacts, and legal skills may prove to be of no value where an emotional public media campaign is waged."

3. This demand has been amply met by an array of high-quality laboratory experiments that often focus on the ability of celebrities to shape audience opinion (e.g., Adkins and Castle 2014; Harvey 2017; Mulligan and Habel 2013; Nownes 2012, 2017).

4. Brockington's main concern is that the college students that compose the sample of most experiments do not constitute a representative sample of society. Consistent with this argument, Atkinson and DeWitt (2016) find that celebrity influence is concentrated in experiments featuring broader audiences that are less politically engaged and informed (see, e.g., Veer, Becirovic, and Martin 2010).

5. The analysis that follows reinterprets some previously published empirical findings in the context of the policy scholarship outlined in this chapter. But in the discussion that follows, I leverage this dataset to implement multiple brand-new tests that will highlight key ways in which celebrities influence the policymaking process.

6. Behavioral measures (as opposed to surveys, focus groups, diaries, laboratory experiments, and so on) are ideal for measuring celebrity influence. Much survey research on the topic of celebrity-motivated political engagement produces results at direct odds with objective reality (Boykoff, Goodman, and Curtis 2009; Markham 2015), thereby highlighting a key finding in psychology that people are not very good judges of their own behavior (Sharot 2017). For this reason, it is necessary to expand the methodological repertoire with a behavioral measure.

7. The absence of clear celebrity influence may be a result of inattentiveness to these dimensions in research design. For instance, Thrall et al. (2008), in the most high-profile study where celebrity advocacy results in null findings, makes no attempt to control for authenticity. Thrall looks at many cases where celebrities do not have authenticity on the issue at hand—their involvement is passive and the product of a publicist. Thus, it is no surprise that these low intensity efforts produce no effect.

8. And many have both. For instance, singer-songwriter Jewel Kilcher, whose chart hits relay her experience as a homeless teenager, spoke about homeless youth on Capitol Hill. To take another example, rapper Usher Raymond IV spoke to Congress about youth volunteerism and public service—after operating, for over a decade, a national non-profit dedicated to building leadership skills among disadvantaged youth through volunteer service. In interviews with committee staffers, Larkin (2009) shows that there is fierce competition among celebrities for seats at congressional hearings and, as a result, only the most active and dedicated celebrities are invited. Thus, celebrities who do show up to Capitol Hill make their political advocacy a central part of their public biography, which should ensure a reasonable level of authenticity, thus opening up the prospect for transformative advocacy.

9. Most of the celebrities invited to Capitol Hill are quite famous (e.g., musician Bill Corgan, coach Dick Butkus, singer Josh Groban, actor Stanley Tucci, boxer Sugar Ray Leonard) and, as a result, the variation that I observe is truncated in the higher echelon of celebrity status.

10. There are mitigating factors in this result—namely, the celebrity associated with energy policy is less famous than the celebrities associated with evaluations of political leaders. But the result is still suggestive that an investigation of issues is necessary.

11. To more convincingly demonstrate the veracity of this claim, review table 5.1 for a list of non-health hearings featuring superstar celebrities—that is, celebrities with ten or more *New York Times* mentions in the 365 days prior to their congressional testimony.

12. Members of Congress would like to contribute to the public good that is good public policy. This requires high-quality information and legislative allies. Hearings effectively provide both of those resources.

13. Upsetting a policy monopoly does not require policy change. If celebrities convince new political actors to pay attention to a policy domain, then a narrow monopoly can no longer dictate public affairs through lawmaking, rulemaking, or other means.

14. This test draws on work presented in Atkinson and DeWitt (2017). That article was an empirical test of the conventional wisdom that celebrities drastically improve hearing attendance from minimal to a full house. In this chapter, I reconsider those results in light of a theoretical frame that allows a more substantive consideration of results.

15. This set of hearings excludes those that are less witness-oriented—markup and treaty—as well as those that take place outside of Washington, DC. Hearing transcripts provide a list of committee members as well as members present at a particular hearing.

16. Since some hearings feature multiple celebrities, star power is the total number of mentions in the *New York Times* for all celebrities at a hearing.

17. See Stewart (2011) for a discussion of the value of various committee assignments in the era under analysis.

18. One would imagine that a member of Congress receives more credit from constituents for attending an appropriation hearing than attending an oversight hearing and, as such, baseline attendance rates will vary.

19. Major topic codes for congressional hearings are provided by the Policy Agendas Project at the University of Texas at Austin. URL: www.comparativeagendas.net. Accessed September 26, 2017.

20. The baseline attendance rate reported in the paper is for a Senate appropriations committee general hearing about macroeconomics. A comprehensive set of attendance rates by committee and subcommittee are reported in the Replication archive available at the author's website. For the interested reader, average attendance rates varies across committees: in the House, from 34.9 percent for the Resources Committee to 77.5 percent for the Rules Committee; in the Senate, from 17.3 percent for the Small Business Committee to 70.4 percent for the Intelligence Committee.

21. For ordinary celebrities, $p = 0.0027$ and for superstar celebrities, $p = 0.050$.

22. A data archive with the full regression table and alternative models is available at http://www.cla.csulb.edu/departments/polisci/faculty-staff/darin-dewitt/.

23. A hearing is counted as being covered by the *New York Times* if the issue discussed at the hearing is reported in direct reference to Congress.

24. Given the smaller number of cases involved in the empirical evaluation of the Celebrity Media Attention Hypothesis, relative to the Celebrity Congressional Attention Hypothesis, I am unable to examine the role that star power plays in generating media attention.

25. Using a chi-square test, the null hypothesis of equal proportions is rejected at the conventional significance level ($p = 0.01$).

26. Celebrities cannot guarantee coverage for political issues but, in a domain such as policy, where most attention is scant, even a small effect represents a change of great political consequence.

27. Wikipedia article traffic statistics for the period December 2007 to present are publicly available. This chapter relies on the public archive accessible at http://dumps.wikimedia.org/other/pagecounts-raw/.

28. When a relevant Wikipedia page exists, search engines tend to place that results prominently (Laurent and Vickers 2009). In particular, Google, which dominates the search market in the period of study, "boosts Wikipedia results toward the pole position" (Höchstötter and Lewandowsky 2009). Since internet users typically click on the first few results (Hindman 2008), this implies that Wikipedia article traffic is a high quality means of empirically measuring mass engagement with policy issues.

29. Hearing transcript lengths, a proxy measure for hearing importance, do not systematically vary across celebrity and non-celebrity cases, thus suggesting that celebrities are not systematically being invited to more, or less, important hearings.

30. For the reader interested in more detail, this endnote provides a more detailed accounting. For each hearing, I seek to identify the main topic of discussion. Fortunately, individual hearings tend to be highly focused, coordinated, and planned exercises held with the goal of drawing attention for a specific topic (see Talbert, Jones, and Baumgartner 1995). To identify the main topic of a hearing, I begin by referring to the opening statement, where the chair (or a designated substitute) reminds committee members of the themes and goals of the hearing. Then, we read the remainder of the hearing transcript to verify that the stated theme appropriately captures the purpose of the hearing and, in particular, the content of the celebrity's testimony. In a hearing titled "Smokeless Tobacco: Impact on the Health of Our Nation's Youth and Use in Major League Baseball" featuring baseball player and television broadcaster Joe Garagiola, Representative Frank Pallone Jr. stated: "The subcommittee is examining the prevalence of smokeless tobacco products, diseases linked to the use of these products and the correlation between smokeless tobacco use by youth and Major League Baseball players. This is an important issue of longstanding interest to this committee, and it is my hope we can continue to raise awareness about the dangers of smokeless tobacco and shape future discussions both in Congress and in Major League Baseball" (Smokeless Tobacco 2010). For this hearing, I use "smokeless tobacco," which was mentioned 273 times in the hearing. This Wikipedia page discusses the main issues raised at the hearing in subsections titled "Safety" and "Carcinogenicity."

31. John Kingdon has called persistence the most important entrepreneurial skill in the policymaking process. Future studies of celebrity political advocacy should look at whether and how celebrities persistently manufacture attention. This chapter shows that celebrities capture issue attention at the agenda-setting stage. But, to extend these insights further, later stages of the policy process will need to be examined. A promising case study opportunity is George Clooney's efforts on behalf of a humanitarian crisis in Sudan, which have consisted of hearing testimony in Congress, an arrest spectacle, think tank reports, and opinion pieces in popular outlets such as *Time*. As scholars examine the full policy process, attention must be paid to how celebrity efficacy might vary according to issue-specific factors such as valence and ideology.

REFERENCES

Adkins, Todd, and Jeremiah J. Castle. "*Moving* Pictures? Experimental Evidence of Cinematic Influence on Political Attitudes." *Social Science Quarterly* 95, no. 5 (2014): 1230–44.

Alexander, Jenny. "The Case of the Green Vampire: Eco-Celebrity, Twitter and Youth Engagement." *Celebrity Studies* 4, no. 3 (2013): 353–68.

Apolloni, Alexandra, Matthew D. Atkinson, and Darin DeWitt. "'Can I Get a Witness?': Musicians Performing Politics in the U.S. Congress." *Ethnomusicology Review* 21 (2017).

Arnold, Douglas R. *The Logic of Congressional Action*. New Haven, CT: Yale University Press, 1990.

Atkinson, Matthew, Maria Deam, and Joseph E. Uscinski. "What's a Dog Story Worth?" *PS: Political Science and Politics* 47, no. 3 (2014): 819–23.

Atkinson, Matthew D., and Darin DeWitt. "Celebrity Political Endorsements Matter." *Celebrity Studies* 7, no. 1 (2016): 119–21.

———. "Snubbing Seth Rogen: Does Celebrity Testimony Increase Congressional Hearing Attendance?" *PS: Political Science & Politics* 50, no. 2 (2017): 354–58.

———. "Does Celebrity Issue Advocacy Mobilize Issue Publics?" *Political Studies* (2018). https://doi.org/10.1177/0032321717751294.

Baum, Matt. *Soft News Goes to War*. Princeton, NJ: Princeton University Press, 2003.

Baumgartner, Frank R., Suzanna L. De Boef, and Amber E. Boydstun. *The Decline of the Death Penalty and the Discover of Innocence*. New York: Cambridge University Press, 2008.

Baumgartner, Frank R., and Bryan D. Jones. *Agendas and Instability in American Politics*. Second edition. Chicago: The University of Chicago Press, 2009.

Boykoff, Maxwell, and Michael Goodman. "Conspicuous Redemption? Reflections on the Promises and Perils of the 'Celebritization' of Climate Change." *Geoforum* 40 (2009): 395–406.

Boykoff, Maxwell, Michael Goodman, and Ian Curtis. "The Cultural Politics of Climate Change: Interactions in the Spaces of Everyday." In *The Politics of Climate Change*, edited by Maxwell T. Boykoff, 136–54. Routledge: London, 2009.

Brockington, Dan. *Celebrity Advocacy and International Development.* Oxon: Routledge, 2014.

———. "Towards an International Understanding of the Power of Celebrity Persuasions: A Review and a Research Agenda." *Celebrity Studies* 6, no. 4 (2015): 486–504.

Brockington, Dan, and Spensor Henson. "Signifying the Public: Celebrity Advocacy and Post-democratic Politics." *International Journal of Cultural Studies* 18, no. 4 (2015): 431–48.

Busby, Joshua William. "Bono Made Jesse Helms Cry." *International Studies Quarterly* 51 (2007): 247–75.

Cobb, Roger William, and Charles D. Elder. *Participation in American Politics: The Dynamics of Agenda-Building.* Baltimore: John Hopkins University Press, 1983.

Cooper, Andrew F. "Beyond Hollywood and the Boardroom: Celebrity Diplomacy." *Georgetown Journal of International Affairs* 8 (2007): 125–32.

———. *Celebrity Diplomacy.* Boulder, CO: Paradigm Publishers, 2008.

Couldry, Nick, and Tim Markham. "Celebrity Culture and Public Connection: Bridge or Chasm?" *International Journal of Cultural Studies* 10, no. 4 (2007): 403–21.

Curry, James M. *Legislating in the Dark: Information and Power in the House of Representatives.* Chicago: University of Chicago Press, 2015.

Daley, Patricia. "Rescuing African Bodies: Celebrities, Consumerism and Neoliberal Humanitarianism." *Review of African Political Economy* 40, no. 137 (2013): 375–93.

Darr, Christopher, and Harry C. Strine IV. "A Pentadic Analysis of Celebrity Testimony in Congressional Hearings." *KB Journal* 6, no. 1 (2009).

Davidson, Roger H., Walter J. Oleszek, Frances E. Lee, and Eric Schickler. *Congress and Its Members.* Sixteenth edition. Washington, DC: CQ Press, 2017.

de Waal, Alex. "The Humanitarian Carnival: A Celebrity Vogue." *World Affairs* 171, no. 2 (2008): 43–55.

———. *Advocacy in Conflict: Critical Perspectives on Transnational Activism.* London: Zed Books, 2015.

Deering, Christopher J., and Steven S. Smith. *Committees in Congress.* Washington, DC: CQ Press, 1997.

Delli Carpini, Michael X., and Scott Keeter. *What Americans Know about Politics and Why It Matters.* New Haven, CT: Yale University Press, 1996.

Demaine, Linda J. "Navigating Policy by the Stars: The Influence of Celebrity Entertainers on Federal Lawmaking." *Journal of Law and Politics* 25 (2009): 83–143.

Den Hartog, Chris, and Nathan W. Monroe. *Agenda Setting in the U.S. Senate: Costly Consideration and Majority Party Advantage.* Cambridge: Cambridge University Press, 2011.

Devereaux, Ryan. "George Clooney Arrested in Planned Protest at Sudanese Embassy." *The Guardian.* March 16, 2012. https://www.theguardian.com/world/2012/mar/16/george-clooney-arrested-sudanese-embassy.

Diermeier, Daniel, and Timothy J. Feddersen. "Information and Congressional Hearings." *American Journal of Political Science* 44, no. 1 (2000): 51–65.

Douglas, Susan J. *Where the Girls Are: Growing Up Female with the Mass Media.* New York: Times Books, 1994.
Doyle, Julie, Nathan Farrell, and Michael K. Goodman. "Celebrity, Climate Change Politics and the Promise of Emotional Witness." In *Oxford Research Encyclopedia of Climate Science*, edited by Matthew Nisbet. Oxford: University of Oxford Press, 2017.
Drezner, Daniel W. "Foreign Policy Goes Glam." *National Interest.* Nov/Dec (2007): 22–28.
Evans, Lawrence C. *Leadership in Committee: A Comparative Analysis of Leadership Behavior in the U.S. Senate.* Ann Arbor: University of Michigan Press, 1991.
Fenno, Richard F. Jr. *Home Style: House Members in Their Districts.* Boston: Little Brown, 1978.
———. *The United States Senate: A Bicameral Perspective.* Washington, DC: American Enterprise Institute, 1982.
———. *Learning to Legislate: The Senate Education of Arlen Specter.* Washington, DC: CQ Press, 1991.
Gamson, Joshua. *Claims to Fame: Celebrity in Contemporary America.* Berkeley: University of California Press, 1994.
Garthwaite, Craig, and Timothy Moore. "Can Celebrity Endorsements Affect Political Outcomes? Evidence from the 2008 US Democratic Presidential Primary." *Journal of Law, Economics, and Organization* 29, no. 2 (2013): 355–84.
Gilligan, Thomas W., and Keith Krehbiel. "Organization of Informative Committees by a Rational Legislature." *American Journal of Political Science* 34, no. 2 (1990): 531–64.
Goodman, Michael, Jo Littler, Dan Brockington, and Maxwell Boykoff. "Spectacular Environmentalism: Media Knowledge and the Framing of Ecological Politics." *Environmental Communication* 10, no. 6 (2016): 677–88.
Hague, Seth, John Street, and Heather Savigny. "The Voice of the People? Musicians as Political Actors." *Cultural Politics* 44, no. 1 (2008): 5–24.
Hall, Richard L. *Participation in Congress.* New Haven, CT: Yale University Press, 1996.
Harvey, Mark. *Celebrity Influence: Politics, Persuasion, and Issue-Based Advocacy.* Lawrence: University Press of Kansas, 2017.
———. "'I'm a Ratings Machine!' Media Coverage and the Celebrity of Donald Trump." In *The Hollywood Connection*, edited by Heather E. Yates and Timothy G. Hill. Lanham, MD: Lexington Books, 2018.
Heitshusen, Valerie. "Senate Committee Hearings: Arranging Witnesses." *Congressional Research Service Report for Congress.* Washington, DC: Congressional Research Service, 2012.
Hindman, Matthew. *The Myth of Digital Democracy.* Princeton, NJ: Princeton University Press, 2008.
Höchstötter, Nadine, and Dirk Lewandowski. "What Users See: Structures in Search Engine Results Pages." *Information Sciences* 179, no. 12 (2009): 1796–1812.
Inthorn, Sanna, and John Street. "'Simon Cowell for Prime Minister'? Young Citizens' Attitudes towards Celebrity Politics." *Media, Culture & Society* 33, no. 3 (2011): 479–89.

Jackson, David J., and Thomas I. A. Darrow. "The Influence of Celebrity Endorsements on Young Adults' Political Opinions." *Harvard International Journal of Press/Politics* 10, no. 3 (2005): 80–98.

Jeffreys, Elaine. "Translocal Celebrity Activism: Shark-Protection Campaigns in Mainland China." *Environmental Communication* 10, no. 6 (2016): 763–76.

King, Gary, Benjamin Schneer, and Ariel White. "How the News Media Activate Public Expression and Influence National Agendas." *Science* 358 (2017): 776–80.

Kingdon, John W. *Agendas, Alternatives, and Public Policies*. Second edition. New York: Longman, 1995.

Krosnick, Jon A. "Government Policy and Citizen Passion: A Study of Issue Publics in Contemporary America." *Political Behavior* 12, no. 1 (1990): 59–92.

Larkin, Kathryn Gregg. "Star Power: Models for Celebrity Political Activism." *Virginia Sports and Entertainment Law Journal* 9, no. 1 (2009): 155–80.

Laurent, Michael R., and Tim J. Vickers. "Seeking Health Information Online: Does Wikipedia Matter?" *Journal of the American Medical Informatics Association* 16, no. 4 (2009): 471–79.

Ledbetter, Carly. "Dior Makes Another Feminist Fashion Statement on the Runway." *Huffington Post*, September 27, 2017. https://www.huffingtonpost.com/entry/everyone-is-going-to-want-to-wear-diors-latest-feminist-fashion-statement_us_59cbb6dfe4b05063fe0e3219.

Leech, Beth L., Frank R. Baumgartner, Jeffrey M. Berry, Marie Hojnacki, and David C. Kimball. 2007. "Does Money Buy Power? Interest Group Resources and Policy Outcomes." Paper presented at the annual meeting of the Midwest Political Science Association, Chicago, IL, 2007.

Markham, Tim. "Celebrity Advocacy and Public Engagement: The Divergent Uses of Celebrity." *International Journal of Cultural Studies* 18, no. 4 (2015): 467–80.

Marsh, David, Paul 't Hart, and Karen Tindall. "Celebrity Politics: The Politics of the Late Modernity?" *Political Studies Review* 8 (2010): 322–40.

Marshall, P. David. *Celebrity and Power: Fame in Contemporary Culture*. Minneapolis: University of Minnesota Press, 1997.

Mayhew, David. *Congress: The Electoral Connection*. New Haven, CT: Yale University Press, 1974.

Meyer, David S., and Joshua Gamson. "The Challenge of Cultural Elites: Celebrities and Social Movements." *Sociological Inquiry* 65, no. 2 (1995): 181–206.

Mulligan, Kenneth, and Philip Habel. "The Implications of Fictional Media for Political Beliefs." *American Politics Research* 41, no. 1 (2013): 122–46.

Netburn, Deborah. "Public is Attentive to Journalism." *Los Angeles Times* (Los Angeles, CA). November 9, 2017.

Nownes, Anthony J. "An Experimental Investigation of the Effects of Celebrity Support for Political Parties in the United States." *American Politics Research* 40, no. 3 (2012): 476–500.

———. "Celebrity Endorsements and Voter Emotions: Evidence from Two Experiments." *American Politics Research* 45, no. 4 (2017): 648–72.

O'Regan, Valerie R., and Stephen J. Stambough. "The Political Influence of Celebrities: Was There a 'Trump' Effect?" Paper presented at the annual meeting of the Western Political Science Association, San Francisco, CA, 2018.

Petersen, Anne Helen. *Too Fat, Too Slutty, Too Loud: The Rise and Reign of Unruly Women*. New York: Plume, 2017.

Ponte, Stefano, and Lisa Ann Richey. "(PRODUCT)REDTM: How Celebrities Push the Boundaries of 'Causumerism.'" *Environment and Planning* 43 (2011): 2060–75.

———. "Buying Into Development? Brand Aid Forms of Cause-Related Marketing." *Third World Quarterly* 35, no. 1 (2014): 65–87.

Price, David E. *The Congressional Experience: Transforming American Politics*. Boulder, CO: Westview Press, 2004.

Richey, Lisa Ann. *Celebrity Humanitarianism and North-South Relations: Politics, Place and Power*. London: Routledge, 2015.

Rojek, Chris. *Celebrity*. Hoboken, NJ: John Wiley & Sons, 2001.

———. "Sports Celebrity and the Civilizing Process." *Sport in Society* 9, no. 4 (2006): 674–90.

Ross, Barbara. "Kelly Cosby, Lawyer Behind 'Notorious R.B.G' Rap Honoring Ruth Bader Ginsberg, Dies from Cancer at 25." *New York Daily News*, November 20, 2015. http://www.nydailynews.com/new-york/notorious-b-g-lawyer-dies-25-cancer-article-1.2441183.

Schattschneider, Elmer Eric. *The Semisovereign People*. New York: Holt, Rinehart and Winston, 1960.

Scott, Martin. "The Role of Celebrities in Mediating Distant Suffering." *International Journal of Cultural Studies* 18, no. 4 (2015): 449–66.

Seymour, Nicole. *Bad Environmentalism: Irony and Irreverence in the Ecological Age*. Minneapolis: University of Minnesota Press, 2018.

Sharot, Tali. *The Influential Mind: What the Brain Reveals about Our Power to Change Others*. New York: Henry Holt and Company, 2017.

Sinclair, Barbara. *Party Wars: Polarization and the Politics of National Policymaking*. Norman: University of Oklahoma Press, 2006.

Smith, Steven S., Jason M. Roberts, and Ryan J. Vander Wielen. *The American Congress*. 9th ed. New York: Cambridge University Press, 2015.

Stewart, Charles. *Analyzing Congress*. Second edition. New York: W. W. Norton & Company, 2011.

Street, John. "Celebrity Politicians: Popular Culture and Political Representation." *The British Journal of Politics and International Relations* 6, no. 4 (2004): 435–52.

Street, John, Sanna Inthorn, and Martin Scott. "Playing at Politics? Popular Culture as Political Engagement." *Parliamentary Affairs* 65 (2012): 338–58.

———. *From Entertainment to Citizenship: Politics and Popular Culture*. Manchester: Manchester University Press, 2013.

Strine, Harry Cornelius. "Stars on Capitol Hill: Explaining Celebrity Appearances in Congressional Committee Hearings." Dissertation, Purdue University, 2004.

Taggart, William A., and Robert F. Durant. "Home Style of a U.S. Senator: A Longitudinal Analysis." *Legislative Studies Quarterly* 10, no. 4 (1985): 489–504.

Talbert, Jeffrey C., Bryan D. Jones, and Frank R. Baumgartner. "Nonlegislative Hearings and Policy Change in Congress." *American Journal of Political Science* 39, no. 2 (1995): 383–405.

Tesler, Michael. "Priming Predispositions and Changing Policy Positions: An Account of When Mass Opinion is Primed or Changed." *American Journal of Political Science* 59, no. 4 (2015): 806–24.

Thrall, A. Trevor, Jaime Lollio-Fakhreddine, Jon Berent, Lana Donnelly, Wes Herrin, Zachary Paquette, Rebecca Wenglinski, and Amy Wyatt. "Star Power: Celebrity Advocacy and the Evolution of the Public Sphere." *International Journal of Press/Politics* 13, no. 4 (2008): 362–85.

Turner, Graeme. *Understanding Celebrity*. London: Sage, 2014.

Uscinski, Joseph E. *The People's News: Media, Politics, and the Demands of Capitalism*. New York: NYU Press, 2014.

van Krieken, Robert. *Celebrity Society*. London: Routledge, 2012.

Veer, Ekant, Ilda Becirovic, and Brett A. S. Martin. "If Kate Voted Conservative, Would You? The Role of Celebrity Endorsements in Political Party Advertising." *European Journal of Marketing* 44, no. 3/4 (2010): 436–50.

Warren, Larry. "The Other Side of the Camera: A TV Reporter's Stint as a Congressional Aide." *PS: Political Science and Politics* 19, no. 1 (1986): 43–48.

Wernick, Andrew. "Promotional Culture." *CTheory* 15, no. 1–3 (1991): 260–81.

West, Darrell M., and John Orman. *Celebrity Politics*. Upper Saddle River, NJ: Prentice Hall, 2003.

Wheeler, Mark. "Celebrity Diplomacy: United Nations' Goodwill Ambassadors and Messengers of Peace." *Celebrity Studies* 2, no. 1 (2011): 6–18.

———. *Celebrity Politics: Image and Identity in Contemporary Political Communications*. Cambridge: Polity, 2013.

———. "The Mediatization of Celebrity Politics through the Social Media." *International Journal of Digital Television* 5, no. 3 (2014): 221–35.

Zaller, John. "What Nature and Origins Leaves Out." *Critical Review* 24, no. 4 (2013): 569–642.

———. "A Theory of Media Politics." Typescript, UCLA, 2017.

Chapter 6

"I'm a Ratings Machine!"

Media Coverage and the Celebrity of Donald Trump

Mark Harvey

On April 3, 2004, celebrity businessman Donald Trump appeared on NBC as the host of *Saturday Night Live*, pretending to fire NBC president and CEO Jeff Zucker in a promotion for his television show, *The Apprentice*. During his monologue, Trump said, "It's great to be here at *Saturday Night Live* but—I'll be completely honest—it's even better for *Saturday Night Live* that I'm here. Nobody's bigger than me. Nobody's better than me. I'm a ratings machine!" (Cary 2015). In December 2017, President Donald Trump made a similar argument in an impromptu interview with Michael Schmidt of the *New York Times,* explaining why he expects to be re-elected in 2020:

> Another reason that I'm going to win another four years is because newspapers, television, all forms of media will tank if I'm not there, because without me, their ratings are going down the tubes. . . . So they basically have to let me win. And eventually, probably six months before the election, they'll be loving me because they're saying, "Please, please, don't lose, Donald Trump." (Borchers 2017; Schmidt and Shear 2017)

Scholars and analysts have argued that Donald Trump's ability to capitalize on free press coverage in lieu of paid advertisements gave him an advantage in the 2016 presidential election (Cary 2015; Patterson 2016a). From the time he announced his candidacy, Trump received the most coverage in the Republican primary: 63 percent compared to his most covered rival at 37 percent. In the general election, Trump received 15 percent more than Clinton did. This gave Trump more opportunities to define his opponent, and to frame the debate (Patterson 2016b).

Granted, some scholars question whether media coverage is a significant variable in determining electoral outcomes at all (Lichtman 2016). This chapter does not seek to demonstrate that level of coverage equals political victory, nor does it presume that more coverage results in positive coverage. Indeed, when Trump tweeted in 2012 that global warming was the result of a Chinese conspiracy, he received a lot of attention. Much was not positive. However, his tweets also did not prevent him from becoming president of the United States. Having said that, it is safe to presume that a high level of coverage is favorable to a political candidate, and that coverage offers options. What was it about Trump that caused this burst of unprecedented media coverage?

One answer is that Trump's lack of experience in public service, use of flamboyant language, proclivity to run against the Republican Party itself, along with the public's distaste for conventional politicians gave him an advantage: he was the ultimate outsider candidate. Of course, many candidates run as outsiders and fail to command that level of attention. Not just any person could win the presidency without the level of attention that Trump was able to garner, and not even Hillary Clinton could command the level of non-paid media attention that Trump received.

Alternatively, recent research has proven that, at times, celebrities are capable of attracting more attention to issues of public importance than public officials can (Harvey 2017, 78–81; Huliaras and Tzifakis 2011; Street 2004).[1] Did Trump's celebrity play a role in garnering media attention that helped to propel him to the White House? If a fundamental element of celebrity is fame, one could argue that Hillary Clinton was every bit the celebrity that Trump was—a famous former first lady, a prominent senator, a generally popular and competent secretary of state, and a lightning rod for controversy (Carpentier 2016). Moreover, Clinton was a high-profile political professional who, by virtue of her position, was routinely covered in international and political news. In that position, one would expect Clinton to have a structural advantage in news coverage. Did the press treat Hillary Clinton as a celebrity as much as a politician, and if so, did it generate the kind of attention that Trump attracted in celebrity news?

While we would expect Clinton to dominate political news before 2016, we would also expect Trump to receive low levels of coverage in political news. Trump's news should highlight his businesses and entertainment career for the most part, since that is what he spends most of his time doing. He has an active interest in promoting them. If Trump's levels of media coverage during this period are comparable to Hillary Clinton's, particularly in the news media or on political issues, it offers support to the thesis that celebrities are as capable of commanding news coverage as politicians are.

In this chapter, I compare Trump's and Clinton's ability to generate media attention and web searches when they were not presidential candidates, from

January 2009 through February 2013. Media attention is measured by the number of stories generated in broadcast news, procured through searches of the Lexis-Nexis database. Level of public attention in response to coverage of these candidates is measured through searches of the Google Trends database. During this time, Hillary Clinton served as secretary of state, while Donald Trump was a television star and businessmen. Both were reported to have presidential ambitions but neither ran for president in 2012. This period offers an opportunity to compare the ability of the politician and the celebrity to gain attention from the media and news consumers.

DISTINGUISHING POLITICIANS AND CELEBRITIES

Before examining the literature on the influence of celebrities in politics, and its implications for media agenda setting and even electoral prospects, some caveats are worth mentioning. First, Donald Trump did not win the popular vote. Thus, it is important not to exaggerate the role of celebrity in electoral outcomes. Even if Trump's ability to attract media attention is attributable to his celebrity status, and that this attention somehow affected the 2016 election, it was not enough for him to win a clear victory.

Second, Trump was a "one of a kind" candidate in a "one-off race." This is the first time that a celebrity with no prior political experience has run for the American presidency. In addition, as we shall see, he may have been a celebrity candidate in 2016, but he still had little in common with other politicians who had backgrounds as entertainers (Vavreck 2016). Another first is a male candidate running against the first female presidential candidate. Further study should be devoted to the question of how gender played a role in this election. Thus, while the analysis in this chapter may be revealing, it is far from comprehensive. What we conclude about Trump prior to the 2016 election may reveal some of the advantages Trump had, but might not tell us whether a similarly positioned candidate could achieve the same result.

Of course, this begs the question: what is a celebrity? Answers to this question are more elusive than they seem at first glance. As suggested above, if fame is an indicator of celebrity, it would be difficult to conceptually differentiate Barack Obama from Oprah Winfrey, let alone Clinton from Trump. In addition, not all public figures are considered celebrities, and how well one is publicly known can be relative (Marwick 2013). The politically aware and voters from his district may be able to recognize Dick Durbin, although few would count him as a celebrity. Thus, fame does not sufficiently distinguish public figures as celebrities, and an operational definition is necessary.

A celebrity "is a person who has a high public profile, usually promoted by appearances in the mass media and they are consequently readily recognized by others . . . characterized by exceptional or extraordinary qualities in terms of their abilities, attractiveness, personalities, and lifestyles" (Gunter 2014, 2). By that definition, famous artists, musicians, actors, and athletes, as well as businesspeople and even politicians can be considered celebrities.

While this definition helps us understand what a celebrity is, it does not offer much help in disentangling the ways in which celebrities interact with the political environment. In a contemporary mass culture society, former entertainers run for public office, politicians have fan bases that rival movie stars, celebrities use their star power to advance political and charitable causes, and all attend to their brand (Corner and Pels 2003). If we are interested in the differences between the impact of politicians on their environment as compared to popular entertainers, we must focus on ways to differentiate them.

West and Orman (2003, 2–8) attempt to make sense of this convergence by specifying four types of celebrities in politics. Those that entertain through political punditry—from Sean Hannity to Rachel Maddow, including former politicians such as Mike Huckabee—are known as "political newsworthies." Those who are famous because of their membership in powerful political families such as the Kennedys, Bushes, and at an earlier time the Roosevelts, are known as "legacies." "Famed nonpoliticos" include elected officials who were formerly entertainers, such as Ronald Reagan and Arnold Schwarzenegger, or celebrity activists/lobbyists such as Bono of U2 and George Clooney. "Event celebrities" are those who become famous due to an accidental or momentary event, such as a tragedy, scandal, or just being at the right place at the right time. Examples may include Anita Hill, Monica Lewinski, or Ken Bone—a man who had a brief burst of fame simply for asking a question at a presidential debate.

West and Orman are fairly comprehensive in their categorization of celebrity. They take into account the multiple ways in which celebrity and politics intersect through individuals who attempt to gain or exercise media and political power. Likewise, they presume that celebrity power relies upon audience recognition. Thus, even Ken Bone—or any individual appearing in a video gone viral—can become a famous name if he gains media attention.

While these definitions are descriptive, they do not offer much help in drawing contrast between politicians and celebrities. For example, this definition does not encompass all forms of celebrity, particularly in the social media age. What about politicians such as Senator Bernie Sanders, whose unsuccessful insurgent presidential run left him with an enthusiastic fan base? In addition, the presumption of fame is problematic, considering that celebrities receive different coverage across different media markets. While American and British celebrities saturate global media markets, some of the most famous celebrities in the world may never be known to Americans because the US media market can be fairly insular, keeping out non-English speaking artists. Fame is relative. Having one's video "go viral" to a broad audience is not necessary to attain celebrity status, although it might create a fan base. Micro-celebrities, people who command great attention within a small, targeted niche community can gain an intense cult fandom without being known to a wider audience (Marwick 2013). Beyond amateur performers on YouTube, obscure comic artists at Comic-Con or local musicians and athletes can command a level of celebrity within their own community of interest.

More importantly, this model offers no insight into the question of power. Can those celebrities who are not legitimately elected or appointed public officials compete for attention and influence with those who are? In order to get at this question, scholars must delineate between politicians and celebrities—and ultimately articulate a theory of celebrity influence—at least for the purpose of conceptual analysis.

CELEBRITIES VERSUS POLITICIANS: SOURCES OF POWER AND INFLUENCE

A good starting point for separating and comparing celebrities and politicians is to revisit French and Raven's bases of power typology (French and Raven 1959; Raven 1993). According to this model, there are six types of power: legitimate, expert, informational, reward, coercive, and referent power.[2] Since people have the potential to access any of these types of power, and because they are not exclusively tied to the exercise of influence by public officials, these bases offer ways to distinguish types of public figures. This section will summarize each of these forms of power and explain how they differentiate politicians and celebrities. The following section will explain how they differentiate Clinton and Trump.

Legitimate power is the idea that people can draw upon power based upon the normatively accepted status of their office. A CEO of a business or a president of the PTA can have legitimate power if others have faith in the office, the chain of command, and the institution itself. When looking at legitimate political power, there is a functional difference between celebrities and public officials. Successful politicians occupy public office, and in that office lies legitimacy—the notion that they have legally vested powers and a bureaucracy to put those powers into action. No entertainer, musician, artist, athlete, or other famous person of note has that. Thus, while the prior definitions offer some insight into what a celebrity is, for the purpose of this study, what separates politicians and celebrities is legitimate power. Following John Street's focus on "entertainers" as advocates, celebrities do not seek or acquire elected office (Street 2004, 438).[3] Ronald Reagan, Barack Obama, Paul Ryan, and Elizabeth Warren have or had legitimate power. Angelina Jolie, Ellen DeGeneres, Willie Nelson, and Oprah Winfrey do not. Put in this context, Barack Obama is more famous than Willie Nelson. Oprah Winfrey is more famous than Paul Ryan. But fame in itself does not necessarily equate to power. Obama and Ryan have or had power that is inaccessible to citizens, including celebrities. While celebrities may have qualities that are similar to that of politicians or activists, the lack of legitimate power make them more like high profile activists. By this definition, Ronald Reagan was a celebrity until he was elected governor of California. He may have kept those celebrity qualities once he came into public office. But earning public office gave him access to power beyond that of a typical celebrity activist, and he no longer organized as an outside activist would. By observing them in this manner, we can begin to meaningfully assess how much influence celebrities wield compared to politicians.

Expertise is a measure of how credible a person is in the minds of others (Andersen and Clevenger Jr. 1963; Hellweg 2004; Teven 2008). For a politician, credibility may be measured by education in a particular issue area, experience on committees or similar bodies, experience in leading the enactment or execution of public policy, or even getting elected to public office. For a celebrity, credibility might come from personal and educational experiences and/or connections to advocacy organizations (Thrall et al. 2008). When George Clooney sneaked into war torn areas of Sudan, he returned with a trove of information he shared in congressional hearings (Straziuso 2012). Angelina Jolie is a UN goodwill ambassador (Bella 2009). Bono studied global economics with Jeffrey Sachs and aligned himself with a network of debt advocacy organizations (Bunting and Burkeman 2002; Jackson 2008). Moreover, celebrities have been shown to be comparably credible or more credible than politicians across a number of policy issues (Harvey 2017, 83–119).

Informational power refers to the ability of an individual to utilize and control information "to quickly and credibly generate politically usable information and move it to where it will have the most impact" (Keck and Sikkink 1998, 16). Government organizations and political campaigns are built for this purpose, from emails to campaign ads; from texts to town hall meetings; from posters to interviews. Activist organizations must achieve the same function. Specifically, they hope to attract media attention to spotlight their issue of concern, and they attempt to frame issues in such a way to persuade the public and politicians to take action on this issue. Since they are frequently less endowed, they are at a relative disadvantage compared to public officials. In the 24-hour news cycle—intense competition, a short attention span, and a drive to produce more content and salacious stories to fill a vacuum of time and web space—celebrities are able to deliver what media organizations demand: "sex, scandal, violence, and celebrity," and by doing so, raise the profile of a political issue where activists and even politicians sometimes struggle (Bennett 2012; Bennett, Lawrence, and Livingston 2008; Cook 2005; Epstein 1973; Suzuki and Dressel 2004, 17).

The agenda-setting literature argues that the media play a role in selecting and framing content, and that it is influential over public attitudes and even over individuals' intention to vote (Dimitrova et al. 2014; Iyengar 1994; McCombs and Shaw 1972). Moreover, the amount of media coverage affects what is salient in the minds of the public, an intense power to direct public attention (Patterson 2016b). It thus follows that individuals, working with organizations and acting as policy entrepreneurs, may attempt to influence the public agenda (Cooper 2008; Fortunato and Martin 2016; Kingdon 2010; Maher 2001). Famous celebrities, acting as high profile activists, already come with financial resources, and brand- and image-building machinery. Moreover, when advocating on political issues, celebrities have the potential to be quite persuasive (Becker 2010; Harvey 2017; Jackson and Darrow 2005; Meyer and Gamson 1995).

A celebrity intervention can take several forms. It could be a charity effort, an endorsement of a candidate or an issue, or even a random statement of political belief. In order to maximize their effect, the most successful celebrities attempt to raise awareness of issues of public concern by working with policy entrepreneurs, as DeWitt argues elsewhere in this volume. Transnational advocacy groups lend celebrities consistency and credibility, access to a network of policy entrepreneurs, experts, and other advocates who can educate celebrities on these issues and connect them to high ranking officials (Harvey 2017, 43–46; Huliaras and Tzifakis 2011; Thrall et al. 2008; Tsaliki, Frangonikolopoulos, and Huliaras 2011). In addition, nearly all celebrity interventions are episodic. Celebrities are not full time professional activists, and they do not hold public office, so they intervene when they have time or when they feel called to do so. Played correctly, the media effect can be substantial.

The definition of *reward* or *coercive power* is fairly obvious. People can offer carrots or sticks to influence the behavior of others. Public officials have the means to reward and punish others through the administration of law, executive orders, public expenditures, offering or denying peers committee appointments, or even blaming, shaming, and holding each other accountable (Cigler, Loomis, and Nownes 2015; Keck and Sikkink 1998; Rodrigues 2004; Shaw 2005). Likewise, activists attempt to hold public officials accountable as they are able, utilizing whatever resources they can gather and affecting public opinion to pressure politicians to change policy (Batliwala and Brown 2006; Keck and Sikkink 1998). Famous and wealthy celebrities operate at another level. Like other big donors, they have the ability to materially coerce and punish by offering or threatening to cut off money. However, an important source of celebrity power is their ability to reward and coerce with informational power. While raising awareness, they can attack politicians or institutions and engage in protest—or make public appearances with politicians, patting them on the back for a job well done. A striking illustration of the power of informational coercion is Donald Trump's use of Twitter to attack and shame rivals, critics, and enemies. He utilized Twitter in this way long before his presidential campaign, and continued to do so once he became president (Blake 2016).

Finally, *referent power* refers to the ability to be liked or admired—a trait much in demand in both political and celebrity circles (French and Raven 1959; Kurzman et al. 2007; Marshall 1997; Tsaliki, Frangonikolopoulos, and Huliaras 2011, 9). Admiration and identification with politicians or celebrities is psychological—a manifestation of a virtual identity community. Public figures interact with their audiences through "parasocial relationships," where people feel a sense of familiarity and even intimacy with celebrities even though they do not personally know them. Thus, audiences relate to these figures while appreciating their art, listening to their music, watching them play a sport, or seeing them speak, act, or perform. This familiarity can become so emotionally intimate that these distant celebrities—or the characters they play—can seem like friends or family (Horton and Wohl 1956; Marwick 2013, 219). In the absence of a real personal relationship, people make judgments about celebrities based upon their subjective perceptions of their art, characters, or information presented in other forms of media.

Thus, identification with public figures is also a social phenomenon. Republicans and Democrats favor their respective politicians in part because of their common social experiences, and because of membership in a political identity group. Likewise, fans of actors and musicians, or athletes and teams share a common social identity and community with people who like those individuals, and separated from those who do not (Caughey 1984; Lammie 2007; Marshall 1997). Social identity theory suggests that people favor their in-groups at the expense of out-groups (Brewer and Schneider 1990; Hinkle and Brown 1990; Hogg and McGarthy 1990; Tajfel 2010). These groups can be activated through the use of symbolic politics, the "ability to call upon symbols, actions, or stories that make sense of a situation for an audience that is frequently far away" (Keck and Sikkink 1998, 23–24). Someone who is successful at this can both unite and divide people around symbols that denote emotional attachment to identity groups, rendering some images and groups as threatening and others as reassuring (Edelman 1985; Marshall 1997). Celebrities may have this ability to bring people together. Republicans find celebrities more credible than Democratic politicians across a host of issues, and Democrats also favor celebrities over Republicans, suggesting that celebrities are able to mediate across party lines (Harvey 2017). Similarly, celebrities tend to get better treatment by members of Congress when they are invited to testify before committees (Strine 2004).

Politicians are particularly good at inciting emotions through the symbolic uses of politics among identity groups (Edelman 1985). However, celebrities also have this capacity, perhaps to a greater degree. One reason is that celebrities often come equipped with emotional content, and are trained to communicate that content through their artistic medium (Darr and Strine IV 2009; Huddart 2005; Tolson 2001). Another is that celebrities are perceived as outsiders in the political system, and thus treated with higher levels of trust. Celebrities are seen as wealthy or popular and unelected, so are perceived to hold no obligations to political faction or moneyed interests—other than the money necessary to finance their next artistic endeavor (Atkin and Block 1983; Crosby and Bender 2000; Harvey 2017; West and Orman 2003). Both emotional artistic content and autonomy from the political system tend to lend authenticity to these individuals (Balliger 1999; Fenster and Swiss 1999; Marshall 1997; Marwick 2013; Trilling 1972).

TRUMP VERSUS CLINTON: COMPARING THEIR POWER AND INFLUENCE

In order to determine whether either of these candidates had particular advantages over the other, it is necessary to review the power model to compare their power and influence, and ultimately to see if the data are consistent with this analysis.

First, Clinton had clear legitimate power compared to Trump. By definition, she was the politician, the former senator, the secretary of state, and she had the ability as secretary of state to make and enact policy through the bureaucracy. Trump did not. He was a famous businessman and host of a reality show—arguably known more for his recognizable brand and for his flirtations with the media than for his success in business. By 2013, Clinton had resigned from her position of legitimate authority. Having said that, when respondents were asked about whether Trump and Clinton were "more of a celebrity than a politician," Trump's celebrity scores were 31 percent higher than Clinton's (Harvey 2017, 22).[4] However, Hillary Clinton's 3.17 score on a 5-point Likert scale puts her in the middle among respondents. People know she is a politician, but she also was not ranked completely on the politician end of the spectrum. Testing whether Trump, the celebrity, is better able to command media attention than Clinton the politician may not be completely straightforward. While there is a functional difference between celebrities and politicians, is this difference meaningful? To what extent is Trump being covered for policy positions, or Clinton covered for her fame? Answers to this question may affirm this distinction or cause us to question it.

On expertise, this delineation is even clearer. Hillary Clinton was a well-connected attorney with extensive experience as a teacher in law school, an advocate on children's issues, and an active attorney. She was involved in organizing election campaigns, worked on the congressional committee that impeached President Nixon, and was appointed by President Carter to the board of directors to the Legal Services Corporation. All of these credentials would have made her an expert candidate for public office, although she chose to remain first lady of Arkansas and the United States while Bill Clinton served as chief executive. Despite some missteps in her leadership of health care policy with the Clinton administration, she managed to garner enough public support to be elected a US senator from New York. After a strong, but unsuccessful bid for the presidency in 2008, she was appointed secretary of state. Her career trajectory was clear and conventional. Based upon her legal, political, and policymaking experience, she was as expert as anyone who ran for public office.

Donald Trump was a real estate professional who carried on the family business. His level of success is highly debated, from the million dollar seed money his father gave him to start his professional life to multiple bankruptcies in his casino and hotel businesses to the mystery behind his net worth. Indeed, his interactions with the media have more closely resembled the kind of coverage reserved for glamorous movie stars on *Lifestyles of the Rich and Famous*. What he was most known for is promoting his businesses through popular entertainment media, affixing his brand name to multiple products, and hosting the hit reality television show *The Apprentice*. Every now and then, Trump would publicly muse about running for president of the United States, and the media would respond with cursory policy questions, accompanied by the typical awe reserved for celebrities that make outlandish statements. The closest he came to a serious presidential run prior to the announcement of his candidacy in 2015 was in 1999, when he announced the formation of an exploratory committee to run as a Reform Party candidate (King 1999). However seriously Trump may have taken this effort, which ultimately fell apart in 2000 due to party infighting, most pundits did not.

As in 2015, observers speculated that the announcement was a publicity stunt to aid Trump's business interests, which is not surprising, considering that practically every celebrity who ran for office prior to that time built a government resume before running for higher office, and then stopped their celebrity business to conduct a campaign (Squitieri 1999). Even Arnold Schwarzenegger had deep connections to the Republican Party and served in roles in the Reagan and George H. W. Bush administration and in California politics before running for governor. Trump did not stop his business or acting careers, and had virtually no experience in politics other than, admittedly, giving money to political candidates in return for favors (Korostelina 2016, 34). Thus, because he was never taken seriously and had never officially announced a presidential run, every mention of his interest in public office was treated as a temporary flirtation.

However, among Republicans surveyed in October 2016, Trump—compared to other politicians and celebrities—was ranked as most credible on the issue of income inequality, an issue related to his economic appeal to the "forgotten people" of America (Harvey 2017, 105; Jackson and Stanglin 2017).[5] A lack of political expert power clearly did not hurt his electoral prospects. However, if one evaluates Trump's expertise in the way that people evaluate celebrity credibility on political issues, this outcome may not be completely surprising. While Trump lacked affiliations with political advocacy organizations throughout most of his professional life, his personal experience likely played a role in the way people perceived his expertise. Many Americans, and particularly Republicans, respect business experience, which translated into credibility for Trump on economic issues, just as Angelina Jolie's experience with the United Nations lends her credibility on international issues (Harvey 2017, 91–95). While this type of expertise may not be comparable to a public official's policy experience, it is sufficient to garner a level of credibility.

In terms of informational power, both had it in abundance throughout the 2016 campaign as well as during the period of this study. Both had access to social media and advertisements throughout the campaign, and both candidates had the support of their respective national committees. Clinton's support in the Democratic National Committee was clearly stronger than Trump's in the Republican National Committee, although both took advantage of the communications infrastructure in those organizations. Considering these similar endowments, differences in informational power may relate to the ability to take advantage of new technologies, to raise money, and to avoid misstatements (Paolino and Shaw 2003; Vavreck 2016). Of course, the 2016 election was unusual in terms of what the candidates could and could not say, particularly given Trump's willingness to make outrageous statements.

As mentioned above, Trump received more coverage than any candidate in the 2016 campaign. Thomas Patterson's analysis is completely consistent with the logic behind coverage of celebrity activism:

> Trump's dominant presence in the news stemmed from the fact that his words and actions were ideally suited to journalists' story needs. The news is not about what's ordinary or expected. It's about what's new and different, better yet when laced with conflict and outrage. Trump delivered that type of material by the cart load. (Patterson 2016b)

Indeed, Trump's own book, *The Art of the Deal*, espoused this as a deliberate media strategy (Blair 2015; Korostelina 2016, 21; Lozada 2015):

> The point is that if you are a little different, or a little outrageous, or if you do things that are bold or controversial, the press is going to write about you. . . . I've always done things a little differently, I don't mind controversy. . . . The result is that the press has always wanted to write about me. . . . I'm not saying that they necessarily like me. Sometimes they write positively, and sometimes they write negatively. But from a pure business point of view, the benefits of being written about have far outweighed the drawbacks. (Trump and Schwartz 2009, 56)

This advantage may have played in his favor long before the 2016 campaign. While Hillary Clinton was secretary of state, she had one of the highest profile positions in the cabinet and command over a large bureaucracy. Reporters routinely followed her and reported on every significant move and meeting, and the US government backed all State Department communications. Clinton had to do virtually nothing to gain easy access to the news media. Trump, on the other hand, had businesses and a television show. The businesses afforded him a reasonable amount of news that he could supplement with occasional attention-getting antics through cameos on television and in movies or various media interviews and pranks. *The Apprentice*, however, was different. While Hillary Clinton had a few moments of media coverage demonstrating her foreign policy competence multiple times a week for four years, Donald Trump visited viewers' living rooms for nearly an hour, demonstrating his opinionated strength and business expertise for fourteen to sixteen straight weeks over fourteen years—not counting promotional spots or reruns.[6] Trump was able to talk to the camera through his conversations with contestants, creating, practicing, and burnishing the image that would eventually propel him to the presidency, nurturing parasocial relationships with a willing audience (Kranish and Fisher 2016, 217).

While Trump clearly had power and reach, he also played politics in a way that was more limited than the tactics employed by other celebrities. Trump rarely appears at benefits, and does not politically organize on behalf of specific issues as a celebrity policy entrepreneur would in cooperation with advocacy organizations. He made political endorsements. During the period of this study, he eventually endorsed Mitt Romney for president. However, the most common form of intervention was the random political comment, which in Trump's hands was a powerful tool. Finally, unlike most other celebrities, Trump had no clear causes—other than advancing the "birther controversy," perpetuating the conspiracy theory that President Barack Obama was not born in the United States. Ultimately, it was difficult for most commentators to determine whether these were sincere efforts to involve himself in public politics, or a crass attempt to gain attention for his businesses and television show.

Clinton and Trump both possessed material forms of reward and coercive power. They had money. Clinton had the power of the US government to reward or coerce allies and rivals around the world. Having said that, if the central question of this study regards their relative ability to command media attention, and thus hold sway over public opinion and potential voters, these sources of power would not have direct bearing on this audience. Clinton, in her capacity as secretary of state, would not have needed to pay for advertisements. The press simply follows the news events dutifully. Trump, likewise, was not interested in spending money on media spots (Vavreck 2016). Indeed, he never saw the need of spending much money on the 2016 campaign if the media was willing to cover him extensively anyway (Peters and Shorey 2016). However, both were able to reward the media, and thus the public, with stories of interest. As the media craves content, both were willing to oblige. Trump's form of news, however, always tended to be more unique because of his celebrity status, and more salacious because of his brazen statements.

Finally, both had a degree of referent power, although the edge on this form of power likely goes to Trump. From the time that Hillary Clinton first emerged on the national stage as wife of candidate Bill Clinton and eventually first lady, she was a woman that the press and the public loved to hate. While she earned the admiration of many, she was vilified by the right wing of the Republican Party (Carpentier 2016). Her tenure as secretary of state brought a mix of praise and criticism, and for a brief time, she was actually perceived as "cool" in the wake of an internet meme portraying her taking care of business on a plane, texting with shades (S. Parker 2012). This "coolness initiative" did not last into the 2016 campaign, where she was covered as much for her awkwardness as for her wonky policy positions (Waldman 2016). Directly prior to the primaries in the so-called "invisible primary" in 2015, Trump got more positive coverage than any potential candidate, and the Republican race received more coverage than the Democratic primary.

Clinton received overwhelmingly negative press during the same time (Patterson 2016a).

However, even negative coverage may have fed constructively into the image he built on *The Apprentice*. In this case, negative perceptions could be converted to respect and authenticity. Trump and other reality stars such as Simon Cowell from *American Idol* revolutionized the assumptions that networks had about the likability of a television character. They presumed that negative authority characters would turn off audiences. What they discovered was that people responded enthusiastically to a character who was, as Kranish and Fisher report, "simultaneously inspiring and negative—a politically incorrect truth teller." Trump's advisors deliberately used the show to build his authenticity quotient: to make him an "unlikely symbol of straight talk, an evangelist for the American gospel of success, a decider who insisted on standards in a country that had somehow slipped into handing out trophies for just showing up." Moreover, Trump's ability to project this image was not innate, but learned on the set. The same kind of training that benefits most celebrities—through coaching and repeated performance—benefitted Trump. According to NBC's head of public relations, Jim Dowd, "People on the street embraced him. He was mobbed. . . . He was a hero and he had not been one before. . . . That was the bridge to the [2016] campaign" (Harvey 2017, 32; Kranish and Fisher 2016, 217–18). In that way, he could be contrasted with "Crooked Hillary." He was perceived by supporters as the honest truth teller who would and could say things that his opponent would never dare. Thus, while both candidates had equal access to traditional and social media, Trump was able to get away with outlandish tweets and statements, while his supporters cheered him on. When Clinton made the slightest outlandish statement—her claim that half of Trump's supporters were a "basket of deplorables"—she was attacked (Blow 2016). Again, this is consistent with the independence people ascribe to celebrities. Celebrities are perceived as autonomous and credible outsiders, particularly in comparison to politicians.

MEDIA IMPACT: OUTSIDE THE CAMPAIGN CYCLE

Thus far, this chapter has presented a theory of celebrity influence and an approach to theoretically differentiate politicians from celebrities. In addition, it has analyzed the prospective ways in which Donald Trump and Hillary Clinton may be compared along this power spectrum. This section will discuss ways to substantiate their relative influence, particularly as it applies to their ability to extend informational power. Previous work on celebrity influence observed how celebrities and politicians comparatively made issues salient in the media (Harvey 2017, 63–82). The ability of an individual to raise consciousness about an issue in the media could be a powerful weapon in an election campaign. And if Donald Trump had this ability in abundance, long before the 2016 presidential campaign, he would come into the campaign with a clear advantage over many other candidates. Moreover, if he were more effective than Clinton at gaining attention before that campaign, then it would give him an even more distinctive edge.

In order to evaluate this prospective "edge," it is necessary to take Trump out of the 2016 election. If we remove the politician and the campaign from Trump and move him back to the time when he was primarily "Celebrity Trump," is there a difference in coverage between Trump and Clinton?

As mentioned above, an optimal time to sample was the period when Hillary Clinton was secretary of state. At that time, she had already lost the Democratic primary to Barack Obama, and had insisted that she would not be a candidate in the 2012 election. Granted, any politician can change his/her mind, and there was speculation about Clinton's interest or prospects in 2016. However, the 2012 election was foremost on the public's mind, and Clinton was a non-factor in that election. For the purpose of this analysis, the effective range of study is Hillary Clinton's full term as secretary of state, January 21, 2009 through February 1, 2013.

This period was more complex in analyzing Trump's coverage. While Trump did not officially announce a presidential run, he toyed with the idea of running for president—just enough to generate significant coverage. CNN first reported his interest during the week of October 3, 2010. Trump declared that he would not seek the nomination during the week of May 15, 2011. Thus, I have separated the data into three series. The first precedes his announcement of interest in running. The second is the period that begins with this statement and ends with his announcement that he would not seek the nomination. The third begins the week after his withdrawal and continues until February 1, 2013. Analyses on factors that may have affected search results on Trump were run separately for the first and third series to compare results before and after the media covered his interest in running for president. The second series was not analyzed in the same way, because it was impossible to determine whether searches during this time were driven by media speculation on the horse race or other variables.[7]

This chapter explores two empirical questions during Hillary Clinton's tenure as secretary of state. First, did she attract more media consumer attention than Donald Trump? Second, what drove media consumers to follow Clinton and Trump's activities? One would expect a politician to attract more media attention on political issues, which would generate more focus among consumers of news. Thus, media consumers should be engaging in more news searches for Clinton on political issues, and have less interest in the kinds of stories that might feature Hillary Clinton's lifestyle or associations with celebrities. It would not be surprising if Trump, on the other hand, drew more attention on stories that were not political. He is a famous celebrity and businessman, so people may respond by seeking general information about him and his lifestyle, or follow his entertainment and business activities. Exceptions to this would raise questions. If so, why did this pattern not play out as predicted, and what does this tell us about the power and influence of celebrities and politicians?

One way to measure the level of interest in Clinton and Trump over time is to look at how many Google searches they generate. Google Trends includes a tool that allows users to compare the number of searches on nearly anything, including these two candidates (Rogers 2016). Trump and Clinton can be compared not only on how many web searches they inspire, but also on news searches. Thus, someone who simply wants to find out more about these people and is not interested in reading news articles might just do a general web search. Someone who wants serious news about them might use the news search feature, which limits results to stories from various news outlets. Likewise, it is possible to cross-reference phrases like Trump and China to track how many times people wanted to know something about Trump in reference to China—perhaps something he said about China, or some kind of business he has done there. Measuring the number of searches Trump and Clinton generate gives us a sense of what is on the mind of the collective public. Thus, it is possible to consider how other variables may affect these potential spikes in coverage. Does a run of Trump's television show generate more searches for Trump? When he appears on Fox News, does it coincide with a jump in searches for Trump and other political issues? When Hillary Clinton's texting meme went viral, did it lead to a surge in searches relative to the political coverage she normally receives? Moreover, we can look at correlations between people's interest in specific issues and overall searches for these individuals. In other words, if people are curious about Clinton's position on same-sex marriage, does that drive searches any more than interest in her international activities? Because the system focuses on searches rather than levels of news coverage, it is possible to see whether levels of news coverage or specific events impact people's levels of interest, rather than presuming that the media's focus on an issue accurately reflects this interest.[8]

What variables might cause surges in searches? First, one would presume that coverage of Clinton would be primarily political. Searches for Trump, on the other hand, might or might not be driven by political coverage. Thus, I contracted two variables. For the first variable, I did a Google search for every week to determine when Trump made political statements.[9] If increases in web searches are correlated with political interventions, we would conclude that Trump's political statements are affecting searches for Trump. Another variable that could affect political interest in Trump is appearances on Fox News, where he appeared as a commentator and interviewee many times. If high web searches for Trump coincide with appearances on Fox News, it might suggest that views of Trump on conservative media drive interest in Trump.[10]

Likewise, one would expect that interest in Trump would be driven by his celebrity feuds, lifestyle, or his show. Two variables were also constructed to measure his celebrity activities. Like the political variable, I did a Google search to determine when Trump gained attention for his celebrity antics.[11] In addition, Trump's show, *The Apprentice*, would likely generate a lot of searches for Trump himself. Five seasons were broadcast during Clinton's tenure as secretary of state—three full seasons and part of a fourth when removing the period when Trump expressed interest in the presidency. A high number of web searches would not be surprising during the show's run, as people may simply be following the intrigue of the reality show.[12]

Another variable is social media. Twitter is Trump's preferred choice of social media. Might Trump's tweets affect coverage? Since Trump has been known to tweet about his show, his celebrity feuds, and political issues, this variable could explain people's interest in Trump, but may not reveal much about his celebrity influence.[13]

Another possibility to consider is the question of Hillary Clinton as a celebrity. As mentioned above, she had nearly universal name recognition and was an instantly recognizable member of Obama's cabinet. What kind of coverage did Clinton receive over this period? Most of her coverage was political, although she also was the subject of lifestyle and personality stories. Did this drive searches for her? To measure this possibility two variables were constructed. One was a measure of how often she was mentioned in a celebrity interest story.[14] The other was a measure of anytime Clinton was referred to as "cool" or "hip."[15] The first variable would indicate whether Clinton was able to generate interest based upon these celebrity-style stories. The second was more of a measure of her potential celebrity referent power. Politicians are not usually considered "cool," although there were a few times during Clinton's tenure as secretary of state where the media communicated that she was. Was this so-called "coolness offensive" able to translate to interest in Clinton (Fallon 2012)? If the data reveal that Clinton unexpectedly benefits from celebrity coverage or seems somehow "hip," it might cause us to challenge the functional separation of celebrity from politician in the first place, or at least force us to examine popular politicians who have celebrity-like characteristics, such as Barack Obama.

MEDIA COVERAGE AND SEARCHES FOR TRUMP AND CLINTON: 2009–2013

When analyzing the results of this study, one observation is clear: Clinton and Trump are on completely different trajectories.[16] Clinton travels in a professional world, speaking cautiously and diplomatically about international issues, free from loose political commentary. Trump plugs his business interests and television appearances, and gains attention for inflammatory insults and shocking political statements. Moreover, while both addressed some of the same issues over Clinton's tenure, they rarely addressed the same issues at the same time. They practically never addressed each other. For example, while Clinton served as secretary of state, Trump had virtually nothing to say about Clinton's role in the Benghazi controversy. Indeed, while Trump was extremely critical of the Obama administration, he was generally complimentary of both Hillary and Bill Clinton in multiple tweets and other public statements.[17] As a result, it is not possible to compare their media impact on a single issue at a single time during this period.[18] However, much can be inferred by looking at media coverage and search data in different ways.

Searching for Trump and Clinton

When comparing indices of Google searches for Trump and Clinton from 2009 through early 2013, a pattern emerges. As predicted, Clinton was the subject of more news searches ($\bar{x}$ = 9.88) than Trump ($\bar{x}$ = 5.61), and Trump prompted more web searches ($\bar{x}$ = 8.96) than Clinton ($\bar{x}$ = 5.88).[19] Thus, media consumers responded to them in different ways. People who searched for Clinton were following the news. People who searched for Trump may have been interested in news about him, but were more likely to seek out general information than information from news outlets.

Figure 6.1 summarizes the pattern of web searches for Clinton and Trump during this time. Trump's dominance over web searches is evident. Predictably, many of the major spikes are driven by salacious controversies or celebrity news. The first major spike in spring 2009 was a controversy in which Miss California, Carrie Prejean, speaking at the Miss USA pageant said:

> Well, I think it's great that Americans are able to choose one or the other. We live in a land where you can choose same-sex marriage or opposite marriage. And you know what? In my country, in my family, I think that I believe that a marriage should be between a man and a woman. No offense to anybody out there but that's how I was raised and that's how I think it should be: between a man and a woman. (Burns 2009; Orr 2009)

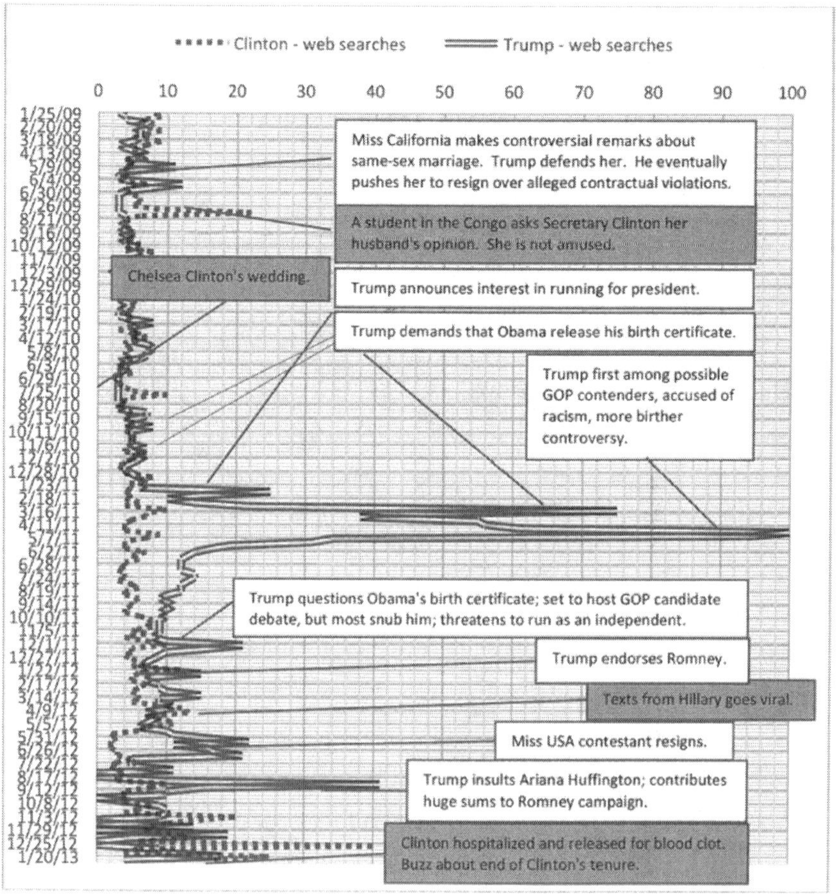

Figure 6.1. Timeline of web searches for Clinton and Trump, January 21, 2009 to February 1, 2013.
Created by the author.

Trump initially sided with her, arguing that her position was the same as President Obama's, which drew further controversy. Eventually, he pushed her to resign on the grounds of alleged contractual violations.

Another 2012 Miss USA controversy involved the resignation of Sheena Monnin, Miss Pennsylvania, from the pageant. She complained that the contest was "trashy" and "rigged and fraudulent," because she had discovered that Trump personally picks up to six of the semi-final contestants without due process. She resigned in protest, citing the unfairness of the competition, and—to make matters even more controversial protesting the organization's decision to allow transgender individuals who are born men to compete in women's beauty pageants. She later qualified that her problem was not with transgender people, but with changes to the rules. Trump, characteristically, sued her (Graves 2016; Prince 2012).

Both of these incidents enmeshed celebrity and politics, but not in a deliberate way. Trump did not initiate either of these actions, and seemed to perceive these as commercial concerns and not political ones. However, two lesser known celebrities—contestants in a beauty contest—took advantage of the high profile event to advance their views. Granted, Carrie Prejean's statement was a weak statement, no doubt intended to "straddle the fence" on the issue, which resulted in offense to many. Sheena Monnin's statement was strong, but almost accidentally political.

While some of Clinton's biggest search results focused on political stories, even those were sensational ones. One story involved an African student in the Congo asking the secretary of state for her husband's advice on a local matter. Clinton's "calm demeanor cracked" with her response: "My husband is not secretary of state. I am" (Clark 2009). Her response dominated the news cycle, and sparked a conversation about double standards applied to women in leadership positions. Clinton also received focused attention on nonpolitical stories, such as daughter Chelsea Clinton's wedding or when she was hospitalized at the end of 2012. Incidentally, these stories drove the biggest individual spikes in news searches for Hillary Clinton. It appears that the kinds of content that people are most likely to search for are the same across platforms.[20] They are just more likely to look for stories about Clinton in one place and Trump in another. Moreover, the same striking spike of attention Trump generated during the birther controversy was just as dramatic in news results as web results.

Clinton and Trump on the Issues: Consistent and Episodic Media Attention

Table 6.1 compares the level of public attention focused on Trump and Clinton in regard to policy issues. Since Clinton was secretary of state, most of her public statements focused on international issues. Thus, for the most part, this list includes references to countries that both Trump and Clinton discussed at some point during her time in office. The table is split into two parts. The first compares broadcast news coverage and Google searches for Trump and Clinton from January 2009 through October 2010, prior to Trump's first statement of interest in running for president in 2012. The second part replicates that comparison, starting in May 2011, right after Trump pulled his name out of consideration, and continuing until the end of Clinton's term.[21] An additional column computes the percentage of attention

Trump earned compared to Clinton. For example, in the first set, Trump only generated 6.73 percent of the searches that Clinton did in reference to China. In the second set, Trump generated 73.24 percent of Clinton's searches.

As expected, Clinton dominated coverage of all political issues surveyed in both broadcast media coverage and total web searches. This finding is consistent with the previous results, illustrating how media consumers tended to follow Clinton as they followed the news. Most of these countries and their accompanying issues are not commonly discussed outside the realm of politics, academia, or current events—a natural mismatch for general web searches about Trump.

Prior to Trump's prospective run, the total amount of media attention Trump received on all sampled issues was 9.89 percent of what Clinton received. That percentage increased to 21.98 percent after he gave up the race. Likewise, comparing both periods, web searches for Trump on these issues also increased from approximately 20 to 40 percent in proportion to Clinton's search results. It appears that the period of his prospective run seemed to affect the way he was perceived both by the media and by people searching

Table 6.1. Broadcast News Coverage and Web Search Results for Trump and Clinton

	Broadcast Transcripts			*Web Search Index*		
Pre-Run	*Clinton*	*Trump*	*%*	*Clinton*	*Trump*	*%*
China	1717	108	6.29%	13.67	0.92	6.73%
Climate Change	855	62	7.25%	3.32	1.10	33.22%
Israel	1384	86	6.21%	10.73	0.61	5.72%
Mexico	1520	135	8.88%	5.07	1.17	23.09%
Syria	235	7	2.98%	2.24	0.00	0.00%
Same-Sex Marriage	903	256	28.35%	9.15	5.07	55.40%
Totals	6614	654	9.89%	44.17	8.875	20.09%
Range: 1/21/2009–10/2/2010						

	Broadcast Transcripts			*Web Search Index*		
Post-Run	*Clinton*	*Trump*	*%*	*Clinton*	*Trump*	*%*
China	1838	44	2.39%	11.00	8.06	73.24%
Climate Change	405	176	43.46%	15.24	0.13	0.88%
Israel	1617	337	20.84%	5.53	1.30	23.58%
Mexico	1137	400	35.18%	13.82	7.20	52.11%
Syria	2223	401	18.04%	9.76	0.44	4.49%
Same-Sex Marriage	1300	515	39.62%	13.00	5.22	40.19%
Totals	8520	1873	21.98%	68.348	22.36	32.71%
Range: 5/16/2011–2/1/2013						

for information about him. At no time did Trump surpass Clinton in media coverage or searches. However, for someone who had no real political experience, the ability to attract a lot of media attention among broadcasters on political issues is still striking. It is also worth noting that he lacked the kind of political organizational and institutional support that many celebrities such as Bono or George Clooney employ in order to raise awareness of an issue. Moreover, because many of these interventions took the form of random statements or political opinions rather than specific issue campaigns or calls to action, the level of attention he attracted is still fairly impressive.

Also striking is the disproportionate number of searches for Trump with some policy issue, compared to actual media coverage. Trump came out against gay marriage in 2011, likely spurring additional interest in this subject, but news coverage appeared to be proportional to the level of interest. In other areas, it appears that Trump's statements may not have connected with reporters nearly as much as they resonated with media consumers. Looking at the search results after his run, it is not surprising that he got the highest search levels on China and Mexico, and that these percentages massively outstripped the level of attention they were receiving in the media.[22] Overall, this analysis confirms a long-standing speculation that there is a disconnect between mainstream media news and the kinds of issues that interest many consumers. The general media seems out of touch with those who followed Trump during this time.

As mentioned before, Clinton has the highest totals in media exposure. However, if we were to look at search results on a timeline as if it were a line graph, it is clear that Trump occasionally eclipses Clinton in discrete periodic coverage. For example, in 2009, Trump had the biggest burst of news coverage compared to Clinton on the issue of same-sex marriage. The coverage, however, directly related to controversies in the Miss USA pageant. In the post-run period, Trump made quite provocative political statements, and inspired large spikes in news coverage. One example was his famous tweet from November 6, 2012: "The concept of global warming was created by and for the Chinese in order to make U.S. manufacturing non-competitive." This statement produced a bigger media impact than any statement Clinton made on China or global warming.

The same generalization can be made about web searches on figure 6.1. Clinton's search results are even and consistent, as one might expect when news organizations routinely monitor the statements and actions of public officials. At that time, Trump did not have a media entourage documenting his political positions. Thus, Trump's results display large, episodic spikes, accompanied by periods of low interest. As is the pattern with most celebrity interventions, Trump did not get involved in politics on a daily basis—he had businesses to run and a television show to promote. However, when he intervened with a political statement, or was at the center of a political controversy, the effect tended to be strong and dramatic. These patterns also play into the news cycle and desires of news organizations. Clinton was doing her job—the day-to-day work of maintaining diplomatic relations with allies and challenging potential rivals. In contrast, Trump's occasional bursts of celebrity activity were entertaining, unusual, and surprising.

The biggest intervention by either Trump or Clinton is outside of the range of table 6.1, because it occurred while Trump considered a run for president. Figure 6.1 reports a huge spike surrounding Trump's advocacy on the birther issue. This is one situation where Trump actually took a single issue—just as many celebrities do—and hammered it in the public spotlight. Even his announcement of a potential presidential run early in October 2010 failed to gain that level of attention. It took him at least three such announcements before people started really searching for him as a possible candidate in February 2011, and only after he made the "birther controversy" one of his main talking points. Coverage increased in the middle of March when he began actively advocating for the release of Obama's official birth certificate. A month of intense news coverage led to Trump rising to first in the polls among possible GOP contenders. He also received additional attention and scrutiny since his actions and some of his statements were construed as racist. The effects of this campaign were not insignificant. Before Trump championed the birther movement, 25 percent of Americans and 51 percent of Republicans doubted Obama's citizenship. By April, 38 percent of all Americans believed that Obama was definitely born a US citizen. As late as August, 72 percent of Republicans believed Obama was not born in the US (Barbaro 2016; Barr 2011; Cheney 2016; Clinton and Roush 2016; Condon 2011; Parker and Eder 2016). Although Trump technically achieved victory by pressuring the president to release his birth certificate, the fact that Obama had legally proven his citizenship slowed Trump's momentum somewhat. That victory, along with Obama's subsequent humorous roast of Trump at the White House Correspondent's Dinner and the killing of Osama Bin Laden likely led to Trump dropping out of contention.

After the run, Trump attempted to make himself a "kingmaker" in the Republican Party. His appearances on Fox News increased. He was allowed to host an early GOP candidate debate on Fox News, but withdrew after most refused to attend. An angry Trump threatened to run as an independent, but ultimately endorsed Mitt Romney and showered money on his campaign. Directly after Obama's victory in November, Trump called for a revolution (Cohn 2012). As table 6.1 illustrates, after his "run," Trump's political interventions became more frequent, and interest in Trump became more pronounced overall.

Correlates of Coverage: What Drives Media Attention?

It is tempting to think that media coverage in general, and coverage of these candidates in particular, is driven by sensationalist "man bites dog" or unusual "fish out of water" stories. There is certainly truth to this, and this theme plays out in some of the analysis. At the same time, that would be an overly simplistic analysis. Ultimately, when it came to overall news coverage, Clinton's structural dominance over the news as a legitimate public figure commanded overall coverage. However, individual spikes in coverage may be characterized by the unusual. Moreover, web searches tend to be more representative of people's interest, while news stories tend to present issues based on what government and media elites think is important—or what they think is likely to sell with their target demographics.

Figure 6.1 illustrates how Trump dominated web searches, and how media consumers took more of an interest in Trump's political activity over time. Additional statistical analysis reveals that interest in Trump prior to his run coincided with his appearance in celebrity news and new episodes of *The Apprentice*. His political activities during this time did not seem to affect total searches for Trump, although his appearances on Fox News did.[23] However, actual broadcast news coverage responded to all of his interests: new *Apprentice* episodes, his appearances on celebrity news, and any political activities or controversies.[24] Thus, even before he considered himself a prospective candidate, Fox News appeared to be a vehicle for advancing his political positions, and news coverage still followed his celebrity and television activities. It appears that Trump's argument, that he is a "ratings machine," may be valid—or at least major broadcast networks believed he had that potential and were willing to give him coverage across a range of his activities.

Trump's presumptive presidential run from 2010–2011 also seemed to be good for his own ratings—specifically on *The Apprentice*. Compared to the previous season with an average Nielsen rating of 1.7, ratings for *The Apprentice* increased to 3.3 during the period when Trump talked about running for president between 2010 and 2011. This implies that *The Apprentice* may not have been generating political interest in Trump nearly as much as the possibility that Trump's non-*Apprentice* activities were keeping the show alive.[25] It also feeds the argument that many in the media made in 2016, that his candidacy was intended more to benefit his businesses and brand than to actually win the presidency. Ratings during this floated candidacy were still low compared to the show's fourteen season average of 4.21. However, the seasonal ratings surge may have saved the show after his weakest season of the entire series, which suffered a precipitous drop after the 2009–2010 season's rating of 3.2.[26] He would never again return to ratings as high as those he had during his prospective run.

His post-run correlations paint a different picture. Only one factor is significantly related to web searches for Trump and coverage of him in broadcast news: his political activities. Celebrity news, Fox News appearances, and even new episodes of *The Apprentice* could not compare, and were not statistically significant.[27]

His Twitter activity was not a significant factor in gaining media attention or generating web searches. While Trump had some political tweets before January 2011, tweets generally correlated with appearances on Fox and new *Apprentice* episodes since so many of them were advertisements for television interviews and *The Apprentice*. Surveying Trump's tweets between January 25, 2009 and May 26, 2012, Fox News appeared 89 times. *The Apprentice* appeared 116 times, with NBC appearing 98 times, mostly in reference to the show. CNN appeared 30 times. None were critical of the news outlets. All were advertising his interviews or appearances. After 2011, his tweets become sporadically more political, but still did not make news. For example, between September 11, 2012 and January 24, 2013, he tweeted 69 times about China. In contrast, the State Department tweeted 19 times about China. A cursory survey of Trump's politically-oriented tweets during this time period demonstrate the obvious: that lots of people follow, like, and retweet Trump's tweets no matter what he posts on Twitter. In contrast, Clinton did not tweet about State Department business. The State Department tweeted modestly and conservatively, and Clinton's name was not generally mentioned in the tweets.

Finally, did celebrity-style coverage of Hillary Clinton affect web searches for her? On several occasions, Clinton was covered for personal stories, such as the aforementioned wedding of Chelsea Clinton. More significantly, in March 2012, a photo of Hillary Clinton sitting on a plane texting with sunglasses on went viral. It became the subject of many memes, some referencing other high profile politicians like Barack Obama, Joe Biden, and Mitt Romney, and famous celebrities such as Justin Bieber, Ryan Gosling, Jay-Z, Beyoncé, Mark Zuckerberg, Jon Stewart, and Stephen Colbert. Even Bill Clinton did a Photoshop parody of the photo for his Twitter profile on April Fool's Day. Hillary Clinton made her own meme to join in on the fun. This began an ongoing celebrity-style interest in Clinton that temporarily transformed the way she was perceived in the media. Prior to this meme, and the accompanying "Texts from Hillary" website, pundits treated her as a typical secretary of state with the regular level of scrutiny associated with the challenges of executing foreign policy. She received criticism for failing to "push the reset button" with Russia, failing to condemn the Chinese for their human rights record, and continuing aggressive anti-terror policies initiated by the Bush administration. After the meme, she was cool. Articles were devoted to the subject, and terms like "hip" and "kick ass" were routinely interjected into the headlines. Meryl Streep talked about the things she had in common with Hillary Clinton in March, and took a selfie with her in December (Doll 2012; McDevitt 2012). One week, Clinton was dancing in South Africa. Another week, she was drinking beer in Colombia (Fallon 2012; Parker 2012). Obama joked at the White House Correspondents' Association Dinner, "Four years ago I was locked in a brutal primary battle with Hillary Clinton. Four years later she won't stop drunk-texting me from Cartagena" (Klatell 2012). Clinton was cool for growing her hair long and not wearing makeup. People suggested that Obama drop Joe Biden as vice president and move Clinton into his place (Cillizza and Weiner 2012). This positive attention seemed to last for the remainder of the year and to the end of the term, even despite criticism over her handling of the Benghazi incident. Did this burst of media attention drive media consumers' attention?

In short, no. Coverage of Clinton as "cool" or personal/celebrity stories about her did not correlate with web search results.[28] Again, Clinton is a politician, and being in the political news is part of her job. Those who were interested in Clinton's "cool offensive" may have been the same people who followed her in the news. It is just as likely that the media elite was attracted by this new image of Clinton and used it to try to attract attention to their broadcasts, perhaps trying to make her a ratings machine, too. Again, low web search results imply an occasional disconnect between what the mainstream media offers and what many people are willing to consume.

Ironically, while Clinton's charm campaign gained little attention, Trump's political activities gained a lot of attention. Trump was able to cross over. He was already popular as a nonpolitical celebrity. When he started making more political statements, he was able to benefit from this diversification in a way that Clinton could not. For Trump, celebrity and business is normal and predictable. When he got political, he got interesting.

WHO WON?

This chapter offered some important findings that reinforce our knowledge of celebrities in politics. Celebrities have a range of options to exercise power and influence in the political realm. This chapter used legitimacy as a conceptual dividing line between politicians who hold public office and celebrities who do not, and illustrated how celebrities and politicians have different sources and expressions of power. Otherwise, this study focused less on reward/coercive power and expert power. Certainly, more can and should be studied about the way that celebrities possess and employ these kinds of power. Instead, this chapter primarily focused on informational power, and to a lesser extent, referent power. Who best utilized informational and referent power in the period while Clinton was primarily a politician and Trump was primarily a celebrity and a part time candidate? Donald Trump may have won the 2016 election, but whether he "won" the contest of media attention between 2009 and 2013 depends upon interpretations of their relative effectiveness in deploying these forms of power. The results offer a mixed picture.

Both Clinton and Trump were able to command media attention effectively, but in different ways. The way that Trump employed informational power was unusual compared to the way other celebrities use it. With the exception of advocacy on the birther issue, he acted more like a candidate—commenting on multiple issues at different times—rather than pushing a single issue at a focused moment. Granted, the birther issue was a significant exception. However, it seems most likely that Trump stumbled into this issue and discovered how well it played with the media and the base as he contemplated a run for president. He was not out to campaign on an issue that was independent of either his desire to become president or his desire to raise the ratings of his television program.

Not surprisingly, his interventions were still more episodic than Clinton's.[29] Over multiple periods, interest in Trump's interventions dwarfed similar peaks of interest in news about Clinton's political activities. Despite a lack of organizational affiliation and assistance from professional activists, interest in his activities was massive. Many celebrities intervene in the news cycle in this way with similar effects (Harvey 2017, 66–76). What effect do these dramatic spikes of coverage have on public discourse in the short and long run? How does it differ from issues, events, and people who do not have the same temporary and intense effect? More research is necessary to understand the effect of different kinds and durations of media coverage.

Content and context are important, too. When does interest in a statement convert to action? Clearly, Trump tapped into angst about Obama in the Republican Party by advancing the birther conspiracy theory, and enough momentum was built to pressure Obama to put the issue to rest. However, when Trump talks about how global warming is a Chinese conspiracy, it may have had some impact on the attitudes of Republicans, just as the birther argument did, but it clearly did not affect any change in public behavior. Future studies should look to determine effects of specific interventions and determine conditions or a threshold where spikes in attention convert to some sort of measurable outcome. These questions are beyond the scope of this study, but knowing more about the results of these kinds of interventions would offer an important contribution to understanding the effect of celebrity interventions.

Moreover, more can be explored about the birther movement and Trump's simultaneous interest in running for president. It appears that Trump's embrace of the birther movement brought about a huge surge of interest in him, starting in March 2011. However, what impact did the Republican horse race play in that coverage? An analysis of the kind of coverage earned by other prospective Republican candidates can help to determine the effect of political movements during this period. If all potential candidates received attention that was proportional to Trump's during this period, we may conclude that the increased intention was not a function of his celebrity or his statements about Obama, but was instead a normal function of the way the press was anticipating the 2012 election.

Clinton dominated coverage and public attention in political news and on political issues. Trump dominated coverage in general web searches, driven by the combination of his celebrity and political activities. So while Clinton had a clear edge in political coverage, Trump still captured an impressive amount of attention on political issues, and seemed to have a broader cultural impact in terms of consumer interest. As a result, the massive demand for Trump likely drove free media coverage in the 2016 election. Jeff Zucker—the man who signed Donald Trump to *The Apprentice*, and was satirically "fired" by Trump on *Saturday Night Live*—subsequently moved to CNN in time for the 2016 election, also literally referred to Trump as a "ratings machine," and has commented on how the free media phenomenon related to Trump's celebrity: "[I] had a unique relationship with Donald Trump, I will acknowledge. . . . [T]here was a little bit of a phenomenon to Donald Trump . . . we did give him quite a bit of coverage" (Gold 2016).

This quotation should offer a reminder that Fox News may have played an active role in the rise of Trump—Fox covered the birther controversy extensively—but other networks followed suit. What remains unexplored here was his relationship to other media organizations. *The Apprentice* was on NBC, and Trump was close to Zucker on CNN and made multiple appearances on CNN broadcasts. What about the rest? Moreover, this study does not address the rise and role of other right wing media outlets such as Breitbart News. How did they cover Trump during this time? At what point did they become influential? An initial survey of these news sources demonstrated that searching and accessing archives of right wing websites in a systematic way is difficult. However, a deep dive into right wing coverage of Trump could offer some insights into their effects on web searches.

This study makes the more limited case that the infrastructure of Trump's television brand, as well as his political activities, drove consumer interest in Trump himself. Trump, the celebrity, had access to the means to feature prominently in the media. The unusual picture of a celebrity advocating political positions was fascinating enough for audiences to respond with interest. Plus, Trump's penchant for making outrageous statements and espousal of controversy made for good television. Trump delivered on sex, scandal, and celebrity during this time, and even included a measure of violence at his rallies in 2016, all of which attract viewers (Bennett 2012; Epstein 1973; Selk 2017; Suzuki and Dressel 2004, 17). Hillary Clinton delivered on none of these, either during the 2016 campaign or during her time in office as secretary of state.

Unlike Clinton, Trump was able to successfully convert cultural capital to political capital. Even after the excitement generated from the "Texts from Hillary" meme, Clinton could not extend her "cool factor" beyond the journalists and political news consumers who followed her in the media. Likewise, no number of celebrity associations or endorsements were strong enough to offer Clinton the referent power that Trump seemed to have. For Trump, cultural impact seemed to override political expertise in the way that consumers, and ultimately voters, perceived him.

Ultimately, this ability to step outside of political norms seemed to be a key factor in determining coverage, and consistent with his media strategy from *The Art of the Deal*, a rephrasing of the quote attributed to P. T. Barnum, "there's no such thing as bad publicity." Indeed, the very fact he was a celebrity was likely a factor in his ability to make statements and engage in behavior that would have normally been outside the political norm. Granted, Trump was not the first to take on the cause of "birtherism," but he was its most prominent and successful advocate. Could—or would—Mitt Romney have done the same if Trump had not? Romney did not, and given political norms, he probably would not. Indeed, much of the Republican Party establishment distanced themselves from Trump's more extreme and salacious arguments and claims throughout the 2016 campaign, and many still have trouble defending his precise statements and actions.

Trump may be even more demonstrative than the average celebrity, but the presumed eccentricity associated with a celebrity, or the unconventionality associated with an outsider, allowed Trump to say and do things most politicians would not. When supporters argue that Trump "tells it how it is," it does not necessarily mean that he tells the truth. Instead, it means that he is speaking authentically, without the filter of a political system dictating what he should or should not do. When asked about the attraction of authenticity in celebrities, respondents argued that they trust celebrities because they do not financially gain from their political statements, that they are passionate about issues and display it in their work, and they are relatable. Ultimately, they are not afraid to speak the truth because they are not afraid of the consequences. When Hillary Clinton lost an election, it mattered a lot to her. Her professional career was politics. Donald Trump was less desperate. He could say what he wanted, because he already had money, fame, businesses, and entertainment interests. He did not need politics, was not a part of politics, and so could logically stand above it. The same logic has been applied to other notable celebrities such as Bono (of the rock band U2), George Clooney, or Angelina Jolie (Greene 2016; Harvey 2017, 57). When they intervene, they are also seen as advocating in a way that is above the normal political fray.

This perceived authenticity often outweighs evaluation of these individuals as normal human beings. All of them take potential commercial risks when making unpopular statements. They also have the potential for positive public relations payoffs if a political intervention improves their social capital and heightens their brand. Plus, while many do not perceive a direct financial gain from celebrity activism, they are certainly concerned with money—as much or more than any politician is (Erb 2013; Harvey 2017, 38–40). In Trump's case, the evidence suggests that his political activities may have saved *The Apprentice* from an otherwise weak season. Trump may have learned from this experience that exciting politics makes for good television—and good business.

Indeed, it seems that many of Trump's activities set the stage for the 2016 campaign. His successful birther campaign may have hurt his chances for seeking the presidency in 2012, but it did illustrate how he could ride controversy to the top of the Republican polls, and essentially get away with it as Celebrity Trump. He would do that over and over again during the campaign—from vicious tweets to name calling, from labeling Mexicans as "rapists" to promising to make Mexico pay to build a border wall, from chastising a Gold Star family to insisting that he could "stand in the middle of Fifth Avenue, shoot somebody, and I wouldn't lose any voters" (Cohn 2016). The formula of being a successful celebrity was the same formula that made him an ultimately successful candidate. It appears that he also believes that it is the formula to make him a successful president.

NOTES

1. For an alternative perspective, see Thrall, et al. (2008).
2. Much of this analysis follows Harvey (2017, 40–57).
3. There is a potential conceptual challenge with Street's definition. His definition of celebrity excludes those who seek office. This is clearly a "grey area." Almost by definition, someone who seeks office is a politician, no matter what their experience. Prior to Trump's 2016 run, there were no examples of a president running for office who had no experience with public office. Absent any past examples of legitimacy or experience, a candidate is essentially left with nothing but their job title, social connections, and in this case, celebrity status. Someone like Trump had no real experi-

ence even in basic policymaking. Thus, while Trump may have been a politician of sorts when he flirted with a 2012 run or actually engaged in a 2016 run, he was more a celebrity running for office than a public official moving up the chain.

4. On a 5-point Likert scale, Clinton's mean score was 3.12, while Donald Trump's mean score was 4.50. This survey was conducted in October 2016. The fact that this survey was conducted within one month of Election Day also challenges Street's definition of a non-celebrity as someone who seeks public office. Clearly, those respondents in the middle of a presidential campaign believed that Trump was not a politician.

5. Trump's score among Republicans was a 3.30 on a 5-point Likert scale, a score that was higher than other select politicians and celebrities ($N = 126$). Rubio was second with 3.14, followed by Obama (3.05), Bruce Springsteen (2.67), and Hillary Clinton (2.37).

6. "Expertise" is a highly subjective term in this context. First, reality shows are constructed in such a way to deliver a plot in the same way as a fictional show does. Nearly anyone can be portrayed as "expert." As for Trump's actual expertise, it is fair to say that many years of experience in real estate certainly implies, if not denotes, a degree of expertise. Many critics might point to the declining net worth of his investments over the period of his life and his multiple business bankruptcies, suggesting that experience does not always correlate with expertise.

7. This was not only necessary from the perspective of removing Trump from campaign mode. It also was a difficult range because of other confounding variables. According to preliminary analyses, the times when Trump played with being a presidential candidate coincided strongly with his advancement of the birther question (б = 0.41; $p \leq 0.001$), likely as a means to gain attention for his candidacy. It also positively correlated with increased coverage of Trump by Fox News, so there was no way to clearly prove that Fox was a unique vehicle for Trump's ambitions (б = 0.40; $p \leq 0.001$). Moreover, it was impossible to tell from the data whether he would have gotten more or less coverage than any other candidate during a cycle where the media may have been focusing on the presidential horse race anyway, and he was just one possible candidate of many. One of the seasons of *The Apprentice* was broadcast during this time, which made the show's run positively correlate with periods where Trump was either teasing or actively declaring his interest as a presidential candidate (б = 0.18; $p \leq 0.05$) and periods where Trump was advancing the birther issue (б = 0.26; $p \leq 0.001$). Trump's overall coverage in media outside of Fox News was also correlated to new *Apprentice* episodes (б = 0.22; $p \leq 0.05$) and Trump's prospective candidacy (б = 0.34; $p \leq 0.001$), but only when including the time range where Trump appears to be talking about the presidency. Likewise, ratings for *The Apprentice* are positively related to coverage of the birther issue and Fox News appearances, suggesting that all of these events together may have improved ratings on *The Apprentice*. When removing this time range, the correlations are different. Thus, it was not possible during this time to determine whether *The Apprentice* was driving web and news searches, or any of these other variables. Thus, the decision to eliminate this range was made not only to separate Trump from the perception of a presidential run, but also to avoid multicollinearity in the model.

8. Using search results found in Google Trends as a dependent variable is a way to gauge interest in public figures and associated stories. There are both advantages and disadvantages to this tool. Advantages include an indexing feature. When comparing Trump and Clinton, it does not measure actual numbers of searches, but randomly samples and indexes them comparatively on a 0–100 scale. It also effectively compares variables over time. There are some shortcomings. It works well with just a few variables, but is less effective when comparing many different kinds of variables. It also may exaggerate the importance of an event if taken out of context. If two variables are compared and both have low coverage, spikes can still look dramatic. Thus, it doesn't work well if the sample is over a relatively short period. This is not a problem for this study, which samples searches for two people weekly over roughly a four year period. Both are high profile individuals, so the implicit sample size is large. In addition, there can be false positives—times when a spike appears to show some level of interest, but it cannot be traced to a specific event that is documented online. So the people searching might be responding to something that was not well documented on the internet, or simple curiosity. This may be amplified if the sample size is low to begin with. I have addressed this challenge in this study by duplicating searches in Google's search engine during the periods of high search results in order to trace a possible cause and effect between searches and results. If an event directly precedes a burst in search activity, we can assume that there is a relationship between an event and a spike in searches (Rogers 2016).

9. If Trump made a political statement that week, a 1 was entered. If not, it was coded with a 0.

10. Trump's appearances on Fox News were tracked using Broadcast Transcripts in the Lexis-Nexis search engine, and recorded as a weekly tabulated total.

11. If Trump was being covered for a lifestyle or celebrity-oriented activity for each week in the series, a 1 was entered. If not, it was coded with a 0.

12. This was constructed as a dummy variable. A 1 was assigned to any weeks when *The Apprentice* was in an original broadcast. A 0 was assigned to any weeks when it was not. Data for reruns was not available. This variable presumes that new episodes may generate more interest than reruns, but this may not be the case. A similar variable was constructed, where the ratings for each respective season were aligned with the original broadcast times. This produced no real difference in overall results.

13. Trump's tweet totals were counted per week to see if the number of tweets would affect the number of searches or the magnitude of coverage.

14. This variable was generated through a Broadcast Transcripts search in Lexis-Nexis in which "Hillary Clinton" and celebrity appeared within the same paragraph. Then I looked through each article to make sure that there were no false positives, and entered the number of articles for each week where Clinton was discussed in the context of a popular celebrity article.

15. This "coolness" variable was created by doing a Google search for the period of the study referencing "Hillary Clinton," and "cool," or "hip." The first ten pages of search results were tabulated. Articles were reviewed for relevance and discarded false phrases like, "cool response."

16. There is no significant correlation between web and news searches for Hillary Clinton and Donald Trump on Google. Thus, whatever news or information that may be driving searches is not affecting them simultaneously. Both seem to attract different sorts of attention, which should not be terribly surprising.

17. See Trump's tweets on September 4, 6, and 21, October 10, 17, and 18, 2012. He also wished her well after being in the hospital on January 3, 2013.

18. My original research design was to compare Trump's and Clinton's statements and actions on the same issues at the same time to determine who was best able to command attention during that period, following Harvey (2017). Since they addressed completely different issues at different times, this design was abandoned.

19. "Donald Trump" and "Hillary Clinton" were entered into Google Trends in two searches: one for web and one for news, and these numbers were indexed, and then divided by the number of days over the period to produce a mean score. The news and web results compare Clinton and Trump within each search, so are not comparable to each other. Thus, one cannot presume that Clinton's news mean ($\bar{x} = 9.88$) is greater than Trump's web mean ($\bar{x} = 8.96$).

20. Indeed, news and web searches for Hillary Clinton ($\beta = 0.77$; $p \leq 0.001$) and Donald Trump ($\beta = 0.94$; $p \leq 0.001$) were correlated, suggesting that those searching for news and those doing general web searches were, in the main, searching for the same sorts of things. Thus, the next section focuses primarily on web searches since the number of observations is higher in that dataset.

21. A Lexis-Nexis search under Broadcast Transcripts, cross-referencing "Hillary Clinton" or "Donald Trump" and the issue listed on table 6.1 provided the total results. Searches were limited to ABC, CBS, NBC, Fox, CNN, and NPR. The search numbers were computed by totaling indexed search numbers for each issue, and dividing by the number of days to produce a mean score as an illustration of the overall level of interest in Trump and Clinton on the various issues. The percentage column divides Trump's numbers by Clinton's to illustrate Trump's attention as a percentage of Clinton's.

22. Searches for Trump on climate change seem to have dwindled compared to media coverage of his opinions. Searches for China exploded. One possible explanation for this mismatch is that the one significant time Trump mentioned global warming was in November 2012, when he insisted that it was created by the Chinese. Thus, people searching for Trump's position on China may have simultaneously been interested in the global warming story, but were cross-referencing China in order to get it. Thus, the level of interest in climate change is likely underreported, and the level of interest in China might be overreported. If we imperfectly assume that both issues received roughly equal coverage, search levels for Trump and climate change, or China, as a percentage of Clinton's searches might still be as high as 37 percent. However, during roughly the same period, Trump appeared on *Late Night with David Letterman*, supporting Mitt Romney's position on China. Letterman reminded him that his ties were made in China—another event that likely raised searches for Trump and China.

23. Appearances in celebrity news ($\beta = 1.65$; $SE = .34$; $p \leq 0.001$) and new episodes of *The Apprentice* ($\beta = 0.79$; $SE = .17$; $p \leq 0.001$) were both significantly correlated to

web searches of Trump, as was Fox News appearances ($\beta = 0.07$; SE = .03; $p \leq 0.05$). These were generated by an OLS regression model (N = 87; R2 = 0.47; SEE = .69). In this case, the dependent variable was Google web search results, pre-run.

24. New *Apprentice* episodes ($\beta = 1.67$; SE = .39; $p \leq 0.001$), Trump's appearance in celebrity news ($\beta = 3.21$; SE = .79; $p \leq 0.001$), and his political activities ($\beta = 5.21$; SE = .79; $p \leq 0.001$) were all statistically significant. The dependent variable was Lexis-Nexis Broadcast Transcript results, pre-run (N = 87; R2 = 0.59; SEE = 1.65). Fox News coverage was dropped from this model.

25. Correlations between the birther controversy ($\beta = 0.30$; $p \leq 0.001$), Fox News appearances ($\beta = 0.28$; $p \leq 0.001$), his candidacy ($\beta = 0.17$; $p \leq 0.05$), and ratings for *The Apprentice* bear out this possibility.

26. Seasonal Nielsen ratings for *The Apprentice* were cited in Maglio (2017).

27. Only his political activities were statistically significant ($\beta = 12.67$; SE = 3.08; $p \leq 0.001$). The dependent variable was Google web search results, post-run (N = 88; R2 = 0.17; SEE = 9.88). The model produced the same directional result ($\beta = 7.47$; SE = 1.44; $p \leq 0.001$). for the Lexis-Nexis Broadcast Transcript results, post-run (N = 88; R2 = 0.37; SEE = 3.90).

28. Several different ways of measuring Clinton's celebrity were correlated to each other. None were correlated to her web search results.

29. We know quite a bit about the results of episodic reporting—that is, reports about the news of the moment, as opposed to thematic reporting, where stories offer broader context of an issue over a longer period of time. People tend to blame individuals more than society for problems, and tend to have less overall context, and limited views of solutions (Iyengar 1994). However, the vast majority of news reports are episodic. What is less known is the effect of episodic moments of intense media impact on people's attitudes toward problems, the urgency of an issue, or even perceptions of the people at the center of that media moment.

REFERENCES

Andersen, Kenneth, and Theodore Clevenger Jr. "A Summary of Experimental Research in Ethos." *Speech Monographs* 30, no. 2 (June 1, 1963): 59–78. https://doi.org/10.1080/03637756309375361.

Atkin, Charles, and Martin Block. "Effectiveness of Celebrity Endorsers." *Journal of Advertising Research* 23, no.1 (1983): 57–61.

Balliger, Robin. "Politics." In *Key Terms in Popular Music and Culture*, edited by Thom Swiss and Bruce Horner. First edition. 57–70. New York: Wiley-Blackwell, 1999.

Barbaro, Michael. "Donald Trump Clung to 'Birther' Lie for Years, and Still Isn't Apologetic." *New York Times*, September 16, 2016. https://www.nytimes.com/2016/09/17/us/politics/donald-trump-obama-birther.html.

Barr, Andy. "51% of GOP Voters: Obama Foreign." *Politico*, February 15, 2011. http://politi.co/fv55e6.

Batliwala, Srilatha, and L. David Brown. "Shaping the Global Human Project: The Nature and Impact of Transnational Civil Activism." In *Transnational Civil Society: An Introduction*, 204–27. Bloomfield CT: Kumarian Press, 2006.

Becker, Amy B. "Fresh Politics: Comedy, Celebrity, and the Promise of New Political Outlooks." PhD, The University of Wisconsin–Madison, 2010. http://search.proquest.com.www2.lib.ku.edu:2048/pqdtft/docview/820616144/abstract/142F21C32652399C4C/2?accountid=14556.

Bella, Laura La. *Angelina Jolie: Goodwill Ambassador for the United Nations*. The Rosen Publishing Group, 2009.

Bennett, W. Lance. *News: The Politics of Illusion*. Upper Saddle River, NJ: Pearson Education, 2012.

Bennett, W. Lance, Regina G. Lawrence, and Steven Livingston. *When the Press Fails: Political Power and the News Media from Iraq to Katrina*. Chicago: University of Chicago Press, 2008.

Blair, Olivia. "People Are Sharing Donald Trump's 1987 Memoir That Outlines His Media Strategy." *The Independent*, December 9, 2015. http://www.independent.co.uk/news/people/donald-trumps-1987-memoir-detailing-media-strategy-is-being-shared-amid-controversy-over-muslim-a6766151.html.

Blake, Andrew. "Megyn Kelly: Trump Threatened to 'Unleash' Twitter Account on Me Prior to GOP Debate." *Washington Times*, November 11, 2016. http://www.washingtontimes.com/news/2016/nov/11/trump-threatened-unleash-twitter-account-megyn-kel/.

Blow, Charles M. "About the 'Basket of Deplorables.'" *New York Times*, September 12, 2016. https://www.nytimes.com/2016/09/12/opinion/about-the-basket-of-deplorables.html.

Borchers, Callum. "Trump Predicts the Media Will Help Him Win in 2020 Because of Ratings." *Washington Post*, December 29, 2017. https://www.washingtonpost.com/news/the-fix/wp/2017/12/29/trump-predicts-the-media-will-help-him-win-in-2020-because-of-ratings/.

Brewer, Marilynn, and Sherry Schneider. "Social Identity and Social Dilemmas: A Double-Edged Sword." In *Social Identity Theory: Constructive and Critical Advances*, edited by Michael A. Hogg and Dominic Abrams, 169–84. New York: Harvester Wheatsheaf, 1990.

Bunting, Madeleine, and Oliver Burkeman. "How Bono Wooed Washington." *The Guardian*, March 18, 2002, sec. US news. http://www.theguardian.com/world/2002/mar/18/usa.debtrelief.

Burns, Alexander. "Trump on Prejean: Same as Obama." *Politico*, May 12, 2009. https://www.politico.com/news/stories/0509/22413.html.

Carpentier, Megan. "Why Do People Dislike Hillary Clinton? The Story Goes Far Back." *The Guardian*, October 18, 2016. http://www.theguardian.com/us-news/2016/oct/18/hillary-clinton-why-hate-unlikeable-us-election.

Cary, Mary Kate. "The Master of Manipulation." *US News & World Report*, November 6, 2015. https://www.usnews.com/news/the-report/articles/2015/11/06/trump-is-a-master-at-manipulating-the-media.

Caughey, John L. *Imaginary Social Worlds: A Cultural Approach*. Lincoln: University of Nebraska Press, 1984.

Cheney, Kyle. "No, Clinton Didn't Start the Birther Thing. This Guy Did." *Politico*, September 16, 2016. http://politi.co/2csXJsc.

Cigler, Allan J., Burdett A. Loomis, and Anthony J. Nownes. *Interest Group Politics*. Ninth edition. CQ Press, 2015.

Cillizza, Chris, and Rachel Weiner. "Hillary Clinton for Vice President: The Rumor That Just Won't Die." *Washington Post*, April 19, 2012. https://www.washingtonpost.com/blogs/the-fix/post/hillary-clinton-for-vice-president-the-rumor-that-wont-die/2012/04/18/gIQASpk8RT_blog.html.

Clark, Andrew. "Bill Clinton's Shadow Darkens Hillary's Mood in Congo." *The Guardian*, August 11, 2009. http://www.theguardian.com/world/2009/aug/11/hillary-clinton-bill-question-congo.

Clinton, Josh, and Carrie Roush. "Poll: Persistent Partisan Divide over 'Birther' Question." *NBC News*. NBC, August 10, 2016. http://www.nbcnews.com/politics/2016-election/poll-persistent-partisan-divide-over-birther-question-n627446.

Cohn, Alicia. "Trump Calls for Revolution, Blasts Electoral College." *The Hill*, November 7, 2012. http://thehill.com/blogs/twitter-room/other-news/266423-trump-calls-for-revolution-blasts-electoral-college.

Cohn, Jonathan. "The Comprehensive Guide to Trump's Most Outrageous Statements." *Huffington Post*, June 9, 2016, sec. Politics. https://www.huffingtonpost.com/entry/worst-trump-quotes_us_5756e8e6e4b07823f9514fb1.

Condon, Stephanie. "Poll: One in Four Americans Think Obama Was Not Born in U.S." *CBS News*. CBS, April 21, 2011. http://www.cbsnews.com/news/poll-one-in-four-americans-think-obama-was-not-born-in-us/.

Cook, Timothy E. *Governing with the News: The News Media as a Political Institution*. Chicago: University of Chicago Press, 2005.

Cooper, Andrew Fenton. *Celebrity Diplomacy*. Boulder: Paradigm Publishers, 2008.

Corner, John, and Dick Pels, eds. *Media and the Restyling of Politics: Consumerism, Celebrity and Cynicism*. Sage Publications, Ltd, 2003.

Crosby, David, and David Bender. *Stand and Be Counted*. New York: HarperCollins World, 2000.

Darr, Christopher R., and Harry C. Strine IV. "A Pentadic Analysis of Celebrity Testimony in Congressional Hearings." *KB Journal* 6, no. 1 (Fall 2009). http://www.kbjournal.org/content/pentadic-analysis-celebrity-testimony-congressional-hearings.

Dimitrova, Daniela V., Adam Shehata, Jesper Strömbäck, and Lars W. Nord. "The Effects of Digital Media on Political Knowledge and Participation in Election Campaigns: Evidence from Panel Data." *Communication Research* 41, no. 1 (February 1, 2014): 95–118. https://doi.org/10.1177/0093650211426004.

Doll, Jen. "How Can You Not Like This Photo of Hillary Clinton and Meryl Streep?" *The Atlantic*, December 3, 2012. https://www.theatlantic.com/national/archive/2012/12/hillary-and-meryls-fabulous-photo-opportunity/320930/.

Edelman, Murray. *The Symbolic Uses of Politics*. Second edition. Champaign: University of Illinois Press, 1985.

Epstein, Edward Jay. *News from Nowhere: Television and the News*. Chicago: I.R. Dee, 1973.

Erb, Kelly Phillips. "Achtung Baby: Bono Defends U2 Tax Moves." *Forbes*, September 24, 2013. http://www.forbes.com/sites/kellyphillipserb/2013/09/24/achtung-baby-bono-defends-u2-tax-moves/.

Fallon, Kevin. "Hillary Clinton's 'Coolness Offensive': 4 Highlights." *The Week*, May 2, 2012. http://theweek.com/articles/475928/hillary-clintons-coolness-offensive-4-highlights.

Fenster, Mark, and Thomas Swiss. "Business." In *Key Terms in Popular Music and Culture*, first edition, edited by Thomas Swiss and Bruce Horner, 225–38. Wiley-Blackwell, 1999.

Fortunato, John A., and Shannon E. Martin. "The Intersection of Agenda-Setting, the Media Environment, and Election Campaign Laws." *Journal of Information Policy* 6 (2016): 129–53. https://doi.org/10.5325/jinfopoli.6.2016.0129.

French, John R. P., and Bertram H. Raven. "The Bases of Social Power." In *Group Dynamics*, edited by D. Cartwright and Alvin Zander, 259–70. New York: Harper & Row, 1959.

Gold, Hadas. "Jeff Zucker Has No Regrets." *Politico*, October 14, 2016. https://www.politico.com/blogs/on-media/2016/10/jeff-zucker-cnn-no-regrets-229820.

Graves, Lucia. "The Miss USA Hopeful Sued by Trump: 'There Are Ways to Stand Your Ground.'" *The Guardian*, September 4, 2016. http://www.theguardian.com/us-news/2016/sep/04/sheena-monnin-donald-trump-miss-usa-lawsuit.

Greene, David. "As November Approaches, Trump Overhauls Campaign Staff." *NPR Morning Edition*. National Public Radio, August 18, 2016. http://www.npr.org/programs/morning-edition/2016/08/18/490440821/morning-edition-for-august-18-2016.

Gunter, Barrie. *Celebrity Capital: Assessing the Value of Fame*. New York: Bloomsbury Academic, 2014.

Harvey, Mark. *Celebrity Influence: Politics, Persuasion, and Issue-Based Advocacy*. Lawrence: University Press of Kansas, 2017.

Hellweg, S. A. "Campaigns and Candidate Images in American Presidential Elections." In *Presidential Candidate Images*, edited by K. L. Hacker, 21–47. Oxford: Rowman & Littlefield, 2004.

Hill, Seth J., James Lo, Lynn Vavreck, and John Zaller. "How Quickly We Forget: The Duration of Persuasion Effects from Mass Communication." *Political* Communication 30, no. 4 (2013): 521–47.

Hinkle, Steve, and Rupert Brown. "Intergroup Comparisons and Social Identity." In *Social Identity Theory: Constructive and Critical Advances*, edited by Michael A. Hogg and Dominic Abrams, 48–70. New York: Harvester Wheatsheaf, 1990.

Hogg, Michael A., and Craig McGarthy. "Self-Categorization and Social Identity." In *Social Identity Theory: Constructive and Critical Advances*, edited by Michael A. Hogg and Dominic Abrams, 13–24. New York: Harvester Wheatsheaf, 1990.

Horton, D., and R. R. Wohl. "Mass Communication and Para-Social Interaction; Observations on Intimacy at a Distance." *Psychiatry* 19, no. 3 (August 1956): 215–29.

Huddart, Stephen. "Do We Need Another Hero? Understanding Celebrities' Roles in Advancing Social Causes." McGill University, Montreal, Canada, May 2005. http://www.cvsrd.org/eng/docs/MMP/Do%20We%20Need%20Another%20Hero%204.pdf.

Huliaras, Asteris, and Nikolaos Tzifakis. "Bringing the Individuals Back in? Celebrities as Transnational Activists." In *Transnational Celebrity Activism in Global Politics: Changing the World?* edited by Liza Tsaliki, Christos A. Frangonikolopoulos, and Asteris Huliaras, 29–44. Bristol, UK: Intellect Books, 2011.

Iyengar, Shanto. *Is Anyone Responsible?: How Television Frames Political Issues*. Reprint. Chicago: University Of Chicago Press, 1994.

Jackson, David J., and Thomas I. A. Darrow. "The Influence of Celebrity Endorsements on Young Adults' Political Opinions." *The Harvard International Journal of Press/Politics* 10, no. 3 (July 1, 2005): 80–98. https://doi.org/10.1177/1081180X05279278.

Jackson, David, and Doug Stanglin. "Trump Is Now President: 'The Forgotten . . . Will Be Forgotten No Longer.'" *USA Today*, January 20, 2017. https://www.usatoday.com/story/news/politics/2017/01/20/donald-trump-inauguration-day-president-white-house/96782700/.

Jackson, Nathan Dwayne. *Bono's Politics: The Future of Celebrity Political Activism*. Saarbrücken, Germany: VDM Verlag Dr. Müller, 2008. http://www.bonospolitics.com/wp-content/uploads/2010/06/Bonos-Politics-The-Future-of-Celebrity-Political-Activism.pdf.

Keck, Margaret, and Kathryn Sikkink. *Activists beyond Borders: Advocacy Networks in International Politics*. Ithaca, NY: Cornell University Press, 1998.

King, Larry. Transcript: Donald Trump announces plans to form presidential exploratory committee, October 8, 1999. http://www.cnn.com/ALLPOLITICS/stories/1999/10/08/trump.transcript/.

Kingdon, John W. *Agendas, Alternatives, and Public Policies, Update Edition, with an Epilogue on Health Care*. Second edition. New York: Longman, 2010.

Klatell, Jamie. "Obama Pokes Fun at the War on Dogs, Drunk Texts from Hillary Clinton." *The Hill*, April 29, 2012. http://thehill.com/homenews/administration/224393-obama-fights-the-war-on-dogs-drunk-texts-from-hillary-with-corespondents-dinner-jokes.

Korostelina, Karina V. *Trump Effect*. Abingdon, UK: Taylor & Francis, 2016.

Kranish, Michael, and Marc Fisher. *Trump Revealed: An American Journey of Ambition, Ego, Money, and Power*. New York: Scribner, 2016.

Kurzman, Charles, Chelise Anderson, Clinton Key, Youn Ok Lee, Mairead Moloney, Alexis Silver, and Maria W. Van Ryn. "Celebrity Status." *Sociological Theory* 25, no. 4 (December 1, 2007): 347–67.

Lammie, Kelli E. "The (Not-so) 'Powerless Elite' Celebrity Endorsements of Political Candidates." PhD, University of Pennsylvania, 2007. http://search.proquest.com.www2.lib.ku.edu:2048/pqdtft/docview/304820769/abstract/142F1B430497BFFD790/3?accountid=14556.

Lichtman, Allan J. *Predicting the Next President: The Keys to the White House*. Lanham, MD: Rowman & Littlefield Publishers, 2016.

Lozada, Carlos. "How Donald Trump Plays the Press, in His Own Words." *Washington Post*, June 17, 2015. https://www.washingtonpost.com/news/book-party/wp/2015/06/17/how-donald-trump-plays-the-press-in-his-own-words/.

Maglio, Tony. "'Celebrity Apprentice': Just How 'Yuge' Were Those TV Ratings Anyway?" *The Wrap*, January 1, 2017. https://www.thewrap.com/celebrity-apprentice-trump-tv-ratings-arnold/.

Maher, T. Michael. "Framing: An Emerging Paradigm or a Phase of Agenda Setting." In *Framing Public Life: Perspectives on Media and Our Understanding of the Social World*, edited by Stephen D. Reese, Oscar H. Gandy, and August E. Grant, 83–89. New York: Routledge, 2001.

Marshall, P. David. *Celebrity and Power: Fame and Contemporary Culture*. Minneapolis: University of Minnesota Press, 1997.

Marwick, Alice E. *Status Update: Celebrity, Publicity, and Branding in the Social Media Age*. First edition. New Haven, CT: Yale University Press, 2013.

McCombs, Maxwell E., and Donald L. Shaw. "The Agenda-Setting Function of Mass Media." *Public Opinion Quarterly* 36, no. 2 (June 20, 1972): 176–87. https://doi.org/10.1086/267990.

McDevitt, Caitlin. "Meryl Streep: Hillary Clinton and I Have Some Things in Common." *Politico*, March 12, 2012. https://www.politico.com/blogs/click/2012/03/streep-compares-herself-to-hillary-clinton-117164.html.

Meyer, David S., and Joshua Gamson. "The Challenge of Cultural Elites: Celebrities and Social Movements." *Sociological Inquiry* 65, no. 2 (1995): 181–206. https://doi.org/10.1111/j.1475-682X.1995.tb00412.x.

Orr, Jimmy. "Miss California Sparks Outrage over Gay Marriage Remarks." *Christian Science Monitor*, April 20, 2009. https://www.csmonitor.com/USA/Politics/The-Vote/2009/0420/miss-california-sparks-outrage-over-gay-marriage-remarks.

Paolino, Philip, and Daron R. Shaw. "Can the Internet Help Outsider Candidates Win the Presidential Nomination?" *PS: Political Science & Politics* 36, no. 2 (April 2003): 193–97. https://doi.org/10.1017/S1049096503002063.

Parker, Ashley, and Steve Eder. "Inside the Six Weeks Donald Trump Was a Nonstop 'Birther.'" *New York Times*, July 2, 2016. https://www.nytimes.com/2016/07/03/us/politics/donald-trump-birther-obama.html.

Parker, Suzi. "Hillary Clinton Is Finally Hip, Thanks to a Meme." *Washington Post*, April 12, 2012. https://www.washingtonpost.com/blogs/she-the-people/post/hillary-clinton-is-finally-hip-thanks-to-meme/2012/04/12/gIQALzOODT_blog.html.

Patterson, Thomas E. (2016a) "News Coverage of the 2016 General Election: How the Press Failed the Voters." *Shorenstein Center on Media, Politics and Public Policy* (blog), December 7, 2016. https://shorensteincenter.org/news-coverage-2016-general-election/.

———. (2016b) "Pre-Primary News Coverage of the 2016 Presidential Race: Trump's Rise, Sanders' Emergence, Clinton's Struggle." *Shorenstein Center on Media, Politics and Public Policy*, June 13, 2016. https://shorensteincenter.org/pre-primary-news-coverage-2016-trump-clinton-sanders/.

Peters, Jeremy W., and Rachel Shorey. "Trump Spent Far Less than Clinton, but Paid His Companies Well." *New York Times*, December 9, 2016. https://www

.nytimes.com/2016/12/09/us/politics/campaign-spending-donald-trump-hillary-clinton.html.

Prince, Rosa. "Donald Trump Furious as Miss USA Contender Labels the Contest 'Trashy,'" June 9, 2012, sec. World. http://www.telegraph.co.uk/news/worldnews/northamerica/usa/9321610/Donald-Trump-furious-as-Miss-USA-contender-labels-the-contest-trashy.html.

Raven, Bertram H. "The Bases of Power: Origins and Recent Developments." *Journal of Social Issues* 49, no. 4 (1993): 227–51. https://doi.org/10.1111/j.1540-4560.1993.tb01191.x.

Rodrigues, Maria Guadalupe Moog. *Global Environmentalism and Local Politics: Transnational Advocacy Networks in Brazil, Ecuador, and India*. Albany: State University of New York Press, 2004.

Rogers, Simon. "What Is Google Trends Data—and What Does It Mean?" *Medium*, July 1, 2016. https://medium.com/google-news-lab/what-is-google-trends-data-and-what-does-it-mean-b48f07342ee8.

Schmidt, Michael S., and Michael D. Shear. "Trump Says Russia Inquiry Makes U.S. 'Look Very Bad.'" *New York Times*, December 28, 2017, sec. Politics. https://www.nytimes.com/2017/12/28/us/politics/trump-interview-mueller-russia-china-north-korea.html.

Selk, Avi. "The Violent Rally Trump Can't Move Past." *Washington Post*, April 3, 2017, sec. The Fix. https://www.washingtonpost.com/news/the-fix/wp/2017/04/03/the-violent-rally-trump-cant-move-past/.

Shaw, Terry V. "Global Environmentalism and Local Politics: Transnational Advocacy Networks in Brazil, Ecuador, and India." *Journal of Sociology & Social Welfare* 32, no. 2 (June 2005): 182–83.

Squitieri, Tom. "Trump Forms Exploratory Committee." *USA Today*, October 8, 1999. http://usatoday30.usatoday.com/news/e98/e429.htm.

Straziuso, Jason. "George Clooney, Sudan; Actor Makes a Quiet Visit to Volatile Region." *Huffington Post*, March 13, 2012. http://www.huffingtonpost.com/2012/03/13/george-clooney-sudan-quiet-visit_n_1342777.html.

Street, John. "Celebrity Politicians: Popular Culture and Political Representation." *The British Journal of Politics & International Relations* 6, no. 4 (2004): 435–52. https://doi.org/10.1111/j.1467-856X.2004.00149.x.

Strine, Harry Cornelius. "Stars on Capitol Hill: Explaining Celebrity Appearances in Congressional Committee Hearings." PhD, Purdue University, 2004. http://search.proquest.com.www2.lib.ku.edu:2048/pqdtft/docview/305153640/abstract/142F23D429952AA8306/13?accountid=14556.

Suzuki, David, and Holly Dressel. *From Naked Ape to Superspecies: Humanity and the Global Eco-Crisis*. Greystone Books, Ltd, 2004. https://books.google.ca/books?id=46m3BAAAQBAJ&pg=PP7&source=gbs_selected_pages&cad=2#v=onepage&q=bo%20derek&f=false.

Tajfel, Henri, ed. *Social Identity and Intergroup Relations*. Cambridge: Cambridge University Press, 2010.

Teven, Jason J. "An Examination of Perceived Credibility of the 2008 Presidential Candidates: Relationships with Believability, Likeability, and Deceptiveness." *Human Communication* 11, no. 4 (2008): 383–400.

Thrall, A. Trevor, Jaime Lollio-Fakhreddine, Jon Berent, Lana Donnelly, Wes Herrin, Zachary Paquette, Rebecca Wenglinski, and Amy Wyatt. "Star Power: Celebrity Advocacy and the Evolution of the Public Sphere." *The International Journal of Press/Politics* 13, no. 4 (October 1, 2008): 362–85. https://doi.org/10.1177/1940161208319098.

Tolson, Andrew. "'Being Yourself': The Pursuit of Authentic Celebrity." *Discourse Studies* 3, no. 4 (November 1, 2001): 443–57.

Trilling, Lionel. *Sincerity and Authenticity*. Cambridge, MA: Harvard University Press, 1972.

Trump, Donald J., and Tony Schwartz. *Trump: The Art of the Deal*. New York: Random House Publishing Group, 2009.

Tsaliki, Liza, Christos A. Frangonikolopoulos, and Asteris Huliaras, eds. *Transnational Celebrity Activism in Global Politics: Changing the World?* Bristol, UK: Intellect Books, 2011.

Vavreck, Lynn. "Donald Trump Is Also an Outlier in Political Science." *New York Times*, January 6, 2016. https://www.nytimes.com/2016/01/07/upshot/donald-trump-is-also-an-outlier-in-political-science.html.

Waldman, Paul. "Hillary Clinton Is Not Cool. That's Okay." *The Week*, October 4, 2016. http://theweek.com/articles/652736/hillary-clinton-not-cool-thats-okay.

West, Darrell M., and John M. Orman. *Celebrity Politics*. Upper Saddle River, NJ: Prentice Hall, 2003.

Chapter 7

Can Celebrity Support Increase Presidential Popularity?

Anthony J. Nownes

President Trump appears to worry more about his popularity (or lack thereof) than most presidents do. But no president is truly unconcerned about the extent to which the public approves of his performance in office. It is now conventional wisdom that popular presidents get more of what they want than unpopular presidents do (more on this below). In addition, popular presidents appear to bring along more of their fellow partisans on Election Day than unpopular presidents (see Bafumi, Erikson, and Wlezien 2010; Campbell 1985; Erikson 2016). And not surprisingly, popular presidents are more likely to win reelection than are unpopular presidents (Lewis-Beck and Rice 1982). In short, presidential popularity matters. Because this is the case, presidents and scholars alike have long wondered what drives presidential popularity. The proverbial usual suspects include economic conditions, international events, "rally events," gas prices, and (more recently) presidential behavior.

In this chapter, I take a first cut at exploring how an additional variable might affect presidential popularity—celebrity support for the president. A spate of recent research suggests that celebrity support for politicians and candidates and political parties affects how voters evaluate them. Thus, there is reason to believe that celebrity support for the president may affect his approval rating among the public at large.

PRESIDENTIAL POPULARITY AND CELEBRITY SUPPORT

Two strands of research inform my work here. The first concerns the drivers of presidential popularity, and the second examines the role of celebrity endorsements in politics.

Presidential Popularity

Presidential popularity matters. It matters primarily because it affects the president's ability to govern. Specifically, numerous studies show that popularity is positively associated with the president's ability to get both members of Congress and members of the general public to support his policy proposals and positions (Bond and Fleisher 1990, 2000; Cranes-Wrone 2001; Hager and Sullivan 1994; Neustadt 1990; Sullivan 1991). Because of its importance, scholars have long sought to understand the determinants of presidential approval. Numerous studies show that economic conditions are strong drivers of presidential evaluations (Achen and Bartels 2004; Alt and Lassen 2013; Bartels 2008; Kinder and Kiewiet 1981; Kramer 1971; Mueller 1970; Peffley and Williams 1985; Sønderskov, Mannemar, and Christiansen 2013). Two indicators of economic conditions—the unemployment rate and the inflation rate—seem especially important, while personal economic well-being is less determinative (Kinder and Kiewiet 1981; Lau and Sears 1981; Niemi, Bremer, and Heel 1999). In addition to economic conditions, specific events appear to affect presidential approval (Brace and Hinckley 1992; Clarke et al. 2005; Mueller 1970; Newman 2002). Among the types of events found to affect levels of presidential approval are diplomatic breakthroughs, international incidents and crises, scandals, domestic unrest, terror attacks, and presidential health scares (Brace and Hinckley 1992; Kelleher and Wolak 2006; Mueller 1970; Newman 2002; Ostrom and Simon 1985; Schier 2009). Scholars who have studied events as drivers of presidential popularity note that for an event to have a substantial impact, it must be covered extensively by major national media (Baker and Oneal 2001; Newman and Forcehimes 2010). Other drivers of presidential approval include time in office (most presidents are more popular early on than they are later in their terms due to a "honeymoon period") (Light 1999), the president's skill or lack thereof at drumming up support by "going public," and (even separate from international crises and incidents) the extent of war casualties (Eichenberg and Stoll 2004; Erikson, MacKuen, and Stimson 2002; Gelpi, Feaver, and Reifler 2006; Mueller 1973; Voeten and Brewer 2006).

This is hardly a comprehensive look at the determinants of presidential popularity. But I have tried to highlight the factors that seem most important. Could other factors affect levels of popular support for the president? Perhaps. After all, President Donald Trump was historically unpopular in the early days of his presidency, despite presiding over a humming economy and relatively low numbers of war casualties, which suggests that factors other than "the usual suspects" may strongly affect presidential approval. So what other factors might matter? Here, based on a spate of research on celebrity politics, I posit that one answer may be celebrity support for the president.

Celebrity Endorsements and Political Behavior

In a recent article, Street (2012) notes that there is a growing body of literature on celebrity politics. One emergent thread in this research examines how celebrity endorsements of politicians and candidates affect citizens' political attitudes and behavior. Several well-executed and widely cited studies indicate that celebrity endorsements do indeed matter. For example, in two formative studies of celebrity effects, Garthwaite and Moore (2008) and Pease and Brewer (2008) demonstrate that Oprah Winfrey's public and voluble endorsement of Barack Obama during the 2008 Democratic primaries improved his standing among Democratic voters. Two other formative studies, both authored by political scientist David Jackson of Bowling Green State University, showed that celebrity support for various causes can increase support for these causes among young people (Jackson 2008; Jackson and Darrow 2005). And more recently, in a study conducted in the midst of the 2008 presidential election, I found that voters' evaluations of the two political parties were affected by their exposure to information about the (actual) partisan leanings of two popular celebrities (Jennifer Aniston and Peyton Manning; see Nownes 2012). In addition, more recently I found that celebrity support for Hillary Clinton during the 2016 presidential election profoundly affected voters' levels of anxiety and anger toward her (Nownes 2017).

Political scientists are not the only academics who study the effects of celebrity endorsements. Researchers in communication studies have long explored the effects of celebrity endorsements, and it is now the received wisdom that when celebrities endorse products, these products become more attractive to consumers (Austin et al. 2008; Inthorn and Street 2011; Street, Hague, and Savigny 2008; Veer, Becirovic, and Martin 2010). In a similar vein, marketing and advertising scholars have consistently shown that celebrity endorsements can increase sales (Agrawal and Kamakura 1995; Butler, Cowan, and Nilsson 2005; Erdogan, Baker, and Tagg 2001; Farrell et al. 2000), and even positively influence stock returns (Elberse and Verleun 2012). There is now a solid body of empirical work in political science and beyond showing that celebrity support affects citizens' attitudes, opinions, and behavior.

Empirical support for celebrity effects is buttressed by theoretical work, especially that of anthropologist and economist Grant McCracken, the scholar behind the well-known "meaning transfer theory." This general theory holds that a celebrity enhances the attractiveness of whatever s/he endorses by transferring her/his meaning to it (McCracken 1986, 1989). To summarize, a celebrity develops a public persona via her/his public behavior or work (for example, "patriot," "tough guy," "sexy woman," or "powerful women"), and over time comes to personify certain traits (e.g., s/he is viewed as tough, responsible, competent, beautiful, powerful, or sophisticated). By endorsing something or someone, a celebrity transfers this meaning to the something or someone s/he endorsed.

Meaning transfer theory has been around for a long time, and as I mentioned above, has received widespread empirical support. But while the theory explains *why* celebrity endorsements might work, and empirical studies show that they *do* indeed work, the exact mechanism by which they work remains somewhat mysterious. However, a recent study gives us a hint. In an ingenious study that received widespread press coverage, Dutch marketing researchers demonstrated that celebrity endorsements of products profoundly affect the brains of people who are exposed to them. In an experiment, Mirri Stallen and her colleagues (Stallen et al. 2010) began by examining fMRI brain scans of twenty-three women as they were exposed to images of attractive celebrities and attractive non-celebrities. The women were then shown hundreds of additional pictures showing different celebrity-shoe, and non-celebrity–shoe combinations—that is, pictures in which a face was paired with a pair of shoes. Essentially, the authors discovered that respondents' brains reacted differently to celebrity-shoe pairings than they did to non-celebrity-shoe pairings. As the authors put it, there was "observed increased activity in the orbitofrontal cortex [a part of the brain involved in appraisal and expression of emotion, as well as in making positive and negative associations (see, for example, Bechara, Damasio, and Damasio 2000; Etkin, Egner, and Kalish 2011)] . . . during the encoding of celebrity-product pairings" (809). This biological response, the authors concluded, "was related to the learning of associations between a famous face and a product" (807). The authors continued:

> The medial orbitofrontal cortex was not activated during the presentation of a famous face alone, which suggests that the medial orbitofrontal cortex did not encode the positive affect associated with the retrieval of implicit memories related to a famous face, but instead represented the learning of associations between an initially neutral product and a positively valenced face. (809)

In support of meaning transfer theory, the authors concluded: "This result provides strong support for the idea that the mechanism underlying celebrity endorsement is a transfer of positive affect from celebrity to product" (809).

Summary: Celebrity Support May Matter

In short, there is now a solid body of work supporting the basic premise that celebrity endorsements matter. Could celebrity endorsements in the form of support for a sitting president affect presidential approval ratings? There are good reasons to believe that the answer to this question is "yes." First of all, the work on presidential popularity shows that voters do, in at least a rudimentarily rational way, respond predictably to real world stimuli such as disasters, wars, and presidential triumphs and accomplishments. Thus, it is entirely possible that the stimuli of celebrity support, especially given that celebrity support for a politician often receives widespread media coverage, may affect voters' opinions of the president. The obvious rebuttal to this view is that a celebrity endorsement is in no way comparable to a natural disaster, a scandal, a war, or a recession. But this rebuttal is a bit facile. There is now a body of credible research, which I cite here, suggesting that voters are indeed affected by the public pronouncements of celebrities. Thus, the second reason to conclude that celebrity endorsements may affect presidential popularity is that there is evidence that such endorsements affect closely related phenomena such as vote choice, party evaluations, and support for specific causes. In other words, extant research on celebrity politics shows that among the sorts of stimuli that voters respond to are celebrity endorsements. Of course, none of this is to say that celebrity support or opposition to a president is a primary determinant of presidential popularity. Indeed, the primary determinants of presidential popularity—economic conditions, events, time in office, and presidential skills—are well established and reasonably well understood. Thus, in examining the effects of celebrity support for the president, we are necessarily working on the margins. But the closeness of our recent presidential elections, coupled with the fact there is still variation in levels of presidential popularity that remains unexplained, makes examining the impact of celebrity endorsements on presidential popularity a reasonable undertaking.

HYPOTHESES AND DATA COLLECTION

Here, based on the research I review above, I contend that celebrity support affects presidential popularity. Specifically, I hypothesize the following:

H1: Individual voter support for the president will increase with exposure to information about popular celebrities supporting the president.

This general hypothesis is based on the basic premise, which flows from extant research, that celebrity endorsements of politicians affect voters' attitudes, opinions, and emotions.

The Experiment

To test this hypothesis, I conducted a survey experiment designed to tease out the effects of celebrity support for the president on individual appraisals of the president. Specifically, I conducted a posttest only, control group experiment. The subject pool comprised 421 university students who participated in exchange for extra course credit. I conducted the experiment during a one week period in late 2017. To begin, I randomly assigned participants to one of two groups—the control group (n = 191), or the treatment group (n = 230). For both groups, I administered a survey containing several items about each respondent's political attitudes and affiliations (e.g., ideology, party identification), and personal characteristics (e.g., age, family income, race/ethnicity, gender). Prior to completing the survey, respondents were told that they were participating in a university-wide study designed to gauge the political attitudes and opinions of young people, and were required to read and sign an informed consent form.

The control group completed a survey with no experimental stimulus. The treatment group survey, however, contained the following instructions: "Now, before I ask you a few more questions, I would like you to read a brief news story about President Donald Trump. Please read this item carefully so you can thoughtfully respond to subsequent survey items." After these instructions came the following text:

> **THE PRESIDENT'S APPROVAL RATING: DONALD TRUMP GETS BY WITH A LITTLE HELP FROM HIS CELEBRITY FRIENDS**
> Being president is not easy. But it is a little easier when you are popular. Indeed, academic studies show that popular presidents have an easier time achieving their policy goals than unpopular presidents do. President Donald Trump's approval rating has varied widely since he took office in January of this year. At one point, close to 60 percent of Americans approved of the way he was handling his job as president, while at another, fewer than 35 percent of Americans did so. But in his quest to remain popular with the American public, President Trump may have a number of "secret weapons"—popular celebrities. News reports indicate that President Trump has the support of several Hollywood celebrities including legendary actor and director Clint Eastwood, longtime action stars Chuck Norris and Bruce Willis, and Oscar-winning actor (and actress Angelina Jolie's father) John Voight. Outside Hollywood, many other celebrities have expressed their support for President Trump, including country singers Trace Adkins, Loretta Lynn, and Brad Paisley, as well as sports figures including NFL star Tom Brady, NASCAR legend Richard Petty, and PGA champion Jack Nicklaus. Many of these celebrities have taken to Instagram and Twitter to show their support for the President.

Both surveys concluded with a series of questions about contemporary political leaders. In that series of questions was this standard presidential approval question: "Do you approve, disapprove, or neither approve nor disapprove of the way President Donald Trump is handling his job?" The possible responses were: "Approve a great deal," "approve a moderate amount," "approve a little," "neither approve nor disapprove," "disapprove a little," "disapprove a moderate amount," "disapprove a great deal."

In sum, respondents in the control group completed a simple, short survey, while respondents in the treatment group completed the same simple, short survey, but with a celebrity support stimulus embedded within it. I administered the experiment via Survey Monkey, the internet-based data collection firm. Web-based survey tools in political science are relatively new, but it appears that the data they produce are as reliable and valid as those collected through more conventional means (Alvarez, Sherman, and VanBeselaere 2003; Cassese et al. 2013; Stephenson and Crête 2011).

To maximize internal validity, I randomly assigned respondents to the two groups. The two groups are very similar on several variables including age (mean for control group = 21.5, mean for treatment group = 20.7), sex (61 percent of respondents in the control group were female, compared to 63 percent in the treatment group), Republican party identification (37 percent of respondents in the control group identified as Republicans, compared to 38 percent in the treatment group), and political knowledge (mean on a six-point political knowledge scale in the control group was 4.66, compared to a mean of 4.57 in the treatment group). There is one glaring difference between the two groups, however: the control group has no non-Caucasian respondents, whereas the treatment group has a substantial number (18 percent). This is unfortunate, and I will control for it in the quantitative analyses that follow. To further safeguard internal validity, I did not reveal the true nature of the experiment to participants until well after the study was complete, informed respondents that their participation was completely voluntary (students could receive extra credit even if they refused to participate), and collected enough data to perform statistical analyses. I maximized external validity by using genuine, accurate information for the stimulus (that is, the celebrities mentioned in the stimulus really had publicly supported President Trump at one time or another), and by limiting my sample to potential or actual voters. In addition, I have done my best here to spell out in some detail my experimental procedures.

One possible threat to the external validity of this study is "the college sophomore problem"—that is, the possible threat to validity posed by using a sample of college students. While I do not dismiss this issue out of hand, there are several reasons to believe that this problem is not all that serious. First, several studies, including Cooper, McCord, and Socha (2010), demonstrate that even though college student samples are not representative of the general adult population, they are similar enough on attitudinal indicators to allow reasonable inferences. Moreover, in comprehension and cognitive skills, college students are quite similar to non-students (Kam, Wilking, and Zechmeister 2007). Second, and perhaps most relevant here, it appears that students respond to political stimuli much as non-students do. As if to highlight this fact, in a recent study, Bol, St-Vincent, and Lavoie (2016) conduct four voting laboratory experiments in which they compare student samples to non-student samples, and conclude, "[t]he difference in behavioral patterns between student-dominated and heterogeneous samples appears to be minimal" (284). Thus, there is reason to believe that student samples pose only a minimal threat to external validity.

Finally, I will explain why I chose the celebrities I did. First, to make my findings more broadly applicable, I chose celebrities from four different parts of the entertainment world—movies, television, music, and sports. Second, to make sure respondents were familiar with the celebrities in question, I avoided celebrities with low "q-scores" (q scores indicate the level of the public's familiarity with celebrities). This was difficult, as many of the celebrities who have publicly supported President Trump over the past one or two years are profoundly unpopular and divisive (for example, Ted Nugent, Dennis Rodman, or Mike Tyson), and many others are simply not very well-known (for example, Robert Davi, Stephen Baldwin, or Tila Tequila). But I did manage to find a handful of celebrities who were indeed somewhat popular and relatively well-known.

THE VARIABLES

The dependent variable here is *level of presidential approval*. It has a range of 1 ("disapprove a great deal") to 7 ("approve a great deal"), with high numbers indicating high levels of support. The overall mean on *level of presidential approval* is 2.86 (s.d. = 1.97). The independent variable of interest is *celebrity treatment*, which takes a value of 0 for respondents in the control group, and a value of 1 for respondents in the treatment group. Because my respondents were randomly assigned to the two groups, controlling for other variables is not strictly necessary. Nonetheless, I decided to control for a few factors that might affect respondents' support for the president. First, mostly because of the disparity in the number of non-White respondents between the two groups (which I note above), I included the variable *White* (0 = non-White race/ethnicity, 1 = White race/ethnicity). Moreover, it is well-known that White voters, on average, have a much more favorable view of the president than do non-White voters, so this seemed necessary. Second, I included *female* (0 = male, 1 = female), primarily because President Trump vanquished the first major party female presidential candidate in history, and also said quite a few derogatory things about her. Third, for obvious reasons, I controlled for party identification by including the dichotomous variable *Republican*. This variable takes a value of 1 for each subject who, in response to the standard party identification survey item, reported being "a strong Republican," or "a not so strong Republican." All other respondents were coded 0 on this variable. Fourth, I included the variable *follow*, which tracks how carefully respondents "follow what's going on in government and public affairs." Responses of "hardly at all" were given a value of 0, responses of "only now and then" were given a value of 1, responses of "some of the time" were given a value of 2, and responses of "most of the time" were given a value of 3. I included this variable to control for the possibility that some respondents were aware of the celebrity endorsements I mentioned before my experiment. For the same reason, I included a variable called *political knowledge*, which has a range of 0–6 based on how many of six political knowledge questions a respondent got correct.[1] Higher numbers on this variable mean more correct answers and thus more knowledge.

I considered including a number of other variables, but decided against it. For example, I considered controlling for ideology, but my measure for ideology is very closely related to my measure of party identification, so I decided to exclude it. I also considered a variable called *discuss*, which measures how often a respondent discusses politics with others. But this variable is quite closely related to *follow*, so I jettisoned it as well. Summary information on all of these variables is found in table 7.1. The results of the models without control variables (which are available from the author) are very similar to those of the models I present below.

Table 7.1. Summary Statistics on Variables

Variable	*Range*	*Mean*	*Median*	*Standard Deviation*
Level of presidential approval (N = 396)	1–7	2.86	2.00	1.97
Celebrity treatment (N = 429)	0–1	.54	1.00	.499
White (N = 382)	0–1	.90	1.00	.307
Female (N = 404)	0–1	.62	1.00	.486
Republican (N = 407)	0–1	.37	0.00	.484
Follow (N = 406)	0–3	2.28	2.00	.838
Political knowledge (N = 429)	0–6	4.61	5.00	1.84

RESULTS

I will begin by examining mean scores on the dependent variable for the two sets of respondents. The mean on *level of presidential approval* is 2.72 for the control group, and 2.98 for the treatment group. This is not a huge difference, about 10 percent, but neither is it insubstantial. A difference of means test does not reveal a statistically significant difference between the two experimental groups (p = .10, one-tailed test) on values of the dependent variable. In all, the raw scores are only partially supportive of Hypothesis 1.

To more fully test Hypothesis 1, I cast an OLS regression model which considers the effects of the celebrity treatment and the other independent variables on the level of approval among exposed respondents. The results of this OLS run are found in table 7.2. The positive coefficient on *celebrity treatment* (.331) indicates that the information about an array of popular celebrities supporting President Trump positively affected exposed respondents' evaluations of the president. Moreover, the t-test for the coefficient is statistically significant, which means we can safely reject the null hypothesis that voter support for President Trump did not respond to exposure to information about popular celebrities supporting his performance as president. In sum, celebrity support for the president increases public support for the president.

As for the other variables, perhaps not surprisingly, the results indicate that being White is positively associated with the dependent variable, as is being a Republican. Being female, following politics closely, and having a lot of political knowledge leads to lower approval ratings. The model has reasonable explanatory power, as the R^2 is .458, which means that the independent

Table 7.2. OLS Regression Results: The Effects of Celebrity Treatment on Level of Presidential Approval

Variable	*B*	*s.e.*
Constant	2.27	.433**
Celebrity treatment	.331	.162*
White	.791	.267**
Female	−.469	.161**
Republican	2.48	.160**
Follow	−.074	.099
Political knowledge	−.160	.061**
N	362	
R^2	.458	
Prob > F	.001	

Notes: (1) ** Coefficient is significant at .01 level (two-tailed test). * Coefficient is significant at .05 level (two-tailed test); (2) Tests indicated that multicollinearity was not a concern.

variables in the model together explain about 46 percent of the variation in the dependent variable.

As a whole, these results provide support for Hypothesis 1—*celebrity support for President Trump had a positive impact on exposed respondents' evaluations of his performance in office*. Just how strong is the impact of celebrity support? To address to this question, I used the Stata add-on Clarify (King, Tomz, and Wittenberg 2000; Tomz, Wittenberg, and King, 2003) to generate expected values on *level of presidential approval* for several different hypothetical voters. For the first scenario, I compared expected values on the dependent variable across the two experimental groups while setting other variables at their means. I found that for respondents in the control group (that is, respondents who did not see the celebrity stimulus), the expected value on *level of presidential approval* is 2.69. The corresponding value on *level of presidential approval* for respondents in the treatment group (that is, respondents who read the celebrity stimulus) is 3.03. This is an increase of 12.5 percent. In the second scenario, I imagined a proverbial "tough nut" who was predisposed to strongly disapprove of President Trump. Specifically, I imagined a non-White, female, non-Republican respondent who has the maximum value on both the political knowledge and discussion variables. Her expected value on *level of presidential approval* in the control group is an abysmal .62. This is below the lowest possible value of the dependent variable, probably because no such person actually exists in the dataset. The corresponding value on *level of presidential approval* for this predisposed "hater" in the treatment group is .947. This is still a very low value, of course, but it represents an increase of 53 percent. Now we will consider a person "on the fence." This hypothetical respondent is a White, female Republican who has a mean score on the discussion and knowledge variables. The expected value on *level of presidential approval* for this person in the control group is 4.11. The corresponding value for the person in the treatment group is 4.44, or an increase of 8 percent. Finally, for the respondent we expect to be most supportive of President Trump—a White, male, Republican with rock bottom scores on our political discussion and political knowledge variables—the expected value on *level of presidential approval* if this person does not receive the celebrity stimulus is 5.53, while the corresponding value for this person if he does receive the celebrity stimulus is 5.86, an increase of about 6 percent.

CONCLUSION

Presidents worry about their popularity, and for good reason—being popular helps presidents get things done. In this chapter, I have taken a first cut at exploring the relationship between celebrity support for the president and individual evaluations of the president. The results of my simple experiment show that popular celebrity support for the president translates into higher levels of approval for the president among voters. In practical terms, this suggests that presidents might want to spend more time either on shoring up celebrity support or on making sure not to run afoul of popular celebrities. As for implications for future research, my results suggest that scholars of presidential approval might want to move beyond just "the usual suspects" when they consider what makes some presidents more popular than others.

This study has several limitations. These limitations point the way to future research. First, mine is a proverbial "one shot" experiment, which means I cannot conclude that the effects I uncover last for any substantial period of time. An obvious plan for future research would be to increase the number of experimental exposures and/or test for effects over time. Second, I used only two experimental groups here—a treatment group and a control group. Thus, one group received a stimulus (the story on celebrity support for the president), while the other group received nothing. This raises the possibility that respondents sussed out what I was up to, and provided me with socially desirable responses to curry my favor. While I have no reason to believe this is true (respondents were given extra credit for showing up to take the survey, but all surveys were completed anonymously, which means I had no idea which survey belonged to which respondent), it points to another direction for future research. Specifically, it calls for an experiment in which there is an additional stimulus group, one that received a stimulus with a news story about the president that did not contain information about celebrity support. This would not fix the possible social desirability problem I mention above, but it would provide another baseline against which to compare the responses of the people in the celebrity stimulus group, which would give us further information about the effects of celebrity support. Third, the celebrity stimulus I use contains information only about celebrity support for the president. Thus, my results cannot speak at all to the effects of celebrity opposition to the president. President Trump appears to be historically unpopular among celebrities (though we have no way of knowing this definitively), and thus it would make sense to explore how widespread celebrity opposition to his presidency affects voters. This limitation of the study also points to an obvious future study, one that contains an additional stimulus group, one that receives a celebrity opposition treatment. Fourth, the celebrities I chose for this study are relatively popular. Thus, my results cannot speak to the effects of support from unpopular or even widely hated celebrities. Again, this points to an obvious future experiment in which the effects of support from unpopular celebrities are examined. Finally, one of the things that my expected value analysis shows is that celebrity endorsements appear to affect some voters much more than others. I did not spend much time on this finding, and thus it calls for additional scrutiny. Additional studies should attempt to tease out the differential effects of celebrity endorsements, perhaps via more sophisticated quantitative analyses.

Despite its limitations, this study further illuminates the effects of celebrity politics. As this volume shows, social scientists are increasingly taking celebrity politics seriously, and this chapter shows that it is reasonable to expand the range of political phenomena that may be affected by the actions and words of celebrities. While no serious scholar would argue that celebrities play a large role in determining how popular the president is, the evidence here suggests that they may play some role.

NOTE

1. Here are the six knowledge questions: 1. Do you happen to know what political office is now held by Mike Pence? 2. Whose responsibility is it to determine if a law is constitutional or not? 3. How much of a majority is required for the US Senate and House to override a presidential veto? 4. Do you happen to know what party has the most members in the US House of Representatives? 5. Which of the two major political parties would you say is more conservative than the other at the national level? 6. How many justices (judges) are there on the US Supreme Court?

REFERENCES

Achen, Christopher H., and Larry M. Bartels. "Musical Chairs: Pocketbook Voting and the Limits of Democratic Accountability." Paper presented at the Annual Meeting of the American Political Science Association, Chicago, Illinois, September 2004.

Agrawal, Jagdish, and Wagner A. Kamakura. "The Economic Worth of Celebrity Endorsers: An Event Study Analysis." *Journal of Marketing* 59, no. 3 (1995): 56–62.

Alt, James E., and David Dreyer Lassen. "Unemployment Expectations, Information, and Voting: Experimental and Administrative Micro-Evidence." EPSA 2013 Annual General Conference Paper 354. Accessed November 15, 2017. http://ssrn.com/abstract=2224816.

Alvarez, R. Michael, Robert P. Sherman, and Carla VanBeselaere. "Subject Acquisition for Web-Based Surveys." *Political Analysis* 11, no. 1 (2003): 23–43.

Austin, Erica Weintraub, Rebecca Van de Vord, Bruce E. Pinkleton, and Evan Epstein. "Celebrity Endorsements and Their Potential to Motivate Young Voters." *Mass Communication and Society* 11, no. 4 (2008): 420–36.

Bafumi, Joseph, Robert S. Erikson, and Christopher Wlezien. "Balancing, Generic Polls and Midterm Congressional Elections." *Journal of Politics* 72, no. 3 (2010): 705–19.

Baker, William D., and John R. Oneal. "Patriotism or Opinion Leadership? The Nature and Origins of the 'Rally 'Round the Flag' Effect." *Journal of Conflict Resolution* 45, no. 5 (2001): 661–87.

Bartels, Larry M. *Unequal Democracy: The Political Economy of the New Gilded Age*. Princeton, NJ: Princeton University Press, 2008.

Bechara, Antoine, Hanna Damasio, and Antonio R. Damasio. "Emotion, Decision Making and the Orbitofrontal Cortex." *Cerebral Cortex* 10, no. 3 (2000): 295–307.

Bol, Damien, Simon Labbé St-Vincent, and Jean-Michel Lavoie. "Recruiting for Laboratory Voting Experiments: Exploring the (Potential) Sampling Bias." In *Voting Experiments*, edited by André Blais, Jean-François Laslier, and Karine Van der Straeten, 271–86. Switzerland: Springer, 2016.

Bond, Jon R., and Richard Fleisher. *The President in the Legislative Arena*. Chicago: University of Chicago Press, 1990.

———. "Congress and the President in a Partisan Era." In *Polarized Politics: Congress and the President in a Partisan Era*, edited by Jon R. Bond and Richard Fleisher, 1–8. Washington, DC: CQ Press, 2000.

Brace, Paul, and Barbara Hinckley. *Follow the Leader: Opinion Polls and the Modern Presidents*. New York: Basic Books, 1992.

Butler, Richard J., Benjamin W. Cowan, and Sebastian Nilsson. "From Obscurity to Bestseller: Examining the Impact of Oprah's Book Club Selections." *Publishing Research Quarterly* 20, no. 4 (2005): 23–34.

Campbell, James E. "Explaining Presidential Losses in Midterm Congressional Elections." *Journal of Politics* 47, no. 4 (1985): 1140–57.

Canes-Wrone, Brandice. "The President's Legislative Influence from Public Appeals." *American Journal of Political Science* (2001): 313–29.

Cassese, Erin C., Leonie Huddy, Todd K. Hartman, Lilliana Mason, and Christopher R. Weber. "Socially Mediated Internet Surveys: Recruiting Participants for Online Experiments." *PS: Political Science and Politics* 46, no. 4 (2013): 775–84.

Clarke, Harold D., Marianne C. Stewart, Mike Ault, and Euel Elliott. "Men, Women and the Dynamics of Presidential Approval." *British Journal of Political Science* 35, no. 1 (2005): 31–51.

Cooper, Christopher H., David M. McCord, and Alan Socha. "Evaluating the College Sophomore Problem: The Case of Personality and Politics." *The Journal of Psychology* 145, no. 1 (2010): 23–37.

Eichenberg, Richard C., and Richard J. Stoll. "The Political Fortunes of War: Iraq and the Domestic Standing of President George W. Bush." London: The Foreign Policy Centre, 2004.

Elberse, Anita, and Jeroen Verleun. "The Economic Value of Celebrity Endorsements." *Journal of Advertising Research* 52, no. 2 (2012): 149–65.

Erdogan, B. Zafer, Michael J. Baker, and Stephen Tagg. "Selecting Celebrity Endorsers: The Practitioner's Perspective." *Journal of Advertising Research* 41, no. 3 (2001): 39–48.

Erikson, Robert S. "Congressional Elections in Presidential Years: Presidential Coattails and Strategic Voting." *Legislative Studies Quarterly* 41, no. 3 (2016): 551–74.

Erikson, Robert S., Michael B. MacKuen, and James A. Stimson. *The Macro Polity*. New York: Cambridge University Press, 2002.

Etkin, Amit, Tobias Egner, and Raffael Kalisch. "Emotional Processing in Anterior Cingulate and Medial Prefrontal Cortex." *Trends in Cognitive Sciences* 15, no. 2 (2011): 85–93.

Farrell, Kathleen A., Gordon V. Karels, Kenneth W. Montfort, and Christine A. McClatchey. "Celebrity Performance and Endorsement Value: The Case of Tiger Woods." *Managerial Finance* 26, no. 7 (2000): 1–15.

Garthwaite, Craig, and Tim Moore. "The Role of Celebrity Endorsements in Politics: Oprah, Obama, and the 2008 Democratic primary." Working paper, 2008. Accessed November 2, 2017. http://www.stat.columbia.edu/~gelman/stuff_for_blog/celebrityendorsements_garthwaitemoore.pdf.

Gelpi, Christopher, Peter D. Feaver, and Jason Reifler. "Success Matters: Casualty Sensitivity and the War in Iraq." *International Security* 30, no. 3 (2006): 7–46.

Hager, Gregory L., and Terry Sullivan. "President-Centered and Presidency-Centered Explanations of Presidential Public Activity." *American Journal of Political Science* 38, no. 4 (1994): 1079–1103.

Inthorn, Sanna, and John Street. "'Simon Cowell for Prime Minister'? Young Citizens' Attitudes toward Celebrity Politics." *Media, Culture and Society* 33, no. 3 (2011): 479–89.

Jackson, David J. "Selling Politics: The Impact of Celebrities' Political Beliefs on Young Americans." *Journal of Political Marketing* 6, no. 4 (2008): 67–83.

Jackson, David J., and Thomas I. A. Darrow. "The Influence of Celebrity Endorsements on Young Adults' Political Opinions." *Harvard International Journal of Press/Politics* 10, no. 3 (2005): 80–98.

Kam, Cindy D., Jennifer R. Wilking, and Elizabeth J. Zechmeister. "Beyond the 'Narrow Data Base': Another Convenience Sample for Experimental Research." *Political Behavior* 29, no. 4 (2007): 415–40.

Kelleher, Christine A., and Jennifer Wolak. "Priming Presidential Approval: The Conditionality of Issue Effects." *Political Behavior* 28, no. 3 (2006): 193–210.

Kinder, Donald R., and D. Roderick Kiewiet. "Sociotropic Politics: The American Case." *British Journal of Political Science* 11, no. 2 (1981): 129–61.

King, Gary, Michael Tomz, and Jason Wittenberg. "Making the Most of Statistical Analyses: Improving Interpretation and Presentation." *American Journal of Political Science* 44, no. 2 (2000): 347–61.

Kramer, Gerald H. "Short-Term Fluctuations in U.S. Voting Behavior, 1896–1964." *American Political Science Review* 65, no. 1 (1971): 131–43.

Lau, Richard R., and David O. Sears. "Cognitive Links between Economic Grievances and Political Responses." *Political Behavior* 3, no. 4 (1981): 279–302.

Lewis-Beck, Michael S., and Tom W. Rice. "Presidential Popularity and Presidential Vote." *Public Opinion Quarterly* 46, no. 4 (1982): 534–37.

Light, Paul C. *The President's Agenda: Domestic Policy Choice from Kennedy to Clinton*. Third edition. Baltimore, MD: Johns Hopkins University Press, 1999.

McCracken, Grant. "Culture and Consumption: A Theoretical Account of the Structure and Movement of the Cultural Meaning of Consumer Goods." *Journal of Consumer Research* 13, no. 1 (1986): 71–84.

———. "Who Is the Celebrity Endorser? Cultural Foundations of the Endorsement Process." *Journal of Consumer Research* 16, no. 3 (1989): 310–21.

Mueller, John E. *War, Presidents and Public Opinion*. New York: John Wiley and Sons, 1973.

———. "Presidential Popularity from Truman to Johnson." *American Political Science Review* 64, no. 1 (1970): 18–34.

Neustadt, Richard E. *Presidential Power and the Modern Presidents: The Politics of Leadership from Roosevelt to Reagan*. New York: The Free Press, 1990.

Newman, Brian. "Bill Clinton's Approval Ratings: The More Things Change, the More They Stay the Same." *Political Research Quarterly* 55, no. 4 (2002): 781–804.

Newman, Brian and Andrew Forcehimes. "'Rally Round the Flag' Events for Presidential Approval Research." *Electoral Studies* 29, no. 1 (2010): 144–54.

Niemi, Richard G., John Bremer, and Michael Heel. "Determinants of State Economic Perceptions." *Political Behavior* 21, no. 2 (1999): 175–93.

Nownes, Anthony J. "An Experimental Investigation of the Effects of Celebrity Support for Political Parties in the United States." *American Politics Research* 40, no. 3 (2012): 476–500.

———. "Celebrity Endorsements and Voter Emotions: Evidence from Two Experiments." *American Politics Research* 45, no. 4 (2017): 648–72.

Ostrom, Charles W. Jr., and Dennis M. Simon. "Promise and Performance: A Dynamic Model of Presidential Popularity." *American Political Science Review* 79, no. 2 (1985): 334–58.

Pease, Andrew, and Paul R. Brewer. "The Oprah Factor: The Effects of a Celebrity Endorsement in a Presidential Primary Campaign." *International Journal of Press/Politics* 13, no. 4 (2008): 386–400.

Peffley, Mark, and John T. Williams. "Attributing Presidential Responsibility for National Economic Problems." *American Politics Quarterly* 13, no. 4 (1985): 393–425.

Schier, Steven E. *Panorama of a Presidency: How George W. Bush Acquired and Spent His Political Capital*. Armonk, NY: M.E. Sharpe, 2009.

Sønderskov, Kim Mannemar, and Martin Bisgaard Christiansen. "Local Experiences with Unemployment and Perceptions of the National Economy." Paper presented at the Annual Meeting of the Danish Political Science Association, Stouby, Denmark, 2013.

Stallen, Mirre, Ale Smidts, Mark Rijpkema, Gitty Smit, Vasily Klucharev, and Guillén Fernández. "Celebrities and Shoes on the Female Brain: The Neural Correlates of Product Evaluation in the Context of Fame." *Journal of Economic Psychology* 31, no. 5 (2010): 802–11.

Stephenson, Laura B., and Jean Crête. "Studying Political Behavior: A Comparison of Internet and Telephone Surveys." *International Journal of Public Opinion Research* 23, no. 1 (2011): 24–55.

Street, John. "Do Celebrity Politics and Celebrity Politicians Matter?" *The British Journal of Politics and International Relations* 14, no. 3 (2012): 346–56.

Street, John, Seth Hague, and Heather Savigny. "Playing to the Crowd: The Role of Music and Musicians in Political Participation." *British Journal of Politics and International Relations* 10, no. 2 (2008): 269–85.

Sullivan, Terry. "The Bank Account Presidency: A New Measure and Evidence on the Temporal Path of Presidential Influence." *American Journal of Political Science* 35, no. 3 (1991): 686–723.

Tomz, Michael, Jason Wittenberg, and Gary King. "Clarify: Software for Interpreting and Presenting Statistical Results." Software package, 2003. Accessed November 13, 2017. https://gking.harvard.edu/clarify.

Veer, Ekant, Ilda Becirovic, and Brett A. S. Martin. "If Kate Voted Conservative, Would You?: The Role of Celebrity Endorsements in Political Party Advertising." *European Journal of Marketing* 44, no. 3–4 (2010): 436–50.

Voeten, Erik, and Paul R. Brewer. "Public Opinion, the War in Iraq, and Presidential Accountability." *Journal of Conflict Resolution* 50, no. 6 (2006): 809–30.

Chapter 8

Attitudes toward Torture

Analyzing the Effects of the Series 24

Heather K. Evans

Initially the field of political communication largely ignored the potential effects of entertainment media on political attitudes since the prevailing thought was that citizens realize they are watching fiction and discount any information that their favorite shows provide. However, as previous scholars have found, it is possible that similar to news media, the topics stressed in entertainment media are more readily accessible to individuals when making decisions. Since the average person spends significantly more time watching entertainment media than news media, we might expect that there would be stronger agenda-setting, priming, and persuasion effects there.

The ability of the news (both hard and soft) media to affect public opinion is well established in research (Baum 2002; Iyengar and Kinder 1987; Miller and Krosnick 2000; Moy et al. 2005; Rogers and Dearing 1988; Young 2004). The major finding of these earlier works is that the news media does a good job telling us what to think about, but not what to think. Over the past fifteen years, media and politics scholars have tested whether these same effects are found with various entertainment media, including television shows and movies (Adkins and Castle 2014; Graber and Navratil 2006; Hill 2009; Holbrook and Hill 2005; Mulligan and Habel 2009; Mutz and Nir 2010).

This chapter tests for whether entertainment media can affect political attitudes using a television series that has received significant attention in the news media for its political undertones: *24*. Criticized for its positive portrayal of torture as an information gathering device, *24*, with its focus on terrorism, allows for a test on whether attitudes regarding US torture policy change after viewing the series. In a 2006 Fox News broadcast, Laura Ingraham claimed that since Americans love *24*, "that is as close to a national referendum that it is okay to use tough tactics as we are ever going to get." The hypothesis put forth by Fox News is that since people enjoy the series *24*, Americans must be pro-torture. The question remains: does watching *24* make individuals more likely to support torture? Using two experiments with undergraduate students, these results show that as suggested by Fox News, those who are exposed to the series become significantly more pro-torture. The effects, however, are not the same for everyone, and vary depending on the year.

ENTERTAINMENT MEDIA EFFECTS

Before Iyengar and Kinder's seminal media effects research, it was assumed that media had very little impact on viewers (Lazarsfeld, Berelson, and Gaudet 1948). Using experiments where the subjects viewed news stories that had been edited to stress particular issues over others, Iyengar and Kinder's results showed that the news media can have a strong agenda-setting and priming effect. The news media does a great job telling viewers what to think about (agenda-setting) and can also change the standards for which viewers evaluate their political leaders (priming). The reason this occurs, according to Iyengar and Kinder, is because when an issue is stressed by the news media, that topic becomes more accessible to viewers in working memory when making decisions.

Beyond these effects, political persuasion studies have also found that the media can affect the attitudes of viewers. Political persuasion studies show that political elites and the news media can affect what citizens believe about various topics, especially among certain segments of the population. Zaller, for instance, has shown that those who are less informed are more susceptible to political persuasion (1996). Other work has also shown that when framed in a particular way, the news media can affect the likelihood that someone will evaluate a topic in a more positive or negative way (Delshad and Raymond 2013; Nelson, Clawson, and Oxley 1997; Sibley, Liu, and Kirkwood 2006).

Early research on these media effects focused primarily on news media and ignored entertainment media. The view was that entertainment media had little impact on politics (Delli Carpini and Williams 1994). Given that the average individual watches more entertainment programming than news media, the lack of research on entertainment media effects was noticeable. It was assumed that viewers are not affected as strongly by these shows because they realize that the shows are fiction. Any information that is provided to the viewer through entertainment media is therefore discounted in the viewer's mind: "viewers presumably discount what is known to be dramatic fiction and rely strictly on information about the real world, using only the latter in forming perceptions and policy preferences" (Mutz and Nir 2010, 197).

Research has revealed that viewers are more affected by entertainment media than previously assumed. Delli Carpini and Williams (1994), for instance, show using focus groups that when people discuss politics, they are just as likely to provide examples from fictional as from nonfictional television shows. Individuals do not discount information that they receive through entertainment media. Viewers do not always make distinctions between entertainment and news.

Other studies focused on an individual show or genre, have found that entertainment media can have the same effects as observed by Iyengar and Kinder. Holbrook and Hill (2005) show in their experiments and survey analysis that people who watch medical dramas and crime dramas are subject to both agenda-setting and priming about health care and criminal justice. People who were exposed to these types of shows were more likely to say that health care and crime were important issues facing the country and were more likely to use health care and crime rates to evaluate the president.

Some studies find that viewers' political attitudes can change after viewing particular shows and fictional movies. For instance, Slater, Rouner, and Long (2006) found that those who watched a crime drama reported more support for the death penalty. Mutz and Nir (2010) also found that individuals exposed to a crime drama with a negative storyline were more likely to express attitudes that were more "anti-criminal justice system" than those exposed to a positive storyline. Mulligan and Habel (2009) also found that individuals exposed to a fictional film about abortion were significantly more favorable toward legalized abortion in the case of incest. Other work by Adkins and Castle (2014) shows that popular movies can also move public opinion, especially when the topic of the movie is not something that has been framed extensively by the news media. As these studies suggest, it seems as though fictional entertainment media can tell us what to think, as well as what to think about.

There is still ample work to be done in the entertainment media effects field, as is evidenced by the chapters in this book. These studies mentioned above have only scratched the surface of the influence of fictional dramas on viewers' attitudes. The following analysis explores the possibility of the series *24* changing viewers' beliefs about terrorism and US torture policy.

THE TELEVISION SERIES *24*

The television series *24* was initially not meant to be about terrorism. According to Joel Surnow, one of the creators of the show, the producers at the Fox network set out to create a dramatic program that would unfold in real time. The idea of using terrorist threats on the country came to the creators only because they thought it would be the best way to keep the main character "going for 24 hours" (Surnow and Cochran 2008). The program debuted less than two months after the 9/11 attacks, when the public still had very raw feelings about terrorism. Due to its timing, the series attracted many viewers in its early seasons: 8.6 million per episode (Nissel 2010). Since 2001, the critically acclaimed series has been nominated for seventy-six Primetime Emmy awards, has won twenty of them, and was awarded the 2004 Golden Globe for Best Television Series–Drama (IMDb 2018).

The series has received public criticism over the years for portraying torture in a positive light. The Parents Television Council, for instance, referred to the show as "the worst offender on television: the most frequent, most graphic, and the leader in the trend of showing the protagonists using torture" (Mayer 2007). The series' main character, Jack Bauer, finds himself in situations throughout the program where he must either physically or mentally torture an individual to gain important information that will keep Americans safe from terrorist attacks. In each season of the show, Jack Bauer saves the country from terrorist activities using questionable tactics that violate national and international law. As Hill (2009) describes, "torture on *24* is not an instrument of the wicked, but a standard tool of interrogation employed by good-hearted people in the defense of the country that they love" (4). The series pits liberty against national security.

The show's success has not gone unnoticed by the US government and think tanks alike. Jack Bauer has become a cultural icon, and for many Americans the characters on the show embody the men and women who are in our counterterrorism agencies (Semel 2008). Each time that Bauer uses some form of torture to get information from individuals, he is able to avert a national disaster. The think tank Heritage Foundation sponsored a conference in 2006 on the US counterterrorism image across the world, and invited both the secretary of homeland security and actors from the series. The secretary praised the actors from the show and said that the perseverance shown on the series would "help America defeat terrorism" (Farhi 2006). Former presidents, Supreme Court justices, and military brass have both praised and critiqued the show (Berlow 2008; Mayer 2007; McAuliff 2007).

The original series aired from 2001 to 2010, and a reboot was brought back for a new season in 2014 (*24: Live Another Day*). Each of the original seasons featured 24 episodes (24 hours), while the show in 2014 only featured 12 episodes. The one-season reboot involved the characters from the original show (Jack Bauer and Chloe O'Brian). Then in 2017, *24: Legacy* was aired as a spin-off of the original show. All of the episodes have followed in the real-time format footsteps of the original series. As of the time of this printing, Fox has decided not to renew *24: Legacy* for a second season and will instead "re-develop the franchise for a new version with a refreshed cast later down the line" (Hibberd 2017).

Due to the constant focus on national security and the positive portrayal of torture in these programs, one might imagine that the series could have an agenda-setting impact on its viewers, and watching the show may have a strong impact on individuals' attitudes toward US torture policy. Hill (2009) finds such an effect in his research, but fails to find that the show changed the attitudes of his participants. This chapter uses a different experimental manipulation to test whether those exposed to the series are more likely to support the use of torture at two points in time.

POLITICAL ATTITUDES ABOUT TORTURE

When it comes to understanding someone's attitudes toward enhanced interrogation tactics, like torture, research has shown that while people tend to oppose torture at a broad level, people are likely to say that torture is justified under certain circumstances (Houck and Conway 2013). The ticking time bomb scenario, which is essentially exactly what happens on the show *24*, is one such example. Homant and Witkowsky (2011) find that 61 percent of undergraduate student participants supported the use of torture if told that a bomb is going to explode soon and there is a person in custody that knows where it is, and we can either torture the suspected terrorist to save lives or allow the bomb to go off. During crisis scenarios, people are simply more likely to support the use of torture.

In terms of demographics, previous research has shown that those who score high on right-wing authoritarianism (Benjamin 2016), social dominance orientation, and political conservatism (Homant and Witkowski 2011; Houck and Conway 2013) are more likely to hold favorable views of torture. Republicans and men are more likely to support the use of torture (Fallahi et al. 2008; Miller, Gronke, and Rejali 2014). Even with these predispositions, however, being presented with a scenario where a loved-one's life is in danger or the ticking time-bomb scenario affects the likelihood that one will agree with the use of torture (Houck and Conway 2013).

Some research also suggests that religion might have independent effects on attitudes toward the use of torture. Noting that partisanship and gender are related to church attendance, Green (2007) shows that those who attend church regularly have more restrictive views on torture once partisanship and gender are taken into account, which is in line with the

"National Religious Campaign against Torture" and the "No2Torture" campaign in 2006 that Catholics and mainline Protestants supported, and the "declaration against torture" issued by the National Association of Evangelicals in 2007.

All of this research suggests that certain demographic factors, like gender, partisanship, church attendance, and ideology, affect attitudes about advanced interrogation tactics, but for all of these subgroups, giving a time bomb scenario can change their minds regarding whether certain tactics are acceptable.

METHOD

To test for the possible effects of *24* on attitudes toward torture, this study uses two post-test experiments. The first took place in the fall of 2010 and the second took place in the fall of 2017. Half of the participants (treatment group) were exposed to one episode of *24* ("Day 7, 11a.m.–12p.m.") and then asked to complete a survey, while the other half (control group) were only asked to complete the survey. In the 2010 experiment, 103 students took part and were offered extra credit for their participation. The second trial had 331 participants who were incentivized to take part in the study by the possibility of winning one of four gift cards. The participants were randomly placed into the two groups and were selected from introductory political science courses at Sam Houston State University.[1]

In both studies, the treatment group watched the same episode of *24*. In this episode, Renee Walker (played by Annie Werching) tortures a sniper that has information about a device that could destroy American lives. The sniper, who was caught on the previous episode and transported to a hospital, is finally awake and Walker arrives before his attorneys to see if she can get any information from him. He taunts her, which leads her to cut off his air supply to get the information about the device. He does not die but does give her the information.

After viewing the episode, the treatment group completed a survey that included several measures investigating attitudes toward terrorism and torture, approval of President Obama or President Trump (depending on the year of the study), and other demographics. First, participants were asked to list what they considered the three most important problems facing the country. The responses were then placed into one of seven categories: economy, foreign affairs, health care, environment, education, social problems, and other. Participants were asked to rank, in order of importance, six different policy areas, including terrorism.

Participants were asked to assess presidential approval for Obama and Trump. Their responses were coded on a five point scale (1 = strongly disapprove, 2 = disapprove, 3 = neither approve nor disapprove, 4 = approve, and 5 = strongly approve). Participants were also instructed to rate the president on his job performance on six other policy items (the economy, education, environment, immigration, terrorism, and the Iraq war).

To determine whether those exposed to *24* have different attitudes about the use of torture, a variety of questions were used. First, participants were asked whether they believe that "using torture to gain information from suspected terrorists is justified." In a follow up set of questions, they were asked whether they favored various types of torture after the following prompt:

> Let's say that the US is holding someone prisoner and intelligence sources say that there is a modest chance that this person has some information about a possible terrorist attack on the US that may prove critical to stopping the attack, but this person denies having such information. Please select whether you would favor or oppose using each of the following methods as a way of trying to get the prisoner to reveal the information he may have.

The methods included after this question were not allowing the detainee to sleep, keeping a hood over the detainee's head for an extended period of time, bombarding the detainee with loud noise for long periods of time, exposing the detainee to extreme heat or cold, applying electric shocks to the detainee, holding the detainee's head under water, and offering detainees a positive incentive for giving information.

Participants were also asked two questions about the government's ban on physical and mental torture with the following prompt:

> The US and most countries in the world have signed a number of conventions—that is, treaties that create international laws—that prohibit certain methods for trying to get information from detainees. Here are some of these prohibitions. For each one, please select whether you favor having it or if you think it is too restrictive.

The first prohibition was that "Governments should never use physical torture." The second one was that "Governments should never use mental torture (such as making someone think that they or their family members will be killed)."

To control for whether students had been previously exposed to the series, they were also asked whether they had previously watched the show. The trial samples were then split into two groups: those who reported never watching the program and those who said that they had watched it. Party identification, ideology, gender, race, and church attendance were also collected.[2]

RESULTS

Agenda-Setting

In the first trial, the most popular response to the question regarding the important problems facing Americans today was the economy, followed by national security and foreign affairs. When separating out these responses by group, the economy continued to be the number one issue concerning the participants, but individuals in the treatment group were significantly more likely ($p \leq .05$) to mention foreign affairs and national security than those in the control group (32.8 percent to 11.1 percent).

In the Fall 2017 trial, the most popular response was social issues, followed by the economy and national security/foreign affairs. Like the previous results, when examining the responses by experimental manipulation, those in the treatment group were more likely to mention national security and foreign affairs than those in the control group (35.6 percent to 28.4 percent).[3]

Responses to this question were also coded specifically for whether terrorism was mentioned by the participant as one of the important problems. In the treatment group in 2010, 31 percent listed terrorism as one of the most important problems facing the country, while only 9 percent of the control group did the same. This difference is also significant ($p \leq .05$). In 2017, however, both the treatment and control group were just as likely to mention terror or terrorism as one of their top three issues (13 percent each).

Participants were also asked how important six different policy areas were to them, including terrorism. Over 65 percent of participants in the control group of the first trial said that terrorism was very important while over 82 percent of those in the treatment group rated terrorism as very important. The difference is significant at the $p = .05$ level. In the second trial, there were no real differences between the two groups on this question, with 78 percent of both groups saying terrorism was very important.

These results illustrate that the show *24* can set the agenda for those watching, especially the groups from 2010. Those who watched *24* were more likely to report that terrorism and national security were the most important problems facing the country. In 2017, those who watched *24* were more likely to mention national security and foreign affairs as the most important problem facing Americans, but the results were not as strong as those in the first trial. This means that *24* can set the agenda for viewers, but that the strength of the series on public opinion has declined over time. This may be due to the national political climate at the time of both of these experimental trials. I will discuss this possibility in greater detail in the conclusion of this chapter.

Priming

Priming is the effect of the media to make certain issues more salient to the viewer when they evaluate a political figure (Scheufele and Tewksbury 2007). Other studies have found that exposure to entertainment programs like crime dramas can prime viewers' evaluations of the president (Holbrook and Hill 2005). To determine whether exposure to *24* can affect viewers' overall approval of President Obama or President Trump, an OLS regression model was calculated. President Obama/Trump's overall job performance was the dependent variable. Exposure to the show was the independent variable of interest. Participants were coded as 1 if they were part of the treatment and 0 if they were part of the control. To determine how exposure to the episode may prime attitudes about how the president deals with terrorism, an interaction term was included. Party identification, gender, and race, were also included in the models. Tables 8.1 and 8.2 present the results.

Approval of President Obama was strongly affected by attitudes regarding his handling of terrorism, party identification, and gender. A one point increase in one's approval of the president's handling of terrorism results in a 0.33 increase in his overall job approval. Being exposed to the *24* episode, however, did not have a significant effect on President Obama's approval rating.

For President Trump, only race and party identification are significant predictors of his overall job approval. Being exposed to the series had no

Table 8.1. The Priming Effect of *24* on President Obama's Overall Job Approval

Independent Variables	*Coefficients (Standard Errors)*
Treatment	0.18
	(0.53)
President's Handling of Terrorism	0.33 *
	(0.13)
Treatment * President's Handling of Terrorism	–0.02
	(0.17)
Party Identification	0.55 **
	(0.12)
Female	–0.51 **
	(0.18)
African American	0.44
	(0.24)
Constant	1.03 *
	(0.44)

* $p \leq .05$, ** $p \leq .01$
Adj R-squared = 0.4954

Table 8.2. The Priming Effect of *24* on President Trump's Overall Job Approval

Independent Variables	*Coefficients (Standard Errors)*
Treatment	0.05
	(0.37)
President's Handling of Terrorism	0.05
	(0.09)
Treatment * President's Handling of Terrorism	–0.10
	(0.11)
Party Identification	–0.20 *
	(0.10)
Female	–0.09
	(0.16)
African American	–0.44 *
	(0.20)
Constant	4.09 **
	(0.36)

* p ≤ .05, ** p ≤ .01
Adj R-squared = 0.0180

significant effect. One's approval of his handling of terrorism did not significantly affect his overall job approval.

In both of these experimental trials, watching *24* did not affect respondent's attitudes toward President Obama or President Trump's overall job approval. The lack of findings here might be due to participants only being tasked with watching one episode of *24*. Other research in this area that has found strong effects has exposed participants to a manipulation over multiple days. For instance, Iyengar, Peters, and Kinder's seminal work (1982) shows that individuals who were exposed to broadcasts over four days became more concerned with the issue they were exposed to (agenda-setting) and were more likely to tie the evaluation of the president about that issue to their overall job performance (priming). The lack of findings here might simply be due to the nature of limited exposure in this study.

Attitude Change

To determine whether those exposed to *24* have different attitudes about the use of torture, a variety of questions were asked of the participants. First, participants were asked whether they believe that "using torture to gain information from suspected terrorists is justified." In the first trial, those who watched *24* were more likely to say that torture is sometimes or often justified but the difference was not significant (65.5 percent to 63.3 percent). In the second trial, the percentage of respondents saying torture is sometimes or often justified were very similar (56.4 percent to 58.4 percent).

In a follow up set of questions, participants were asked whether they favored various types of torture such as not allowing the detainee to sleep, keeping a hood over the detainee's head for an extended period of time, bombarding the detainee with loud noise for long periods of time, exposing the detainee to extreme heat or cold, applying electric shocks to the detainee, holding the detainee's head under water, and offering detainees a positive incentive for giving information.

When comparing the control group and treatment group's answers to these questions in the first trial, there are significant differences between the two. The frequencies are listed in table 8.3. Those exposed to the episode of *24* were more likely to favor the use of tough tactics including not allowing the detainee to sleep and bombarding them with noise. While the coefficients for these two methods are not significant at the $p = .05$ level, both of these measures approach significance ($p \leq .10$). On the other hand, participants in the treatment group were significantly more likely to favor the *more extreme* torture tactics, such as exposing the detainee to extreme heat, applying electric shocks, and holding their head under water. Over three times as many individuals in the treatment group favored holding a detainee's head under water, and over twice as many approved of applying electric shocks to the detainee to acquire information than those in the control group.

In the second experiment, those exposed to the show were also more likely to approve of each of these forms of interrogation, but the differences were not statistically significant.

Participants were also asked two questions about the government's ban on physical and mental torture. Over 58 percent of the participants in the first treatment group said that they thought the statement "governments should

Table 8.3. Participants' Approval of Interrogation Tactics in First Experiment

Method	*Control Group*	*Test Group*
Sleep deprivation	56.8	70.7
Keeping a hood over the detainee's head	50	46.5
Bombarding the detainee with loud noise	47.7	63.8
Exposure to extreme heat or cold *	22.7	39.7
Applying electric shocks *	11.4	31
Holding head under water *	9	29.3
Offering a positive incentive for giving information	86.4	93

Numbers listed are percentages.
* $p \leq .05$

never use physical torture" was too restrictive, while 43 percent of the control group participants agreed (correlation = 0.16). This difference approaches significance at $p \leq .10$.

In the second trial, 60 percent of the manipulation group said "governments should never use physical torture" was too restrictive, compared to 56 percent of the control group, but the difference was not significant.

Overall, these results show that while those watching the series may not be more likely to say that torture is justified than those that do not watch, those who watch are more likely to favor certain types of torture, especially tactics that are more extreme, and be more "pro-physical torture" than those not exposed to *24*.

Previous Exposure to *24*

Participants in both trials were also asked how often (if ever) they watch *24*. 55 percent of the respondents in the first trial said that they had never watched the show. In the second trial, 80.97 percent said they had never watched the show. The effects found earlier in this chapter may be stronger for individuals that have not been previously exposed to the show, but given that so many said they had never watched the show in 2017 and the small and insignificant effects found that year, such might not be the case. The test and control group samples were divided into two groups: those who reported never watching the program and those who said that they had watched it. In the first trial, more individuals who were previously exposed to the program listed terrorism as one of the three most important problems facing America and said that the issue of terrorism was "very important" than those not exposed to the series in both the control group and the treatment group. In terms of overall attitudes toward torture tactics, those who were previously exposed were also more likely to find extreme tactics acceptable. When comparing the exposure/non-exposure samples, those who were not previously exposed were affected more by watching *24* than those who reported that they had watched the series before, although the differences were not statistically significant. In the second trial, there were no real differences between the "hadn't been previously exposed" and "had been previously exposed" groups in their attitudes toward torture or whether they listed terrorism as one of the three most important problems in America.

DEMOGRAPHIC FACTORS

Like previous work on attitudes toward torture, the data from 2017 show that those who are more religious (those who say that they go to church regularly) are more likely to favor tougher interrogation tactics than those who do not go to church as often. Women are also significantly less likely than men to be in favor of those tactics. Republicans and those defining themselves as conservatives are also more likely to be in favor of torture.

To see the cumulative effect of these variables as well as the effect of watching the program, a logit model was calculated for each type of torture present in the questionnaire. To recap, variation between these groups was examined for the following types of torture: not allowing the detainee to sleep, keeping a hood over the detainee's head for an extended period of time, bombarding the detainee with loud noise for long periods of time, exposing the detainee to extreme heat or cold, applying electric shocks to the detainee, and holding the detainee's head underwater. The independent variables were female (1 = female, 0 = male), Republican (1 = Republican, 0 = otherwise), conservative (1 = conservative/very conservative, 0 = otherwise), attend (1 = don't attend often, 0 = attend often), and experiment (1 = in test group, 0 = in control). Each of the dependent variables is coded such that a score of 1 means the person is opposed to that type of interrogation. The results are presented in table 8.4.

As these results show, when all of the demographic variables are controlled for, only gender and partisanship are significant predictors of attitudes toward torture. Women are significantly less likely to support the use of aggressive interrogation tactics, while Republicans are more likely to support them. Ideology is significant in only one model, with conservatives being significantly more likely to approve of waterboarding. Being part of the treatment group had no significant effect on any of these attitudes.

Table 8.4. Logit Models of Types of Torture

	Sleep	*Hood*	*Noise*	*Shock*	*Water*
Female	0.85**	1.23**	1.07**	1.22**	1.59**
	(0.25)	(0.25)	(0.24)	(0.26)	(0.28)
Republican	−0.57†	−0.91**	−0.65*	−0.75*	−0.70*
	(0.30)	(0.30)	(0.29)	(0.32)	(0.33)
Conservative	−0.30	0.09	−0.25	−0.11	−0.68*
	(0.31)	(0.31)	(0.30)	(0.33)	(0.33)
Attend	0.26	0.02	0.30	0.24	0.31
	(0.24)	(0.24)	(0.24)	(0.27)	(0.28)
Experiment	−0.13	0.02	−0.20	−0.34	−0.18
	(0.24)	(0.24)	(0.24)	(0.27)	(0.28)
Constant	−0.99*	−0.66	−0.64	0.41	0.22
	(0.47)	(0.47)	(0.46)	(0.50)	(0.52)

** $p \le 0.01$, * $p \le 0.05$, † $p \le 0.10$

DISCUSSION AND CONCLUSION

These results suggest that entertainment media should not be ignored in the media effects literature. While viewers may realize that fictional television programs are not real, these story lines can have effects on viewers' attitudes. Specifically, the results in this chapter show that watching *24* can affect what viewers believe is the most important problem facing America today and can change their attitudes about US torture policy, but is somewhat time specific. Those who watched the episode in 2010 became significantly more pro-torture and were more likely to agree with the use of extreme information gathering tactics. In 2017, while those watching the episode were more likely to report that foreign affairs and terrorism were one of the top three issues facing Americans, and were more likely to agree with tougher interrogation tactics, the differences were not significant.

The differences in the results between these experimental years deserve further discussion and analysis. In 2017, viewers were not as affected by watching the episode as they were in 2010, and I believe this has everything to do with the state of the political world at the time of the study. As Bjering (2017) explains, the original version of *24* became an important part of our discussion regarding torture and security in the years following 9/11. Essentially, the show, "played into the fear-driven political climate of the time" (656). As Bjering describes, it is very interesting to note that the original series ended around the same time as the Bush administration, and the reboot was aired around the same time as the publication of the *Senate Intelligence Committee Report on Torture.*

The first experiment took place at the conclusion of the first series. At the time of the second experimental trial, no national discussions were taking place regarding the use of extreme interrogation tactics. What was being discussed daily, as is evidenced in these survey results, was racial injustice and police brutality. And as this data bear out, a large percentage of the respondents had never watched *24* before.

Like all work in experimental methodology, this study is not without its limitations, like generalizability. Participants who take part in the experiment are undoubtedly more focused on the program during the experiment than the average person watching in their living room. Thus, any experimental data should be interpreted with caution unless they are paired with additional data analysis (such as survey data).

Comparing the first experimental results to survey data collected at Sam Houston State University in 2010 that includes questions about the show *24* and attitudes about torture, this study finds that those who watch more often are more likely to approve of the use of torture. Students were asked how often (if ever) they watched *24* and whether they thought using torture to gain information from suspected terrorists was justified. Over 69 percent of those who said they watched the show often said that using torture was often or sometimes justified, while only 59 percent of those that never watch agreed. Using this survey data alone, one could make the case that watching the show makes people more pro-torture, but individuals who approve of these tactics may be drawn to this type of programming in the first place. This is where experimental results are useful in media research. Through experiments, we can determine causality.

Another limit to the generalizability of this study is in the recruitment of participants. College students were used in this study. As Carl Hovland suggested years ago, college students may not represent "real people." Future work in this area should recruit individuals from outside the university setting. Having a larger sample that is more representative of the US population would be useful for seeing the scope of the effects found here.

Finally, there is the remaining question regarding how long these effects last. Both of these trial experiments have shown that *24* can set the issue agenda for those watching and that participants become more pro-torture after viewing the program. It is possible that after multiple viewings the effects would be stronger. Whether the effects last for weeks after the experiment is still unknown.[4] This is another avenue for future research on entertainment media.

Despite these limitations, this study has given us additional reasons to investigate the effect of entertainment media on political attitudes, and not to ignore the political context when we evaluate research findings. Those who were part of the first test group were significantly more likely to list terrorism as one of the most important problems facing the United States, and were significantly more likely to favor the use of tough tactics when dealing with detainees. The anchors at Fox News were somewhat correct. Those who were exposed to *24* in 2010 did favor tough tactics more often than those not exposed to the show, but not everyone who watched the show believed that using torture to gain information from suspected terrorists was justified.

NOTES

1. Sam Houston State is typical of many state universities in the nation. It is a large public university with a racially/ethnically diverse student body, with students coming from modest family backgrounds. The students are fairly representative of students at nationwide colleges and universities.

2. In the first trial, the largest demographic difference between the treatment and control group was party identification: 32.8 percent of the treatment group identified

themselves as Republicans while 37.8 percent of the control group said the same. This difference, however, is not statistically significant. Approximately the same proportion of the two groups were female, White, liberal, and attended church regularly. In the second trial, the proportions of Republicans, females, liberals, Whites, and regular church attenders was equal. Comparing the samples, the second treatment group was more White and male.

3. This difference is not statistically significant using a difference of means t-test: $p = 0.17$.

4. During the second study, participants were contacted a second time to see if the effects lasted. So few respondents took part in the second wave of the survey ($N = 32$) that the data is unable to be used to test this question. This is an area for future research.

REFERENCES

Adkins, Todd and Jeremiah J. Castle. "Moving Pictures? Experimental Evidence of Cinematic Influence on Political Attitudes." *Social Science Quarterly* 95, no. 5 (2014): 1230–43.

Baum, Matthew A. "Sex, Lies, and War: How Soft News Brings Foreign Policy to the Inattentive Public." *American Political Science Review* 96, no. (2002): 91–109.

Benjamin, Arlin James Jr. "Right-Wing Authoritarianism and Attitudes toward Torture." *Social Behavior and Personality* 44, no. 6 (2016): 881–88.

Berlow, Alan. "Who Would Antonin Scalia Torture?" *Salon*. January 2, 2008.

Bjering, Jens Christian Borrebye. "A Bipolar Machine: Sovereignty and Action in *24*." *Television and New Media* 18, no. 7 (2017): 655–69.

Delli Carpini, Michael X. and Bruce A. Williams. "Methods, Metaphors, and Media Research: The Uses of Television in Political Conversation." *Communication Research* 21 (1994): 782–812.

Delshad, Ashlie and Leigh Raymond. "Media Framing and Public Attitudes towards Biofuels." *Review of Policy Research* 30, no. 2 (2013): 190–210.

Fallahi, Carolyn R., Carol Shaw Austad, Lisa L. Leishman, Michael Gendron, and Rebecca M. Wood. "Gender Differences in the Perception of Prisoner Abuse." *Sex Roles* 60, no. 3/4 (2008): 261–66.

Farhi, Paul. "Calling on Hollywood's Terrorism 'Experts.'" *Washington Post*, June 24, 2006.

Goldthwaite Young, Dannagal. "Late-Night Comedy In Election 2000: Its Influence on Candidate Trait Ratings and the Moderating Effects of Political Knowledge and Partisanship." *Journal of Broadcasting & Electronic Media* 48, no. 1 (2004): 1–22.

Graber, Doris and Kevin Navratil. "Experiencing Politics through Experiments—Evidence from Experiments." *Paper prepared for the Midwest Political Science Association Annual Meeting*, 2006.

Green, John C. "Religion and Torture: A View from the Polls." *The Review of Faith and International Affairs* (Summer 2007): 23–27.

Hibberd, James. "*24: Legacy* Canceled; Fox Plans New Version." *Entertainment Weekly*. June 7, 2017.

Hill, Timothy G. "Terror, Torture, and 24: Does Jack Bauer Raise Your Personal 'Threat Level'?" *Paper prepared for the Midwest Political Science Association Annual Meeting,* 2009.

Hill, Timothy G. and R. Andrew Holbrook. "'Doctor Dramas as Political Cues': ER and the Priming of Health Care as a Political Issue." *Paper prepared for the National Communication Association,* 2004.

Holbrook, R. Andrew and Timothy G. Hill. "Agenda-Setting and Priming in Prime Time Television: Crime Dramas as Political Cues." *Political Communication* 22, no. 3 (2005): 277–95.

Homant, Robert P. and Michael J. Witkowski. "Support for Coercive Interrogation among College Students: Torture and the Ticking Time Bomb Scenario." *Journal of Applied Security Research* 6, no. 2 (2011): 135–67.

Houck, Shannon C. and Lucian Gideon Conway. "What People Think about Torture: Torture Is Inherently Bad . . . Unless It Can Save Someone I Love." *Journal of Applied Security Research* 8, no. 4 (2013): 429–54.

IMDb. *24 Awards*. 2018. https://www.imdb.com/title/tt0285331/awards.

Iyengar, Shanto and Donald R. Kinder. *News that Matters* Chicago: University of Chicago Press, 1987.

Iyengar, Shanto, Mark D. Peters, and Donald R. Kinder. "Experimental Demonstrations of the "Not-So-Minimal" Consequences of Television News Programs." *American Political Science Review* 76 (1982): 848–58.

Lazarsfeld, Paul F., Bernard R. Berelson, and Hazel Gaudet. *The People's Choice*. New York: Columbia University Press, 1948.

Mayer, Linda. "Whatever It Takes: The Politics of the Man behind 24." *The New Yorker*. February 19, 2007.

McAuliff, Michael. "Torture Like Jack Bauer's Would Be Ok, Bill Clinton, Says." *Daily News*. October 2, 2007.

Miller, Joanne and Jon A. Krosnick. "New Media Impact on the Ingredients of Presidential Evaluations: Politically Knowledgeable Citizens Are Guided by a Trusting Source." *American Journal of Political Science* 44, no. 2 (2000): 295–309.

Miller, Peter, Paul Gronke, and Darius Rejali. "Torture and Public Opinion: The Partisan Dimension." In *Examining Torture: Empirical Studies of State Repression*, edited by Tracy Lightcap and James C. Pfiffner, 11–41. New York: Palgrave MacMillan, 2014.

Moy, Patricia, Michael A. Xenos, and Verena K. Hess. "Communication and Citizenship: Mapping the Political Effects of Infotainment." *Mass Communication & Society* 8, no. 2 (2005): 111–31.

Mulligan, Ken and Philip Habel. "A Test of the Effects of Fictional Framing on Attitudes." *Paper prepared for the Southern Political Science Association Annual Meeting*, 2009.

Mutz, Diana C. and Lilach Nir. "Not Necessarily the News: Does Fictional Television Influence Real-World Policy Preferences?" *Mass Communication and Society* 13 (2010): 196–217.

Nelson, Thomas E., Roaslee A. Clawson, and Zoe M. Oxley. "Media Framing of a Civil Liberties Conflict and Its Effect on Tolerance." *The American Political Science Review* 91, no. 3 (1997): 567–83.

Nissel, Magnus. "The Ever-Ticking Time Bomb: Examining 24's Promotion of Torture against the Background of 9/11." *Aspeers* 3 (2010): 37–51.

Rogers, Everett M. and James W. Dearing. "Agenda Setting Research: Where Has It Been, Where Is It Going?" In *Communication Yearbook 11*, edited by James A. Anderson, 555–94. Thousand Oaks, CA: Sage Publications, 1988.

Scheufele, Dietram A. and David Tewksbury. "Framing, Agenda Setting, and Priming: The Evolution of Three Media Effects Models." *Journal of Communication.* 57 (2007): 9–20.

Semel, Matthew D. "24 and the Efficacy of Torture." Criminal Justice Faculty Publications. Paper 11 (2008).

Sibley, Chris G., James K. Liu, and Steve Kirkwood. "Toward a Social Representations Theory of Attitude Change: The Effect of Message Framing on General and Specific Attitudes towards Equality and Entitlement." *New Zealand Journal of Psychology* 35, no. 1 (2006): 3–13.

Slater, Michael D., Donna Rouner, and Marilee Long. "Television Dramas and Support for Controversial Public Policies: Effects and Mechanisms." *Journal of Communication* 56, no. 2 (2006): 235–52.

Surnow, Joel, and Robert Cochran. "*24*'s Creators Explain the Show's Origins." 2008. http://sky1.sky.com/24s-creators-explain-the-shows-origins.

Zaller, John. "The Myth of Massive Media Impact Revived: New Support for a Discredited Idea." In *Political Persuasion and Attitude Change*, edited by Diana C. Mutz, Paul M. Sniderman, and Richard A. Brody, 17–28. Ann Arbor: University of Michigan Press, 1996.

Chapter 9

Jump Scare Politics

The Political Impact of Nonpolitical Horror Films

Timothy G. Hill and Ashley R. Van Fleet

Since roughly the turn of the millennium scholars who study the effects of fictional media have labored to bring those effects out of the long shadow cast by its considerably older sibling, the literature examining the impact of news media. Theorizing that viewers of fictional media both experience more exposure (since the average viewer watches more entertainment programming than news) and is more susceptible to its effects (since they are not expecting political argument, and so are less likely to adopt a defensive posture), they have demonstrated an influence on attitudes from crime (Holbrook and Hill 2005; Mutz and Nir 2010), to conspiracy theories (Mulligan and Habel 2013), to the availability of abortion and contraception (Swigger 2017). However, this growing literature has been largely confined to those pop culture artifacts which tie directly to politics (e.g., *Wag the Dog*) or to political issues (e.g., crime or the death penalty). We suggest that such a lens provides too narrow a field of view for examining the full scope of the potential effects fictional media may have on the electorate.

One possible means of widening that field of view is provided by the literature on the effect of emotion on politics, and specifically by Affective Intelligence Theory (AIT). AIT posits that all emotion is the result of just three questions which the brain is continually, and preconsciously, asking itself. These questions are the hard-wired result of evolution, and have pronounced political consequences. Fear, for instance, makes one less likely to support military aggression, while anger makes one more likely to do so. Since film and television often evoke and even invite emotional reactions, it seems reasonable to us to examine the potential impact of those emotions on attitudes for certain political issues. If we are correct, there would be political consequences to a much broader array of film and television, because even the programming with no particular political valence may be altering viewers' mood or emotion, and viewers' emotional states would bridge the gap between the nonpolitical stimulus and the political issue content. Moreover, there is ample evidence (e.g., Healy, Mahotra, and Mo 2010) that citizens are regularly influenced by events that have no visible connection to politics; any connection we find, then, is well in line with existing literature.

Before describing our specific hypotheses, however, we should first sketch at least the outline of the literatures from which we are pulling to make our argument. After our theory, we will describe our experiment, recount our results (which indicate a relationship that is more complex than we originally anticipated), and then close by discussing what our data might mean and a few possible ways forward.

LITERATURE

Our study exists at the confluence of two streams of political science research. One tributary is the work done on media effects on public opinion, and particularly those of fictional media. The other is the research into the impact of emotions on politics, specifically the framework known as Affective Intelligence Theory. While we do not have the space to fully explicate either of these literatures, we should begin this chapter with at least an outline of how each flows into our own work.

Media and Public Opinion

Media's influence on politics has been studied for decades (Chaffee and Hochheimer 1985). For most of that time, however, the focus has been almost exclusively turned to news media specifically. Little evidence exists that news media can actually persuade citizens to change their minds about policy (though, see Zaller 1992). However, starting with the work of Iyengar, Peters, and Kinder (1982), news was demonstrated experimentally to have both agenda-setting and priming effects—news media attention to a story can push viewers to both see it as an important issue and to give it an outsized role in their assessments of the job performance of politicians—which have been amply replicated in the ensuing thirty years (e.g., Iyengar and Kinder 1987; Iyengar, Kinder, Peters, and Krosnick 1984; Krosnick and Brannon 1993; Krosnick and Kinder 1990). Framing, or the notion that the central theme of a news story can affect the way citizens think about the underlying issue, has also been demonstrated to have a measurable impact (e.g., Iyengar 1991; Nelson, Clawson, and Oxley 1997; Nelson, Oxley, and Clawson 1997; Price and Tewksbury 1997).

In recent years, though, scholars have begun examining a wider array of media artifacts for their political impact. Baum (2002) set off a cottage industry of scholarship surrounding the notion of "soft news" when he suggested that news-adjacent entertainment programs ranging from *Oprah* to *Entertainment Tonight* to *The Daily Show with Jon Stewart* were increasing knowledge about a variety of scandals and foreign policy crises among their viewership. The lattermost, as well as its spin-off, *The Colbert Report*, were particularly fertile ground for scholars while they were on the air (Baym 2005; LaMarre, Landreville, and Beam 2009; Morris 2009). While these programs are important to study, however, they are daily and topical in much the same way the nightly news is, and so are not dramatically different from traditional sources of media scholarship.

A larger break with the traditional emphases of the discipline exists in the growing number of studies that eschew nonfictional media sources entirely. Entertainment media was long considered a trivial intellectual pursuit, and the chance of it being important in the development of political opinions was judged to be low. It follows, then, that some of the earliest work in this field (Feldman and Sigelman 1985; Lenart and McGraw 1989) examined politically-minded TV miniseries that were covered by various news sources as cultural events worthy of notice—if there was "buzz" around a pop cultural offering, that might make it more likely that viewers would use it as an ingredient in their opinions on the topics discussed in the show. However, that also meant they were not representative of the bulk of the programming on television, either then or now. Additionally, their findings were only vaguely suggestive that such media might be a force that mattered in the shaping of viewers' political opinions, thus generally reinforcing the field's pre-existing bias about the utility of examining entertainment media in this context.

It has only been more recently that scholars have begun looking more seriously at the potential political consequences of fictional media offerings, despite the solid theoretical reasons to expect them to have an impact. First, the bulk of programming on television is non-news-based, so there are simply more raw hours available in a programming schedule for entertainment programs to influence viewers than there are for those focused around the news. And second, the purpose of fictional television tends to be entertainment rather than information. As a result, viewers watch with their guard down—they are less likely to counter-argue with the implicit and explicit arguments made than they would be while watching news programming, a time when they feel more need to be vigilant (Mulligan and Habel 2013). The scholars that have explored this area have found evidence for agenda-setting, priming, and even persuasion (e.g., Holbrook and Hill 2005; Mutz and Nir 2010; Swigger 2017).

Evidence of the first two of these effects comes from Holbrook and Hill (2005), who found that participants who were randomly selected to watch crime dramas were more likely to list crime as an important issue facing the country and more likely to judge the president disproportionately on his performance on crime than were those who watched family dramas. The experimental findings were confirmed by an examination of NES data, indicating that the effect was both causally valid and existed in the world beyond the laboratory.

Other experimental work showed even more dramatic effects. Mutz and Nir (2010), for example, demonstrated that by randomly showing participants episodes of *Law and Order* with a negative or positive portrayal of the criminal justice system, they could affect how people saw that system, and even if they approved of capital punishment or not. Adkins and Castle (2014) showed that a film with a "strong message" about health care can move viewers' preferences leftward and maintain the shift for at least a week. Glas and Taylor (2018) found that the movies *300* and *V for Vendetta* could activate participants' latent authoritarian and antiauthoritarian tendencies respectively, thereby influencing a host of political attitudes, including immigration and whether military service should be required for US citizenship.

It was Mulligan and Habel (2013), however, who took this form of experiment to what is perhaps its logical extreme when they randomly exposed half their sample to the film *Wag the Dog*, a 1997 satire about a Washington PR flack (Robert DeNiro) who, to distract the country from a presidential sex scandal, orchestrates a fake war with the help of a Hollywood producer (Dustin Hoffman). They then asked participants how likely it was that a conspiracy like that in the movie might actually occur sometime in the future, and how likely it is that it has already occurred. Viewers of *Wag the Dog* found both more likely than did the participants in their control group.

The common thread through all these studies is that the stimulus, while fictional, is overtly political in some way. In the case of *Wag the Dog*, the movie is focused on a presidential advisor producing a fake war; in the case of the crime drama studies, it is the political valence of the various issues around the criminal justice system. Swigger (2017) takes a different approach, examining the political impact of situation comedies that are not only fictional, but uninterested in politics entirely. By randomly showing participants an episode of either *Parks and Recreation* or *How I Met Your Mother*, Swigger examines the impact of a show's feminist or misogynist attitudes toward dating on the audience's support for access to abortion and contraception.[1] He concludes that his findings suggest that "there may not be such a thing as nonpolitical programming" (1).

Thus, fictional media have demonstrated their political relevance across a variety of domains and issue areas, even when the programming itself does not have an obvious tie to the political world. As such, it follows other stimuli far afield of politics, yet which have nevertheless been demonstrated to have political effects. For instance, Bassi (2015) demonstrated that inclement weather not only has the potential to depress turnout on Election Day, it also induces citizens to vote for the candidate that is perceived to be less risky. Additionally, Healy, Mahotra, and Mo (2010) found that incumbents do slightly better if the area college team won its game in the ten days prior to the election, and that cities doing well in the "March Madness" tournament were more likely to approve of the president's job performance. It is Achen and Bartels (2016) who may have the most to say in this area, however, tracing irrational electoral behavior to a variety of nonpolitical causes, including "droughts, floods, and shark attacks" (116). Thus, it is not farfetched to suggest that viewers might not be scrupulous about keeping the emotions engendered by their entertainment separate from their political judgments. To explore that possibility, however, we must first lay out an understanding of how emotions interact with politics more generally.

Emotions, Public Opinion, and Affective Intelligence Theory

One way the political effects of fictional media remains unexplored is through the emotions it elicits in its viewership. As entertainment, fictional media exists in part to provoke an emotional reaction from the audience. If those emotions have political consequences, Swigger's remark about there being no such thing as nonpolitical programming may be more true even than he realized. In order to form coherent hypotheses about the way in which fictional media might affect viewers' political attitudes by way of their emotions, however, we must first examine what the existing literature has to say about how emotions interact with political beliefs and behavior.

One of the earliest articles in that regard is Conover and Feldman's work on emotional reactions to the economy (1986). In their survey of the citizens of Lexington, Kentucky, they found that affect is at least as important in discussions of the economy as is cognition.[2] Specifically, while cognition about one's personal economic situation had little bearing on one's overall assessment of the economy or the president's job performance, one's emotional state about the situation did have a statistically significant effect. Affect, then, provides information about voters' beliefs and preferences that a focus merely on cognition would miss. Indeed, affect and cognition about economic conditions appear to be only weakly correlated, indicating that the two processes operate somewhat independently of each other. Finally, Conover and Feldman found distinct dimensions among emotions, noting that positive and negative emotions are orthogonal rather than oppositional, and further dividing negative emotions into angry/disgusted on the one hand and uneasy/afraid on the other. This lattermost distinction seems to derive from a perception of whether economic events are under the control of political actors or not: a negative perception of the economy accompanied by a belief that events are controllable tends to lead to anger or disgust, while the same perception coupled with a belief that events are beyond an actor's control is more likely to lead to fear or uneasiness. Thus, those who feel the latter emotions are less likely to use their perception of the economy in their evaluations of political leaders, so even though they are unhappy with economic conditions, they do not punish their leaders as those who are angry would.

This tripartite understanding of emotion is at the heart of what has come to be known as Affective Intelligence Theory (AIT). As explained by one of its creators, George Marcus (2017), AIT argues that humans are constantly, and pre-consciously, updating their appraisals of three questions: the success of current goal-seeking behavior, the level of norm violation taking place in the environment, and the amount of uncertainty present. In other words, our brains are constantly asking: *Am I getting what I want?*, *Are there people around me breaking the rules?*, and *How sure am I about what's going to happen?* These questions correspond with the three major emotional states: enthusiasm, anger, and anxiety. The first two of these states are designed for preconscious action, while the third allows room for more deliberate thinking to take place if our preconscious brains deem it necessary.

The evidence for this theory spans a number of issue areas (Clore and Isbell 2008; MacKuen et al. 2007; Marcus 2002), but Huddy, Feldman, and Cassese's 2007 examination of attitudes toward going to war in Iraq is particularly pertinent to our own research. Anxiety increased citizens' desire to attend to the risks of going to war, while anger inclined citizens to less reflection and greater action. And while both emotional states heightened the perceived risk Saddam Hussein posed to the United States, anger downplayed the perceived risk of the war itself. Anger thus made supporting the war easier, while anxiety made it more problematic. Lerner et al. (2003) found a similar pattern when asking respondents to reflect on what made them angry, sad, or afraid about the 9/11 terror attacks. Anger-induced participants perceived less risk across a variety of indicators than fear-induced participants. Anger-induced participants were also significantly more likely to support policies centered around vengeance and significantly less likely to support policies centered on conciliation.

Marcus et al. (2005) found that inducing anxiety in a civil liberties context has significant, if complicated, effects. For instance, anxiety about a white supremacy rally becoming violent led participants to become significantly less tolerant of the group's right to assemble, but only if participants did not claim white supremacists as their "least-liked group" (955). Moreover, in a second experiment, those who received an anxiety-inducing prime became more receptive to both the pro- and anti-free speech framing of a news story about anti-immigrant protests in Germany.[3]

Brader (2006) uses this work to examine the impact of campaign advertisements on potential voters, bringing the two literatures we are exploring closer together. In a series of experiments, he randomly showed participants one of four ads embedded in a local news broadcast: an ad with an enthusiasm valence, the same ad with music and images to heighten the emotional appeal, an ad with a fear valence, or the fear-based ad with nonverbal cues to heighten its level of emotion. Similar to the studies mentioned above, he found that those participants primed with emotional content toward enthusiasm were less inclined to change their pre-existing preferences even than those who saw the same ad without the heightened emotional content. Similarly, those who were primed with fear content were more likely to change their minds than those who saw the enthusiasm ad, and even those who saw the fear ad without the additional emotion. Moreover, enthusiasm and fear each encouraged certain forms of participation, including willingness to volunteer in both cases. These findings square with AIT's suggestion that while any emotional state can spur action, only fear also incentivizes cognition.[4]

Perhaps the most relevant study to our own, however, is Renshon, Lee, and Tingley's 2014 exploration of the relationship between film-induced emotion and attitudes toward immigration. Using skin conductance equipment to measure levels of physiological arousal, participants were randomly assigned to a calming condition in which they watched a short meditation video, a neutral condition in which they watched an abstract screen saver, or an anxiety-inducing condition in which they watched a short clip from the 1993 Sylvester Stallone film *Cliffhanger*, in which Stallone's character attempts to save a young woman from a fatal fall into a ravine. While they did not find a difference in self-reported feelings of fear between the conditions, there was a significant difference in the skin conductance measures, which in turn predicted a more restrictionist approach to immigration.

Political science, then, has found evidence that fictional media can have a variety of impacts on the attitudes of viewers; it has found evidence that attitudes and even vote choices can be shaped by exogenous, unrelated events; and it has found evidence that emotions, and particularly the three emotional states identified by Affective Intelligence Theory, are key to understanding citizens' political attitudes. We propose that there is fertile ground to be explored at the intersection of those three established phenomena. In the next section, we will elaborate on this connection and use it to develop testable hypotheses.

THEORY

One of the hallmarks of storytelling is the emotional connection it can create between art and audience. It's not surprising, then, that fictional media offerings often come with an emotional valence. For instance, sports stories and other tales of triumphing over adversity provoke a reaction that feels much like enthusiasm. Tales of betrayal allow audiences to experience vicarious anger. And horror films in particular are designed to induce a sense of fear and anxiety. Those emotional reactions, of course, have nothing to do with politics. However, the research above shows that the human psyche is generally a fairly poor compartmentalizer. Thus, it is plausible that these emotional states may have political consequences despite not containing any overtly political content.

Many genres of film and television, however, mix elements of various emotions to tell their stories. To take one example from literature: *The Count of Monte Cristo* (Dumas 1844/1997) is a story of betrayal but also of revenge and of overcoming a desperate situation. Thus, it is not clear on the surface what emotional reaction is primed by the tale, as it elicits various emotions throughout. Horror stories, by contrast, are designed primarily to scare, so priming fear through the use of a horror film is a more straightforward task. While we would like to reach a point of sophistication that would allow us to examine more emotionally complex material, then, for now we focus strictly on the horror genre to establish a baseline understanding of what effects may or may not exist.

Specifically, we examine the results from two experiments to explore the role fear plays in the issue domains of war and immigration. Following Brader, we also examine in our second experiment a hypothetical primary campaign to see if horror movie-watchers will be more likely to pick the "safe" choice. Affective Intelligence Theory would predict 1) that those primed with fear by watching a horror film will have a heightened sense of threat, and so be more likely to see America's adversaries as dangerous than those in the control condition; 2) that they will nevertheless be less likely to endorse aggressive action toward America's adversaries than their counterparts in the control condition; 3) that the heightened sense of threat induced by the horror prime will cause viewers to endorse more restrictive immigration measures; and 4) that they will be more likely to choose a "safe" candidate over a "risky" one. These, then, are the hypotheses we set out to test. Our results suggest a complicated picture that points toward the need for further research. In neither case was there a main effect of the experimental treatment by itself, but in both experiments the treatment did seem to have some effect. That said, the first experiment showed more tenuous results than the second, and neither replicated the findings of the other, suggesting to us that we should interpret these results with a fair amount of caution.

EXPERIMENT 1

In the summer of 2017, we recruited 200 participants from Amazon's Mechanical Turk to watch a short video and answer questions about what they saw. Mechanical Turk is a service offered by Amazon.com which pairs workers (known colloquially as "Turkers") with those who need work done ("requesters") in the form of what Amazon calls "human intelligence tasks"—the sort of tasks for which computers are not reliable but human beings are. These can be as simple as identifying whether a photograph depicts a dog or a cat, and can pay as little as one cent per task. Requesters provide a description of their task and amount they will pay, and Turkers decide which tasks they will do. Researchers use the service as a low-cost way of testing hypotheses with a relatively diverse sample. Diverse, however, is not the same as representative, and Mechanical Turk is not representative of the American population at large (Huff and Tingley 2015). However, a fair amount of research does tend to validate it as a research tool (e.g., Bartneck et al. 2015; Clifford, Jewell, and Waggoner 2015; Yang et al. 2015). Moreover, there is significant evidence that broad critiques of non-representative samples—even those of the much maligned "college sophomores"—are at best oversimplified (e.g., Landers and Behrend 2015; Roulin 2015). The appropriateness of a sample should be judged within the context of the variables of interest; blanket statements about any sampling technique should be taken with a grain of salt. Thus, we are confident that our sample is representative in the ways which are important for our study.[5]

The experiment began with a cover story about our study in order to maintain the purity of the manipulation. Participants were told they were part of a study examining the effect of their political views on memory. When we debriefed subjects at the end of the experiment, it seems as if this story largely held up. While several suspected they had not been told the full story, only two suggested that we were studying the impact of fear on political attitudes. For the most part, then, our cover story seems to have done what we wished.

Once participants consented to take part, they were randomly shown one of two short videos. Those in the treatment condition watched *Lights Out*, a short horror film which depicted a woman being stalked by a monster as she prepares for bed. Those in the control condition watched a video about Sammie, a golden retriever puppy who was receiving his first bath. Participants then answered questions about their political attitudes and demographic characteristics, as well as about the video itself. Those in the treatment condition were also asked how frightened the video made them and how often they watched horror films. Finally, they were debriefed and provided a code they used to claim their payment.

The experimental manipulation, of course, is the independent variable that is most relevant to our hypotheses. However, we also collected information about all the standard demographic controls (sex, race, ethnicity, age, education, income, religiosity, party, and ideology) which might play a part in telling the story. Some of these control variables proved important in teasing out the relationships we observed, which we will report in the next section.

Since our dependent variables are multiple, we operationalized them with seven specific questions. Regarding opinions about America's adversaries, we asked participants how threatened they felt by, and their position on taking military action against, two countries that represented significant political trouble spots in the summer of 2017—North Korea and Syria. President Trump had gone as far as to order a missile strike against Syria the preceding April, and took to Twitter several times during 2017 to denounce the North Korean regime in particularly bellicose language. Thus, they serve as the best proxies for war available at a time when domestic politics dominated headlines.[6] For attitudes about immigration, we used three questions: one that measured participants' opinions regarding President Trump's proposed border wall, one which gauged their opinions about the fate that should befall unauthorized immigrants, and a final question which asked about the president's refugee ban which, at the time of the study, was the subject of both controversy and litigation.[7] Exact wording of these questions is available in table 9.1.

An important caveat to both this study and the one that follows is that, unlike Reshon et al. (2014), we had to rely on a self-reported measure of fright. Our results should be read with that limitation in mind.

Results

First, as one might expect, partisanship plays an enormous role in attitudes on both of these issues. Indeed, if we simply isolate Republicans and compare them to the rest of the sample using one-way ANOVA, without any regard to the experimental condition, four of the seven dependent variables are significant at the .01 level or greater, and a fifth at the .1 level. The immigration questions do particularly well here: all are significant at the .001 level (data not shown).[8] This is despite there being only thirty-five participants, or 17.5 percent of the sample, who identify as Republicans or Republican-leaning independents.

The experimental condition does not display results that are nearly so dramatic. Indeed, none of the relationships between the condition and the de-

Table 9.1. Question Wording for Dependent Variables

North Korea	Do you think North Korea is a major threat to the security of the United States, a minor threat, or no threat at all?
	In dealing with North Korea, should the US mostly use diplomacy or military action?
Syria	Do you think Syria is a major threat to the security of the United States, a minor threat, or no threat at all?
	Should the US take an active role in removing Syrian President Assad, not take an active role but support his removal, or should the US not be involved at all?
Immigration	All things considered, would you favor or oppose building a wall along the entire border with Mexico? (five-point Likert scale)
	Which of the following comes closest to your view about unauthorized immigrants who are living in the US? • They should be allowed to stay in the US and eventually apply for citizenship. • They should be allowed to stay in the US legally, but not be allowed to apply for citizenship. • They should be required to leave the US.
	Do you favor or oppose Donald Trump's executive order to limit entrance to the United States of non-American citizens from six majority Muslim countries? (five-point Likert scale)

pendent variables come anywhere near traditional levels of statistical significance, nor are there even any clear patterns in which questions are relatively more affected than the others. In trying to explain this lack of any clear effect, we first considered that some of those in our treatment condition might not be afraid enough to exhibit the hypothesized reaction, which could be artificially deflating the overall effects. Therefore, we ran our analysis again, this time looking at the interaction effect that compared those in the treatment condition who reported being "very much" or "somewhat" frightened by the video to everyone else. This interaction provided only the slightest hint of a relationship: of the seven dependent variables, only two were significant, even below the very relaxed standard of $p < .2$, with the greatest t-value being a 1.4 (on the question regarding the threat posed by Syria).

As partisanship is such an integral part of the story of these issues, however, it is important to account for it in the analysis. And in fact, in addition to being a major determinant of attitudes on its own, it appears in this first experiment to have something of a moderating effect between the treatment and the dependent variables.[9] This relationship is most evident when we look at the war questions while dividing the sample into those who identify or lean Republican and everyone else. Those affiliated with the GOP are considerably more likely to see North Korea as a threat when exposed to the treatment, though it does not reach traditional levels of significance. Importantly, though, they are considerably less likely to take an aggressive stance on that feeling if they have seen the horror film than if they have not. (See tables 9.2a and 9.2b.) This finding is particularly notable because, again, Republicans were not well represented in our sample. We should note, however, that Republican affiliation does not have a similar impact on attitudes regarding military action in Syria, perhaps indicating that Syria was simply not seen as enough of a threat to the United States to make the aggression seem worthy of consideration. (In fact, twice as many respondents overall listed North Korea as a "major threat" than Syria; fewer than half as many called it "no threat at all.")

There is a similar story to be told if we isolate Democrats: those exposed to the treatment are significantly less likely to say that unauthorized immigrants should be allowed to stay in the country and apply for citizenship ($F = 4.146$, $p < .05$). These are not especially robust effects—one could have more confidence in them if they extended to other variables—but in both cases the treatment is moving partisans away from their usual postures in ways that AIT would predict. It is possible that partisanship is strong enough that its effect overwhelms the treatment in the aggregate, but we can still observe the treatment's impact in its ability to lessen a visceral partisan reaction in the face of a countervailing stimulus.

These results suggest that the relationship between our independent and dependent variables may be more complicated than we initially hypothesized. First, the length of the stimulus may not have been enough to see the effect of fear on these political attitudes. And second, we may need to take more care in accounting for partisanship and its potentially moderating effects.

Table 9.2a. North Korean Threat by Condition (GOP Participants Only, Exp. 1)

	Control Cond.	*Treatment Cond.*
Major Threat	47.1%	61.1%
Minor Threat	52.9%	16.7%
No Threat at All	0%	22.2%

$N = 35$; $\chi^2 = 7.451$, $p < .05$; $F = .117$, $p > .25$

Table 9.2b. North Korean Action by Condition (GOP Participants Only, Exp. 1)

	Control Cond.	*Treatment Cond.*
Diplomacy	23.5%	66.7%
Military Action	76.5%	33.3%

$N = 35$; $\chi^2 = 6.556$, $p = .01$; $F = 7.606$, $p < .01$

With those considerations in mind, we set out to redesign our experiment to provide us with what we hoped would be a more valid and reliable data set.

EXPERIMENT 2

One concern we had about the design of the first experiment is that, due to budgetary constraints, we used only a short film to induce fear in the treatment condition. While Renshon et al. (2014) were able to induce political attitude change with only a brief film clip, we nevertheless wondered if exposure to a feature-length horror movie would increase the intensity of the stimulus. Given that people are much more likely to watch feature-length films than film shorts, such an exposure also provides a more valid test of the hypotheses than was possible in Experiment 1.

Thus, in the fall and winter of 2017/2018, we recruited ninety-seven undergraduates at our small, private liberal arts college to watch a film and fill out a questionnaire in exchange for extra credit in one of their classes. Half the students were randomly assigned to watch *The Babadook*, a horror film about a widowed mother who is possessed by a demon as a result of reading a book to her six-year-old son.[10] The other half watched *Invincible*, a biopic about Vince Papale, an improbable player for the NFL's Philadelphia Eagles. The two films are roughly equal in length, and neither is overtly political. As before, when the film was complete, participants filled out the questionnaire via the online survey software Qualtrics.

In addition to our concerns about the length of the treatment, given the role partisanship appeared to play in Experiment 1, it seemed necessary to provide participants with a context which neutralized their political allegiances. Remembering the work of Brader (2006), we created a false primary campaign scenario that the software automatically coded to the partisan preference of each participant.[11] The question asked participants to choose between two candidates within their party for a race in a different state:

> There is a race for the [Republican/Democratic] nomination for governor in Indiana between Scott Burns, a member of the state Senate, and Roy McDaniel, a wealthy businessman. Scott Burns is preferred by the political establishment as the "safe" choice. Roy McDaniel has made popular promises to shake up Indiana politics, but is seen as more risky. If you were voting in the election, would you prefer Scott Burns or Roy McDaniel?

According to Affective Intelligence Theory, those in the treatment condition should be more drawn to Scott Burns, the safe choice, relative to those who have not been induced into a state of anxiety. And since the choice takes place within their chosen party, their partisanship cannot play a role in that decision.

As before, participants were told that the study was about the way their political beliefs affected what they remembered about the film, and as before the deception seems to have held up. While 35 percent of participants in Experiment 2 reported suspecting that the study was about something other than our cover story, only one person guessed that it was about "mood and how that would view political things," and no other guess came close. Thus, we feel confident that the results have not been contaminated by participants guessing the true nature of our hypotheses.

Results

As in Experiment 1, the main effect of our experimental condition appeared to have little significant effect on our independent variables. Of the eight dependent variables, only the question regarding the threat posed by North Korea is significant at the $p < .05$ level. Another, the question regarding how to handle the threat of Syria, is significant at the $p < .1$ level, but in the opposite direction from what Affective Intelligence Theory would predict. Interestingly, though, all three of the immigration questions are in the right direction, and two come close to the $p < .1$ level of significance. While this is not solid evidence, it does plausibly suggest a relationship.

It is notable, however, that the election variable is not among those that show any promise at all at this stage.[12] Unlike Brader (2006), then, we did not find that increasing fear cues could, on their own, influence participants to choose the "safer" choice. Perhaps this is the result of differing contexts, but whatever the reason, his findings did not seem to replicate here.

When we run an analysis that examines only members of one party or the other as we did in Experiment 1, we see none of the same differences obtained in the earlier experiment. Specifically, neither the intra-GOP split on the question of North Korea nor the intra-Democratic split on the question of citizenship for unauthorized immigrants is large enough across conditions to suggest any relationship at all. That these findings are not robust suggests that we must be limited and cautious in our interpretation even of those in Experiment 1. While the moderating effects of party here are an interesting question, we consider that question very much still open to inquiry.

Ironically, while the avenue that seemed most promising in Experiment 1 turned out to be a blind alley in Experiment 2, it was a dead end from Experiment 1 which, in Experiment 2, provided the strongest evidence for the hypotheses that we have yet encountered, while also providing some results that are counterintuitive given the AIT literature. As before, we considered that simply dividing participants by their randomly assigned conditions might not provide a full picture of the treatment's effects, since the treatment is likely to make some participants more afraid than others. Thus, we once again created an interaction effect isolating those who both saw *The Babadook* and reported being "somewhat" or "very much" frightened by it from everyone else regardless of which film they saw.

While Renshon et al. (2014) find self-reported anxiety to be an unreliable measure, our results here suggest it might nevertheless prove useful under the right conditions. Of our eight dependent variables, four are significant at the $p < .05$ level and two more at $p < .1$ despite there only being twenty-eight cases that are positive on both criteria of the interaction effect. (See table 9.3.) Moreover, all three of the immigration variables are in the hypothesized direction and two of the three are significant. This last finding confirms the work of Renshon and his colleagues that inducing fear via nonpolitical entertainment media can impact the immigration preferences of participants.

However, the other variables behave more counterintuitively, or even chaotically. The campaign variable is significant at $p < .1$, but in the direction opposite to Brader's findings and the expectations of AIT. That is, those who report being frightened by *The Babadook* are actually slightly *more* likely to choose the risky candidate, not less. The variables regarding identifying and dealing with foreign threats provide some similarly puzzling results. While the frightened participants are more likely to see North Korea as a threat, as AIT would predict, they are also marginally more likely to use military force than diplomacy to deal with that threat, contra the previous findings of the theory. As in Experiment 1, Syria does not seem to be enough of a danger to sponsor a reaction one way or another when it comes to identifying it as a threat, which makes it all the more surprising that the frightened participants are significantly more likely to support military action to remove Syrian dictator

Table 9.3. T-Tests and ANOVAs, Experiment 2

	Interaction Effect			*Gender (male)*		
	T-test	*ANOVA*	*N*	*T-test*	*ANOVA*	*N*
Campaign: risky choice	1.701†	2.893†	83	−1.951†	3.805†	82
N. Korea: threat	−2.408*	5.798*	94	0.430	0.184	93
N. Korea: action	1.770†	3.133†	94	−2.172*	4.716*	93
Syria: threat	0.556	0.309	94	−0.675	0.456	93
Syria: action	−2.295*	5.269*	94	−0.401	0.161	93
Immigration: wall	−2.215*	4.907*	94	4.711**	22.190**	93
Immigration: unauthorized	0.815	0.664	94	−3.636**	13.222**	93
Immigration: refugee ban	−2.496*	6.230*	94	5.023**	25.230**	93

†p < .1; *p < .05; **p < .001

Bashar al-Assad from power. These are reactions AIT would be more likely to associate with anger than with anxiety. Clearly, there is a need for more study in this area to discover why these results might obtain under these conditions.

Of course, as with the results from Experiment 1, the fact that these findings do not replicate across both experimental contexts means that we should be careful when drawing any conclusions. Additionally, at the risk of feeding an arcane stereotype, it is worth noting that fully two-thirds of those who claimed to have been frightened by the horror film identified themselves as female. Bivariate analysis of our dependent variables with gender demonstrates that gender has a strong relationship with those variables, and in at least two cases (North Korea and the fake campaign) the gender confound may be at least a partial explanation for the counterintuitive results mentioned above. For that reason, we executed a series of ordinary least squares regressions designed to adjudicate the question of whether our results were being driven by the gender imbalance in our groups (data not shown). Since we could rely on random assignment to equalize variables, such as partisanship, that we would generally have to control for, our model was simple: we included just the interaction variable and a dichotomous variable coded 1 for male and 0 for any other response. In no case did the presence of the gender variable significantly reduce the statistical power of results regarding the interaction variable, so we are confident that while gender surely plays a role in this story, it is not the role of spoiler.

DISCUSSION AND CONCLUSIONS

By now, scholars of fictional media have a fairly lengthy track record of demonstrating that non-news media can have political effects, even pushing people to change their minds on hot-button emotional issues like abortion (Swigger 2017) or convince them that wildly implausible conspiracies have taken place in our government (Mulligan and Habel 2013). Meanwhile, the work by George Marcus and others to develop Affective Intelligence Theory strongly suggests that our emotional states also affect our political attitudes. Finally, there is work within the subfield of political behavior (e.g., Healy, Mahotra, and Mo 2010) which suggests that events unrelated to politics in any way nevertheless can have political consequences. Since movies and television often traffic in emotional manipulation, these literatures would seem to suggest that fictional media's impact on our emotions could be having pronounced effects on our political attitudes and opinions.

The results we have reported above suggest that such effects are indeed plausible, but also that identifying them may not be as straightforward as we initially suspected. The lack of replication across the two experiments suggests the effect could be smaller and subtler than we first anticipated. Meanwhile, the results in Experiment 2 (see table 9.3), which run counter to the established theory within AIT, suggest the relationship might be a more complicated one than it first appeared. What accounts for the odd pattern in our results? We do not have enough data to answer the question with confidence, but we have a few speculative thoughts.

First, to put it plainly, we could be wrong; the results above could be spurious and the relationship merely a phantom. This option is one that no researcher likes to contemplate, especially after many months' work, but it is one that is always lurking. And if we are to take the "science" in *political science* seriously, it is one we should never discard lightly. However, we believe there are enough patterns in the data above to be confident that we are documenting an actual phenomenon. But what else could be driving our results?

One possibility is that despite our attempt to induce greater fear in Experiment 2 by showing participants an entire feature-length film, perhaps we have still not found a strong enough stimulus to isolate the effects in a reliable way. It could be, for instance, that it is not the length of the treatment that is the important variable in this manipulation but its intensity. Renshon and his colleagues (2014), after all, report a clear effect at the conclusion of a two-and-a-half minute film clip. In plain English, then, perhaps the film we chose simply was not scary enough. With our current data, it is hard to tell whether this is true or not, however, as this is a question that points to the limitation of the self-report data we relied on for this project. While some participants claimed they were "very much" afraid, we do not have any way to measure how that translates into direct physiological arousal, so we cannot tell for certain how scared our participants were.[13]

The question of gender is also one which should be examined more closely. Experiment 2 suggests an impact for gender on the relationship, but the precise shape of that impact is as yet unclear. It does not appear to be the case that it is driving a spurious relationship between our variables of interest: in most cases, gender and the experimental manipulation work in opposite directions. For instance, women are more likely to report being frightened by *The Babadook*, but they are also strongly more inclined to a forgiving immigration policy. If anything, the impact of gender may be artificially deflating the relationship between our variables of interest. Nevertheless, a fuller exploration of the ways in which gender may moderate this relationship should clearly be a priority.

More broadly, there is plenty of room to explore how fictional media-induced emotion affects politics beyond fright. Most obviously, there are two other emotional states which AIT suggests may be affected by interaction with our environment; finding ways to test the pop culture versions of these states would be useful if, as stated in our theory section, somewhat more complicated. Additionally, it may be that there are Big Five personality traits which moderate a person's susceptibility to these kinds of effects, either by making them less susceptible to the emotional tug of the stimulus or by making them better able to build walls between their immediate environment and their political attitudes.[14] Finally, whatever effects researchers may find are only as interesting as their ability to impact behavior. If the effects are ephemeral or transitory, they may satisfy academic curiosity, but they are of little consequence in politics. Thus, discovering the duration of their influence is vitally important. This is generally true of all fictional media research,[15] but it is perhaps especially true here, given the potentially fleeting nature of emotions.

Fictional media research has long endeavored to demonstrate that popular culture has an impact on politics. Over the past decade and a half, it has generally been successful at doing so, though the extant literature can seem a bit patchwork, with scholars often examining the effects of films or TV shows they find personally compelling, rather than contributing to a larger theoretical model. One cost of doing so is that, while there is little doubt that fictional media influences public opinion under the right circumstances, those circumstances have been confined almost exclusively to forms of popular culture that have some obvious connection to politics or political issues. To move this literature forward, we must think about ways in which fictional media may have influence that are not necessarily tied up in the traditional understanding of politics. Swigger (2017) points to one method of doing just that when he examines the impact of situation comedies when they send signals regarding gender roles. We have proposed another path here. Others may discover yet more of them.

Regardless of the specific path, finding ways to bring the literature past its current limitations is important to bringing it to the maturation it deserves. There are good theoretical reasons to believe that fictional media affects a much broader range of opinions with a much broader range of stimuli, perhaps even that Swigger is right when he speculates that there is no such thing as nonpolitical programming. The labor of the empirical work is likely to be more challenging when we "color outside the lines" in this way, but the results are likely to be that much more rewarding as a consequence.

NOTES

1. Viewers of *Parks and Rec* will note that it is not truly "nonpolitical," in that it is set in the offices of a small-town municipal government department. However, while many episodes of the show do explore the way government interacts with citizens and the nature of elections, much of the show is simply a workplace comedy. Swigger

chose his episodes carefully to avoid political content, so this is a smaller issue than it might first appear.

2. In psychological parlance, affect is the emotional component of an attitude and cognition is the rational component.

3. Note that while anxiety encourages cognition, it does not necessarily encourage critical thinking in the classic sense.

4. Enthusiasm is generated from a positive answer to the question about whether goal-seeking behavior is succeeding. Since the preconscious answer is affirmative, there is no need for the conscious mind to take over.

5. A more serious concern is that of the ethics of using Mechanical Turk at all, or at least as using it to recruit a large sample as cheaply as possible. The power dynamic inherent in the set-up raises important ethical concerns about the amount of money Turkers are paid for their time and labor: since they are paid by the task, it is fairly common for requesters to end up paying an hourly rate that is less than the national minimum wage. Since many Turkers rely on these tasks as an important source of income (Williamson 2016), the temptation to stretch a paltry research budget runs up against the well-being of one's participants. In this debate, we come down in favor of paying as well as circumstances will allow. As such, we estimated our study to take about 12 minutes and offered $1.80, or an hourly rate of nine dollars, well above the federal minimum wage. (For slower respondents who took 15 minutes, the hourly rate was still $7.20, just a whisker under the federal minimum wage of $7.25.) While not ideal—we agree with those who would respond that the minimum wage itself is currently too low—we feel we have done the best we can to treat our participants fairly.

6. Of course, during this time the US was *actually prosecuting* a war in Afghanistan, which has been ongoing since 2001. The tragic irony is that the fighting there has been going on so long, and falls on the backs of so few Americans, that it seems a less useful means of measuring this attitude.

7. Only one of the three questions mentioned Trump by name.

8. Comparable, though slightly less dramatic, results obtain when isolating Democrats in a similar way.

9. Ideally, we would also examine these numbers by who experienced fear, rather than simply by exposure to the treatment. However, with such a small number of Republicans in the sample, the cell size does not allow for reliable analysis.

10. It's scarier than it sounds.

11. Pure independents (n = 11) were thus excluded from this portion of the analysis.

12. For purposes of analysis, we dichotomized this choice such that 1 was a preference for the risky choice and 0 was either a preference for the safe choice or no preference at all.

13. This works both ways, of course. Some participants may have put on a brave face but secretly have been terrified.

14. The Big Five personality traits—openness to experience, conscientiousness, agreeableness, extraversion, and neuroticism—are well established in psychology as the fundamental building blocks of human personality (e.g., McCrae and Costa 1999). They have also been linked to political attitudes (e.g., Gerber et al. 2010). Certain

of these traits may make one more or less susceptible to the effects discussed in this paper, though it would be imprudent for us to speculate more specifically.

15. Kudos to Adkins and Castle (2014) for beginning this work in earnest.

REFERENCES

Achen, Christopher H., and Larry M. Bartels. *Democracy for Realists: Why Elections Do Not Produce Responsive Government*. Princeton, NJ: Princeton University Press, 2016.

Adkins, Todd, and Jeremiah J. Castle. "*Moving* Pictures? Experimental Evidence of Cinematic Influence on Political Attitudes." *Social Science Quarterly* 95, no. 5 (2014): 1230–44.

Bartneck, Christoph, Andreas Duenser, Elena Moltchanova, and Karolina Zawieska. "Comparing the Similarity of Responses from Studies in Amazon's Mechanical Turk to Studies Conducted Online and with Direct Recruitment." *PLOS One* 10, no. 4 (2015). http://journals.plos.org/plosone/article?id=10.1371/journal.pone.0121595.

Bassi, Anna. "Weather, Risk, and Voting: An Experimental Analysis of the Effect of Weather Beyond Turnout." 2015 Working paper. http://www.unc.edu/~abassi/Research/weather-mood-voting.pdf.

Baum, Matthew A. "Sex, Lies, and War: How Soft News Brings Foreign Policy to the Inattentive Public." *The American Political Science Review* 96, no. 1 (2002): 91–109.

Baym, Geoffrey. "*The Daily Show*: Discursive Integration and the Reinvention of Political Journalism." *Political Communication* 22, no. 3 (2005): 259–76.

Brader, Ted. *Campaigning for Hearts and Minds: How Emotional Appeals in Political Ads Work*. Chicago: University of Chicago Press, 2006.

Chafee, Steven H., and John L. Hochheimer. "The Beginnings of Political Communication Research in the United States: Origins of the 'Limited Effects' Model." In *The Media Revolution in America and Western Europe*, edited by Everett M. Rogers and Francis Balle, 267–96. Norwood, NJ: Ablex, 1985.

Clifford, Scott, Ryan M. Jewell, and Philip D. Waggoner. "Are Samples Drawn from Mechanical Turk Valid for Research on Political Ideology?" *Research & Politics* 2, no. 4 (2015): 1–9.

Clore, Gerald L., and Linda M. Isbell. "Emotion as Virtue and Vice." In *Citizens and Politics: Perspectives from Political Psychology*, edited by James H. Kuklinski, 103–26. New York: Cambridge University Press, 2008.

Conover, Pamela J., and Stanley Feldman. "Emotional Reactions to the Economy: I'm Mad as Hell and I'm Not Going to Take It Anymore." *American Journal of Political Science* 30, no. 1 (1986): 50–78.

Dumas, Alexandre. *The Count of Monte Cristo*. London: Wordsworth, 1844/1997.

Feldman, Stanley, and Lee Sigelman. "The Political Impact of Prime-Time Television: 'The Day After.'" *Journal of Politics* 47, no. 2 (1985): 556–78.

Glas, Jeffrey M., and J. Benjamin Taylor. "The Silver Screen and Authoritarianism: Popular Films Activate Latent Personality Dispositions and Affect Political Attitudes." *American Politics Research* 46, no. 2 (2018): 246–75.

Gerber, Alan S., Gregory A. Huber, David Doherty, Conor M. Dowling, and Shang E. Ha. "Personality and Political Attitudes: Relationships across Issue Domains and Political Contexts." *American Political Science Review* 104, no. 1 (2010): 111–33.

Healy, Andrew J., Neil Malhotra, and Cecilia Hyunjung Mo. "Irrelevant Events Affect Voters' Evaluations of Government Performance." *Proceedings of the National Academy of Sciences of the United States of America* 107, no. 29 (2010): 12804–12809.

Holbrook, R. Andrew, and Timothy G. Hill. "Agenda-Setting and Priming in Prime Time Television: Crime Dramas as Political Cues." *Political Communication* 22, no. 3 (2005): 277–95.

Huddy, Leonie, Stanley Feldman, and Erin Cassese. "On the Distinct Political Effects of Anxiety and Anger." In *The Affect Effect: Dynamics of Emotion in Political Thinking and Behavior*, edited by W. Russell Neumann, George E. Marcus, and Ann N. Crigler, and Michael MacKuen, 202–30. Chicago: University of Chicago Press, 2007.

Huff, Connor, and Dustin Tingley. "'Who Are These People?' Evaluating the Demographic Characteristics and Political Preferences of MTurk Survey Respondents." *Research & Politics* 2, no. 3 (2015): 1–12.

Iyengar, Shanto. *Is Anyone Responsible?* Chicago: University of Chicago Press, 1991.

Iyengar, Shanto, and Donald Kinder. "Psychological Accounts of Agenda-Setting." In *Mass Media and Political Thought*, edited by Sidney Kraus and Richard M. Perloff, 117–40. Beverly Hills, CA: Sage, 1985.

———. *News That Matters.* Chicago: University of Chicago Press, 1987.

Iyengar, Shanto, Mark D. Peters, and Donald R. Kinder. "Experimental Demonstration of the 'Not-So-Minimal' Consequences of Television News Programs." *American Political Science Review* 76, no. 4 (1982): 848–58.

Iyengar, Shanto, Donald R. Kinder, Mark D. Peters and Jon A. Krosnick. "The Evening News and Presidential Evaluations." *Journal of Personality and Social Psychology* 46, no. 4 (1984): 778–87.

Krosnick, Jon A., and Laura A. Brannon. "The Impact of the Gulf War on the Ingredients of Presidential Evaluations: Multidimensional Effects of Political Involvement." *American Political Science Review* 87, no. 4 (1993): 963–75.

Krosnick, Jon A., and Donald R. Kinder. "Altering the Foundations of Support for the President through Priming." *American Political Science Review* 84, no. 2 (1990): 497–512.

LaMarre, Heather L., Kristen D. Landreville, and Michael A. Beam. "The Irony of Satire: Political Ideology and the Motivation to See What You Want to See in The Colbert Report." *The International Journal of the Press/Politics* 14, no. 2 (2009): 212–31.

Landers, Richard N., and Tara S. Behrend. "An Inconvenient Truth: Arbitrary Distinctions between Organizational, Mechanical Turk, and Other Convenience Samples." *Industrial and Organizational Psychology* 8, no. 2 (2015): 142–64.

Lenart, Silvo, and Kathleen M. McGraw. "America Watches 'Amerika': Television Docudrama and Political Attitudes." *Journal of Politics* 51, no. 3 (1989): 697–712.

Lerner, Jennifer S., Roxana M. Gonzales, Deborah A. Small, and Baruch Fischhoff. "Effects of Fear and Anger on Perceived Risks of Terrorism: A National Field Experiment." *Psychological Science* 14, no. 2 (2003): 144–50.

MacKuen, Michael B., George E. Marcus, W. Russell Neuman, and Luke Keele. "The Third Way: The Theory of Affective Intelligence and American Democracy." In *The Affect Effect: Dynamics of Emotion in Political Thinking and Behavior*, edited by W. Russell Neumann, George E. Marcus, Ann N. Crigler, and Michael MacKuen, 124–51. Chicago: University of Chicago Press, 2007.

Marcus, George E. *The Sentimental Citizen: Emotion in Democratic Politics*. University Park: University of Pennsylvania Press, 2002.

———. "How Affective Intelligence Theory Can Help Us Understand Politics." *Emotion Researcher*, February 2017. http://emotionresearcher.com/how-affective-intelligence-theory-can-help-us-understand-politics/.

Marcus, George E., John L. Sullivan, Elizabeth Theiss-Morse Daniel Stevens. "The Emotional Foundation of Political Cognition: The Impact of Extrinsic Anxiety on the Formation of Political Tolerance Judgments." *Political Psychology* 26, no. 6 (2005): 949–63.

McCrae, Robert R., and Paul T. Costa Jr. "A Five-Factor Theory of Personality." In *Handbook of Personality: Theory and Research*, second edition, edited by Lawrence A. Pervin and Oliver P. John, 139–53. New York: Guilford, 1999.

Morris, Jonathan S. "*The Daily Show* with Jon Stewart and Audience Attitude Change during the 2004 Party Conventions." *Political Behavior* 31, no. 1 (2009): 79–102.

Mulligan, Kenneth, and Philip Habel. "The Implications of Fictional Media for Political Belief." *American Politics Research* 41, no. 1 (2013): 122–46.

Mutz, Diana C., and Lilach Nir. "Not Necessarily the News: Does Fictional Television Influence Real-World Policy Preferences?" *Mass Communication and Society* 13, no. 2 (2010): 196–217.

Nelson, Thomas E., Rosalee A. Clawson, and Zoe M. Oxley. "Media Framing of a Civil Liberties Conflict and Its Effect on Tolerance." *The American Political Science Review* 91, no. 3 (1997): 567–83.

Nelson, Thomas E., Zoe M. Oxley, and Rosalee A. Clawson. "Toward a Psychology of Framing Effects." *Political Behavior* 19, no. 3 (1997): 221–46.

Price, Vincent, and David Tewksbury. "News Values and Public Opinion: A Theoretical Account of Media Priming and Framing." In *Progress in Communication Sciences: Advances in Persuasion*, vol. 13, edited by George A. Barnett and Franklin J. Boster, 173–213. Cambridge, MA: MIT Press, 1997.

Renshon, Jonathan, Jooa Julia Lee, and Dustin Tingley. "Physiological Arousal and Political Beliefs." *Political Psychology* 36, no. 5 (2014): 569–85.

Roulin, Nicolas. "Don't Throw the Baby Out with the Bathwater: Comparing Data Quality of Crowdsourcing, Online Panels, and Student Samples." *Industrial and Organizational Psychology* 8, no. 2 (2015): 190–96.

Swigger, Nathaniel. "The Effect of Gender Norms in Sitcoms on Support for Access to Abortion and Contraception." *American Politics Research* 45, no. 1 (2017): 109–27.

Williamson, Vanessa. "On the Ethics of Crowdsourced Research." *PS: Political Science and Politics* 49, no. 1 (2016): 77–81.

Yang, Hung-Chia, Sally M. Donovan, Scott J. Young, Jeffrey B. Greenblatt, and Louis-Benoit Desroches. "Assessment of Household Appliance Surveys Collected with Amazon Mechanical Turk." *Energy Efficiency* 8, no. 6 (2015): 1063–75.

Zaller, John. *The Nature and Origins of Mass Opinion*. Cambridge, UK: Cambridge University Press, 1992.

Chapter 10

The Hollywood Connection

A Roadmap for Future Research

Timothy G. Hill and Heather E. Yates

We are witnessing an extraordinary time in American politics. Our ongoing democratic experiment entered a new phase when Donald J. Trump was elected in November 2016. The New York real estate mogul and reality television personality was an unconventional presidential candidate, and his electoral victory rattled the Washington political establishment. This political reality has opened paths of inquiry about the kinds of lingering effects the celebrity of Donald Trump will have on American politics.

It is not just Trump's election that has the potential to change how celebrity interacts with politics, however. It is also his presidency. As a candidate for the highest political office, Trump had no previous experience that would have prepared him for the demands of the job. As the president, he has achieved little legislative success and his overall approval rating has consistently been among the lowest (and very often, the lowest) of any president for which such data exists. Yet his job approval among his co-partisans remains high, and there are signs he is moving the Republican Party toward him on his signature issues of immigration and trade. The next few years, therefore, will be instrumental in understanding how Americans judge celebrities who take up politics as a second career.

Trump's presidency is only one reason that this book is neither the first nor the last inspection of how celebrity culture and fictional media intersect with politics. Recent developments in the literature (discussed more completely in the introduction) have also exposed new questions that are relevant to inquiry by political science. The studies in a work like this one move that inquiry forward by providing a survey of research that shows in what ways political institutions, norms, and behavior are interacting with celebrity culture more frequently. At the end of such a survey, it is worth taking a step back to see if there are any thematic lessons to be learned from the research as a collective. This wider view is what we will attempt in the next section.

LESSONS LEARNED

The studies in the foregoing pages, while broadly related thematically, are diverse in their approaches and content. They examine both mass and elite politics, they cover a wide methodological range, and they draw on literatures from across political science and beyond. Yet their very diversity demonstrates some important lessons for future researchers in these areas to consider.

First, *the findings expand the scope of inquiry and curiosity.* While the Hollywood connection has historically been limited to demonstrations that fictional media and celebrity forays into politics had an impact, there are actually a multiplicity of questions to ask, requiring a multiplicity of research methods. The studies collected here have shown that there is much more to say in these areas. These studies have demonstrated an impact on both mass and elite audiences, have employed both qualitative and quantitative methods, and have gone well beyond the bubble of the most obviously political fare. The results show that scholars should feel free to think much more broadly about these questions than they generally have to date.

Second, *questions of identity and representation matter*. Included in the pages here are three chapters focused on questions of feminism, gender, and representation. Yates examined the portrayal of women in political satire, Kirkpatrick and Stoutenborough explored celebrity influence on feminist identity, and Mulligan explored identity questions more broadly in asking whether representation suffered as a result of media consolidation. Those are hardly revolutionary steps, and yet they represent what may be the strongest focus on identity issues to date in the research areas represented in this volume. As above, the research presented here indicates that an even stronger focus on these issues would be fruitful ground for scholars moving forward. This exploration might include questions of representation such as Mulligan and Yates both explore; questions of interaction between celebrities who discuss matters of identity and their fans, as Kirkpatrick and Stoutenborough examine; questions of how fictional media aimed at black, queer, or other minority audiences shape opinions about identity inside (and outside) their core demographic; or even how more mainstream pop cultural offerings may carry different messages to audiences of different identity makeups. Marrying the literature from one or more of these identity areas with that of the Hollywood connection could by itself keep scholars busy for many years to come.

Third, *fictional media yields influence*. Despite television news' incentives to be entertaining, fictional media is not simply the less-informative sibling of news media, and scholars should not approach it as if it is. While fictional media will always be less immediately relevant to politics, there are also effects apparent in the fictional media literature that suggest an impact that is in at least one way more powerful than hard news. Specifically, there is relatively little evidence of a persuasion effect from news media, but the potential for persuasion in fictional media is well documented. Celebrities also seem to have a persuasive impact on the public even when they are not portraying a character on the big or small screens. We do not claim to have made this discovery here; even a cursory read through the extant literature would bring one to the same conclusions. However, we would suggest that, given these literatures being still fairly marginal within political science, it is important to be explicit about why they deserve to come out of the shadow of what has come before.

Fourth, *there are new applications for concepts and theories*. Just as we do not need to see this work merely as an extension of research on news media, we do not need to limit ourselves to the theoretical perspectives that have serviced our studies in the past. Kirkpatrick and Stoutenborough's use of narrative policy framework and Hill and Van Fleet's use of affective intelligence theory demonstrate that our understanding of both celebrities in politics and fictional media can be enhanced by exploring theoretical constructs beyond the traditional ones we are used to seeing. The ways in which the Hollywood connection could be affecting American politics are myriad, and they almost certainly have not all been explored yet. Finding new ways to think about these questions is sure to be rewarding both to the scholars that pursue them and to the larger community.

Finally, *the celebrity factor matters in politics*. This research illustrates that celebrity influence has a measurable effect on audiences, and we suggest that this is a salient research pursuit in political science. This collection stands on the shoulders of a well-documented literature showing the ways in which entertainers have used their public platforms to promote political positions. The work presented in this volume suggests there is much more to explore in this area, and that continuing that work is important to our understanding of public opinion more generally.

These lessons provide us with some ideas about how to move forward. They do not, however, set anything like an agenda for what that research might look like. In the next section, we hope to provide a few broad questions that, when combined with the lessons above, might give scholars a roadmap for what could come next in these research areas.

FUTURE DIRECTIONS

We hold that the studies collected in this volume provide an important set of voices in the ongoing conversations of the Hollywood connection. Nevertheless, questions remain which will help those conversations move forward. Some of those questions were raised by the studies themselves. Others are more general, but we would be remiss not to mention them. While this edited collection expands some corridors of future exploration, we make no claim that these are the only questions scholars should tackle within these areas, or even that they are the most critical ones. However, we would argue that they all represent logical "next steps" considering the state of the literature as it currently exists.

First, *what are the limits to fictional media effects?* As with any scientific undertaking, now that the effects themselves are reasonably well established, it is important to discover the scope of the conditions under which they exist. The limits that remain largely obscure are threefold: limits of salience, limits of content, and limits of persistence.

By limits of salience, we mean that it is unclear how the broader salience of an issue in society affects fictional media's ability to influence attitudes and behavior. Evans's findings are consistent with the idea that, as terrorism retreated as a priority issue in American society, portrayals of terrorism on television became less influential on audiences. However, one might also expect that an issue which was not well-known by audiences would be the most ripe for attitude change, since for a large portion of the audience, it would likely not be attitude *change* at all, but attitude *formation*. How these two pressures interact, and whether it varies by issue, remains to be worked out.

Limits of content are those explored here by Hill and Van Fleet, and elsewhere by Swigger (2017). As we mentioned in the introduction to this volume, most study in the area of fictional media has revolved around media content that has an overt connection to politics. As Hill and Van Fleet suggest, there is good reason to believe that such compartmentalization on the part of audiences is incomplete at best. Whether it be through emotions as Hill and Van Fleet suggest, through the subtle cues of the story and characterization as Swigger proposes, or through some other, as yet undiscovered mechanism, there is good reason to explore how ostensibly nonpolitical entertainment may nonetheless have political consequences. What forms of content are more or less able to communicate these influences, what mechanisms are at work under what conditions, and which members of the audience are the most susceptible to these influences are all questions that currently have no clear answers.

Finally, limits of persistence refer to the question Adkins and Castle (2014) provided a preliminary window into: the "half-life" of fictional media effects. While experimental methodology has proved an excellent tool for demonstrating fictional media effects, be they agenda-setting, priming, or persuasion, the bulk of experiments so far have been one-shot affairs that involve exposure to a stimulus followed immediately by measurement of the effect. With the exception of Adkins and Castle's work, to our knowledge no published study has attempted to demonstrate any continued impact of that stimulus beyond the moment of the study itself. While Adkins and Castle demonstrated that it is at least possible to find a measurable effect up to a week after the initial exposure, scholars require a great deal more data on this question before we can responsibly make any conclusions. The questions of how and at what pace these effects decay remain key deficits in our knowledge of fictional media effects.

Second, *how do fictional media effects manifest in, to borrow a phrase from William James, the "blooming, buzzing confusion" of the real-world media environment, with its multiple, possibly conflicting signals?* (1890, 488). This question is directly related to the previous query about persistence. One reason persistence is so important to understand is that, once participants leave the laboratory, they re-enter a world that is constantly influencing them in innumerable unmeasurable ways. The buffeting of this constantly shifting set of forces inevitably reduces the power of any one media artifact. And even leaving aside the rest of the world, the media environment itself will not necessarily always deliver signals that hold the same valence on a given issue. A crime procedural in which the justice system largely works might be followed by one in which the results are more messy. A situation comedy that portrays women as prizes might play immediately before or after one in which the female protagonist is competent and responsible. In the laboratory, such dichotomies might provide the fodder for the separate conditions of an experiment. In real life, it is entirely possible for viewers to encounter them within close proximity to each other, and we have no good sense of what happens when they do. Perhaps they cancel each other out, and leave the viewer back where s/he was initially on the relevant issue. Perhaps the viewer pays attention to the message that s/he already agreed with and discards the other, making her/his own opinion that much stronger. Perhaps hearing multiple perspectives leaves her/him cross-pressured and ambivalent. Without data in this area, any given speculation is equally as useful as any other.

Third, *when celebrities are becoming politicians and politicians are often celebrities, where is the line between the impact of celebrities on politics and politics more generally?* Several of our authors dealt with the question of whether politicians counted as celebrities. Invariably, they decided in the affirmative. Politicians now carefully cultivate their brands on social media, take selfies with voters who behave a great deal like fans, and inspire memes and other online social activity. Conversely, celebrities are increasingly mentioned as political figures, including presidential candidates, without any prior political experience. No doubt the success of Donald Trump's candidacy is largely responsible for the latter trend. Since his election, other major celebrity personalities have either associated themselves or had others associate them with a presidential run, including rapper Kanye West, actor Dwayne "The Rock" Johnson, reality television personality Kim Kardashian, and media queen Oprah Winfrey. In such an environment, does it even make sense to try to pull apart celebrity influences in politics from more traditional ones? And if so, how do we go about doing so?

Finally, *how has the presidency of Donald Trump challenged our understanding of celebrity influence in politics, and how will it continue to do so?* As mentioned above, Trump succeeded in attaining the highest office in American politics without doing any of the work previously thought necessary to be considered a serious contender. It would not be appropriate, of course, to suggest that his celebrity alone won him the nomination, much less the presidency. Learning how much of a role it played will be instrumental in understanding how that lack of experience has altered American electoral politics.

For now, it remains unclear if Trump's brand of celebrity politics is an anomaly or if the celebrity factor will become a more common factor in American politics. If Trump wins a second term, continues to preside over an expanding economy, and finds a way to improve on his generally mediocre approval numbers, both elites and the mass public may find in him a template for political success. The name recognition, the telegenic charisma, the ability to connect to a crowd: each of these is a desirable quality in a presidential candidate. Should it become clear that "on-the-job training" is acceptable for learning the nation's highest political office, we would expect both parties to recruit from their pool of ideologically-aligned celebrities with considerable alacrity. If, on the other hand, Trump's limitations as a politician lead to his defeat in 2020 and to an America that is weaker economically and is reduced in its global influence, this experiment with inexperience could very well sour the American public on celebrities parlaying their fame into political power. The one thing that seems assured is that some kind of change in how Americans understand this relationship is underway, and will continue. In either case, scholars who study the interaction of celebrities and politics will have their work cut out for them.

LOOKING AHEAD

The fields of fictional media and celebrity influence in politics are in something of an adolescence.[1] They have passed the infancy of demonstrating their viability as ideas, but have not yet reached the adulthood of diversified, nuanced fields of research as have other areas within public opinion. That process of growing up necessarily entails risk, and the temptation can be strong to return to familiar patterns. The easy path for researchers would be to continue to publish variations on the same themes: fictional media with obvious political overtones can be demonstrated to have certain effects under certain, tightly controlled conditions. Celebrities can impact attitudes or behavior through the mechanisms that are by now well documented. However, the research in this volume suggests to us, as we hope it does to the reader, that what remains unknown is both big and exciting. We are confident that this concluding chapter has raised only a fraction of the questions researchers could ask in these areas. As the context in which people consume fictional media changes, and the lines continue to blur between celebrity and politician, the work for students of these areas will be more voluminous than ever. We eagerly await the scholarly conversations that will result.

NOTE

1. We refer here to the literatures in America specifically. The celebrity politics literature in the UK is more developed, but is beyond the scope of our current project.

REFERENCES

Adkins, Todd, and Jeremiah J. Castle. "*Moving* Pictures? Experimental Evidence of Cinematic Influence on Political Attitudes." *Social Science Quarterly* 95, no. 5 (2014): 1230–44.

James, William. *The Principles of Psychology*. New York: Henry Holt and Company, 1890.

Swigger, Nathaniel. "The Effect of Gender Norms in Sitcoms on Support for Access to Abortion and Contraception." *American Politics Research* 45, no. 1 (2017): 109–27.

Index

About the Contributors

Darin DeWitt is assistant professor of political science at California State University, Long Beach. He studies American political institutions, conspiracy theory politics, and celebrity politics.

Heather K. Evans is associate professor of political science at Sam Houston State University. She has a PhD from Indiana University, Bloomington, and a BA from Berea College. Her research interests include American politics, particularly public opinion, competitive elections, political communication, social media, the status of women in the discipline, Congress, and the effect of entertainment media on political attitudes. Her research has appeared in journals like *American Politics Research*; *PS: Political Science and Politics*; *Electoral Studies*; and the *Journal of Elections, Public Opinion, and Parties*. She is the author of *Competitive Elections and Democracy in America: The Good, the Bad, and the Ugly* (2014). She is also the editor of two recent volumes from Rowman & Littlefield: *Community Engagement Findings across the Disciplines: Applying Course Content to Community Needs* and *Community Engagement Best Practices across the Disciplines: Applying Course Content to Community Needs*.

Mark Harvey is director of graduate and undergraduate programs at the University of Saint Mary. He has published articles on human rights, economic development, democratization, the politics of innovation in the music industry, and learning teams in the classroom. His book, *Celebrity Influence*, discusses the way celebrities have affected our political environment. He also has two ongoing projects on the effect of music on perceptions of political candidates and the use of games and simulations to teach classroom concepts.

Timothy G. Hill is professor of political science at Doane University in Crete, Nebraska, where he teaches courses in American government and co-hosts the podcast *Impolite Conversation: Religion and Politics*. His research interests include the political impact of fictional media and the political attitudes and behavior of America's minority religious traditions.

Kellee J. Kirkpatrick is assistant professor in the Department of Political Science at Idaho State University. Her research agenda examines issues of women's health and reproductive policy. Specifically, her research focuses on questions that concern how and why governments regulate private, social issues.

Kenneth Mulligan joined the Political Science Department at Southern Illinois University, Carbondale, in 2006. His research and teaching interests include mass communication, media effects and regulation, and public opinion.

Anthony J. Nownes is professor of political science at the University of Tennessee, Knoxville. His research interests include interest groups, lobbying, public policy, and celebrity politics. He coedited the volume *Interest Group Politics* (ninth edition). His most recent book is *Organizing for Transgender Rights: Collective Action, Group Development, and the Rise of a New Social Movement*.

James W. Stoutenborough is assistant professor in the Department of Political Science at Idaho State University and senior research fellow with the Institute of Science, Technology, and Public Policy in the Bush School of Government and Public Service at Texas A&M University. His research interests include public policy, public opinion, and political behavior. Specifically, his research examines how public opinion influences the formation and adoption of public policy in the United States.

Ashley R. Van Fleet is a 2018 graduate of Doane University with a major in psychology and a minor in political science. She is a senior coach at College Possible in Omaha, Nebraska.

Heather E. Yates is assistant professor of political science at the University of Central Arkansas. Her research interests include American political behavior, the role emotions have in politics, and gender and identity politics. Yates's book, *The Politics of Emotions, Candidates, and Choices*, concentrates on how voters' emotions influence their preferences for presidential candidates and, in turn, underscore appraisals of substantive campaign issues. She has also contributed to edited and reference volumes on interest groups and advocacy and political behavior, and contributes regular public affairs analysis for the Utica College Center for Public Policy and Elections Research.